CHURCH OF THE HOLY SPIRIT

GOD IN YOU

GOD *in* YOU

RELEASING THE POWER
OF THE HOLY SPIRIT IN YOUR LIFE

David Jeremiah

GRASON

Minneapolis, MN

GOD IN YOU
published by Multnomah Publishers, Inc.

and in association with the literary agency of Yates & Yates
505 S. Main, Suite 1000, Orange, California 92668
© 1998 by David Jeremiah

International Standard Book Number: *1-57673-233-9*

Design by Kevin Keller
Cover photograph by Don Fogg/Workbook Co/op Stock

Scripture quotations are from:
The Holy Bible, New King James Version ©1984 by Thomas Nelson, Inc.
Used by permission.

Also quoted:
The Holy Bible, New International Version (NIV) © 1973, 1984 by
International Bible Society, used by permission of Zondervan Publishing House.

The Living Bible (TLB) © 1971 by Tyndale House Publishers, Inc.,
Wheaton, Illinois 60189. All rights reserved.

The New Testament in Modern English (Phillips) © 1958 by J. B. Phillips.

New American Standard Bible (NASB) © 1960, 1977, 1994 by The Lockman Foundation,
used by permission.

Printed in the United States of America

MULTNOMAH PUBLISHERS, INC.•POST OFFICE BOX 1720•SISTERS, OREGON 97759

Library of Congress Cataloging-in-Publication Data:
Jeremiah, David.
    God in you: understanding the ministry of the Holy Spirit/David Jeremiah.
        p.cm.   ISBN 0-89066-312-2 (alk. paper)
    1. Holy Spirit. 2. Spiritual life—Christianity. I. title.
BT121.2.J47   1998   98–27934
231'.3—dc21   CIP
This special edition is published with the permission of Multnomah Publishers, Inc.,
Sisters, OR.

99 00 01 02 03 04 — 10 9 8 7 6 5 4 3

To my first grandson
David Todd Jeremiah
Born August 25, 1997

With the prayer that he will
love God with all of his heart
and walk with Him all the days of his life.

(I tried, but they wouldn't let me include his picture on this page!)

ACKNOWLEDGEMENTS

For they refreshed my spirit and yours;
therefore acknowledge such...
1 CORINTHIANS 16:18, NKJV

Donna Jeremiah: As I completed this project, Donna and I were celebrating our thirty-fifth wedding anniversary. For three and a half decades, she has been my greatest cheerleader and has shown by her consistent example the Spirit-filled lifestyle that is described in this book.

Sealy Yates: What a great friend and partner in ministry he has become! I acknowledge with great appreciation his tireless efforts on my behalf. We pray together.

Ken Nichols: For over twenty years we have been best friends. Many of the things that I have written about in this book have come into sharp focus through our many hours of fellowship. He gives me honest feedback on my ideas and my life.

Glenda Parker and Helen Barnhart: That's right; it takes two people to keep me on track! Without the faithful administrative assistance of these two women, I would never have had the quiet times to write down the thoughts that have been formalized in this book.

Charles Ryrie and Stanley Toussaint: Two men whose teaching about the Holy Spirit at Dallas Seminary helped me understand the importance of this doctrine.

Bill Bright: His message on "spiritual breathing," which I heard over twenty years ago, challenged me to integrate into my life that which I had learned about the third person of the Trinity.

Be proud that you have people like this among you.
1 CORINTHIANS 16:18, THE MESSAGE

CONTENTS

Chapter One

THE PROMISE
OF THE SPIRIT

DREAMS GREATER THAN
OUR MEMORIES

We all need dreams. We all need those moments when we lift our eyes from the long, winding trail and catch sight of the shining, snow-capped peaks on the horizon. Without such a vision of the peaks, without such dreams, life becomes a weary tramp through the lowlands.

As I look back on the recent years of my pastoral ministry, however, I must honestly admit that what has happened is beyond what I had even dreamed. The peaks are higher, brighter, and more glorious than I could ever have imagined. There have been Sundays when my wife and I have been on our way home after a wonderful day of ministry, and I have turned to her and said, "As far as a pastor is concerned, it doesn't get any better than this."

What a joy—what an incredible thrill—to be a part of what God is doing in the hearts and lives of so many people and to see His work grow faster and further than I could have conceived. Sometimes the excitement and gratitude well up within me to overflowing, and I don't have words to express how I feel.

But at the same time, God keep me—and all of us—from feeling that we have "arrived." I'm not sure at what age it sets in, but there is a temptation as we get older and have enjoyed some accomplishments and achievements to begin letting up on the accelerator a little. We find ourselves more and more inclined to pop life into cruise control, sit back a little, and watch the scenery go by. We content ourselves with our press clippings and scrapbooks and don't go out of our way to exert ourselves or launch into something new.

Some people call it a "retirement mind-set," and it can show up in people from their midforties to their midnineties. (If we make it beyond that, maybe we really have earned a little break!) Nevertheless, I have to tell you that I have scoured the Word of God from beginning to end and have not found one place where a believer is given permission to retire. *Retire* doesn't seem to be part of God's vocabulary. That realization is both unsettling and challenging to me.

Now, that doesn't necessarily mean that things won't change for us as the years go by. And no one is saying we ought to keep the same routines or do the same things we've always done to bring home the bacon or occupy our time. But it *does* mean that we never become too old to serve the Lord Jesus Christ with all our heart and soul and strength. He will never downsize His kingdom and put us out of work. He never gives us permission to check out of life. He never gives us permission to coast. Becoming a Christian is a *lifetime* commitment of service and ministry.

I believe it is the same for a church.

I believe that our dreams should be greater than our memories.

I would like you to think with me for a moment about a group of people who had every reason to cling to the past. And yet they were challenged by Jesus Christ Himself to let go of their memories...to put away their press clippings...and to embrace a dream beyond their comprehension.

In John 14, Jesus was in the midst of His final address to the eleven disciples. He was preparing them for the ultimate shock of His arrest and death. He had told them in John 13:33 that He was going away. As we come to chapter 14, our Lord's purpose is clearly defined in the first phrase of the chapter. *"Let not your heart be troubled...."*

He wanted to encourage the troubled hearts of His disciples. He wanted to comfort them with the truth of His ultimate destiny. But as He conversed with them, two of His disciples ventured to voice their insecurities and fears.

Thomas asked Him about the future.

"Lord, we do not know where You are going, and how can we know the way?" (John 14:5)

Can you hear the emotion tremble in this man's question? "Lord, how can we get to where You're going if You are *leaving* us? How will we know what to do, where to go, or which way to turn?"

Thomas, you'll remember, was the doubter. He wanted all the details in hand before the journey began. He wanted a road map with the route highlighted in yellow marker. Many of us are like that, aren't we? The Lord patiently answered Thomas's question. When He had finished, Philip put something else on the table. Philip's request, however, didn't concern the future; Philip was concerned about the here and now.

"Lord, show us the Father, and it is sufficient for us." (John 14:8)

Philip was saying, "If You're going away, Lord, and we're not going to have You here anymore, the least You can do is show us the Father, and then we'll be okay while You're gone. *Lord, where is the Father?*"

Now, that seems like a legitimate question. In truth, it is one of the most important questions in all of Scripture. The answer to that question is the secret to all ministry in the church today. It is the ongoing secret for every one of us who knows the Lord. It is the very guarantee that our dreams will always be greater than our memories.

Listen to what the Lord replied.

"Have I been with you so long, and yet you have not known Me, Philip? He who has seen Me has seen the Father; so how can you say, 'Show us the Father'? Do you not believe that I am in the Father, and the Father in Me? The words that I speak to you I do not speak on My own authority; but the Father who dwells in Me does the works. Believe Me that I am in the Father and the Father in Me, or else believe Me for the sake of the works themselves." (John 14:9–11)

Philip said to Jesus, "Show us the Father," as though he had never seen the Father. And Jesus insisted to Philip that he *had* seen the Father—he just didn't realize it! Every time he watched Jesus heal a leper, he saw the Father. Every time he saw Jesus do a miracle of any kind, he saw the Father.

But it was all so difficult for these shell-shocked, brokenhearted men to grasp. In that moment, the disciples were hung up on their memories. And who wouldn't be, after the three years they had just spent at the side of Jesus of Nazareth! A thousand images must have flashed across their minds. Jesus on the mountainside…Jesus walking on the sea…Jesus teaching from a boat…Jesus in the synagogue...Jesus with the little children. *And now He was going away?*

They didn't understand that Jesus was about to give them the very secret of that ministry they had closely observed for three years. They didn't understand that their Lord was about to reveal a truth that would sustain them, keep them, empower them, and fill them with overflowing joy in the face of everything the world could throw at them.

To poor, perplexed Philip, Jesus was saying, "I am not the source of My own sufficiency. The things I said and the works I accomplished did not initiate with Me. It was the Father, accomplishing His purposes in and through Me." Jesus disclaimed any credit for the words He spoke or the works He performed. They all flowed from His Father in heaven.

This perspective helps us to understand a number of similar passages. In John 5:19 Jesus said, "Most assuredly, I say to you, the Son can do nothing of Himself, but what He sees the Father do; for whatever He does, the Son also does in like manner." In verse 30 He said, "I can of Myself do nothing. As I hear, I judge; and My judgment is righteous, because I do not seek My own will but the will of the Father who sent Me."

You will find this same truth in John 8:28 and again in John 12:49. The Father spoke through the voice of Jesus. The Father healed through the touch of Jesus. The Father worked His will through Jesus. So Jesus was saying, "Listen to Me, Philip. *The secret of these works is not My physical presence. And if the secret is not My physical presence, then My physical absence isn't going to make any difference!*"

Do you see what He was saying? "Philip, you must try to understand. I'm going away, that is true. But the secret of My working while I was here was never My physical presence anyway. It was the Father working through Me. As a matter of fact, if you will trust Me, the works that I have done you will continue to do. And hear Me—you will do even *greater* works than I have done!"

What was Jesus saying to His men that evening? He was certainly trying to lift their downcast eyes and give them a glimpse of the shining mountain peaks on the horizon. Yes, there was a very deep valley that must come first—darker than any moment in the history of the world. But after that, mountain peak after mountain peak! He was telling them, "Don't look back! Your dreams are greater than your memories."

The temptation to look back, of course, was very strong. What wonderful years of ministry they had enjoyed, walking with the Nazarene. The wonders!

The miracles! The crowds! The excitement! Yet Jesus was telling them, "Yes, life for you is changing. It won't be the same. But don't be afraid! *The future is brighter than the past.*"

Years ago, when I first read those words about "greater works than I have done," I remember being completely mystified. How could He say that? What could He mean? How could the disciples' works ever be greater than His mighty works?

Deep down, I wondered if the Lord—because He loved these men and wanted so much to encourage them—might have been, well, overstating things just a bit for their sakes. He knew He was leaving, His followers were full of sorrow, and Jesus wanted to make them feel good. Most of us have done something like that in times past, haven't we? We go a little bit beyond reality to please someone or lift someone's sagging spirits.

But that could have never happened with the Son of God. He is truth incarnate. What He spoke was absolute reality and never "stretched" or "elaborated" for emphasis. No lie—whether white, black, or gray—could ever be found on His tongue.

THE POSSIBILITY OF GREATER WORKS

What, then, is the significance of His words for you and me? How could the disciples do greater works than Jesus did while He was on this earth?

And wasn't He speaking of you and me as well? Wasn't He saying that *we* could do greater works than His?

Could it be? Could it actually be true that you and I—all of us who belong to Jesus Christ—have the potential to do greater works than Jesus did? Isn't that a little outrageous? Isn't that almost…blasphemous?

No, it is neither outrageous nor blasphemous. It is truth. Jesus, whose name is Truth, said so Himself.

The works Jesus performed during His public ministry were mind-boggling. He banished diseases…cast out demons…raised corpses to life…created wine, fish, and bread with a word and a touch…calmed mighty storms with a single command. How could it be said by any stretch of imagination that the works of the disciples and that our works—we who belong to His church—are greater than Jesus' works? Has this promise ever been fulfilled? Can we point to anything that would help us understand that in our world today?

Some have said, "Well, you have to understand that the 'greater works' are related to *belief.*" In other words, the reason we don't do these greater works is because we don't believe enough. Is that true? The problem with this understanding is that if our ability to do such works depends on our faith, then we would have to have greater faith than Jesus! Jesus didn't say, "He who believes in Me with sufficient faith," or "He who believes in Me with all his heart," or "He who believes in Me intensely and with great sincerity shall do greater works."

He simply said, "He who believes in Me, the works that I do he will do also; and greater works than these he will do" (John 14:12).

But that makes no sense…does it? Greater works? Greater miracles than He performed? What could that mean?

> In John 2, at the wedding feast in Cana, Jesus converted the simple molecular structure of water into the far more complex molecular structure of wine. *Can we do more than that?*
>
> In John 4, by a word uttered over ten miles from the scene, Jesus instantly reversed the decay process and restored to full vigor and activity the cellular structure destroyed by a mortal illness. *Can we do more than that?*
>
> In John 6:1–14, Jesus took five loaves and two fish and created out of them enough bread and meat to feed five thousand hungry men and their families. *Can we do more than that?*
>
> In John 6:15–21, Jesus created an antigravitational force of an unknown nature that enabled Him to walk along the surface of a stormy sea. *Can we do more than that?*
>
> In John 11, Jesus stood at the mouth of an opened grave and called through the veil of death to His friend Lazarus. Not only was Lazarus dead, his limbs, eyes, brain, and internal organs were already in a state of decay. This man had been dead for four days; putrefaction was well under way. And yet at the creative word of Jesus Christ, all the cells and functions of that body were instantly restructured, and the departed spirit was summoned again to the body. Lazarus lived and spoke and thought and remembered. Awesome! *What could possibly qualify as a greater work than that?*[1]

Great works? Marvelous miracles? Yes, beyond all question. And yet think about it: every one of those acts was only superficial and temporary. I am not discounting what Jesus did. I am simply making the point that no one was *permanently* helped by these miracles. None of men's deepest needs were met by these works of power.

Yes, He created food for a single meal; but the people just got hungry again.

Yes, He stilled the raging sea; but only until the next storm.

Yes, He healed bodily ailments; but every person he healed eventually died anyway.

I don't know what you think about Lazarus, but I really feel bad for him. How would you like to die twice? That's what happened to him. He had already passed into Glory. He was already walking the streets of heaven, talking to Abraham, Moses, and David, filling his eyes with heavenly splendor and gazing on the very throne of God. And what happened? *Jesus brought him back.* Years later, Lazarus had to repeat the whole process. He had to die again. The miracle of bringing Lazarus back was no favor to Lazarus! Jesus did it as a sign miracle for all who watched.

Dr. John Mitchell, preeminent Bible teacher for many years at Multnomah Bible College, used to tell the story of sitting at the bedside of a dying friend. The man seemed to be slipping out of this life. His breathing grew very, very shallow until, finally, it seemed to stop.

Well, Dr. Mitchell thought, *he's gone now.*

Suddenly, the man's eyes popped open and he looked up at the craggy face of Dr. Mitchell. "Who's there?" the man said.

"It's all right," Dr. Mitchell soothed. "It's just me."

"Oh," the man groaned, "I'm *so* disappointed!"

The dying man had anticipated looking into the face of Jesus—or at least an angel. Instead, he saw the same old hospital room and the face of the old Scotsman Mitchell. If *he* was disappointed, just imagine how Lazarus had felt! What a letdown to find himself back in his grave clothes lying on a slab in a dark tomb.

Yet the Author of Life called him back, and he stepped once again into the lesser light of the sun. And you and I can do a greater work than *this?* How so?

THE PROMISE OF GREATER WORKS

The fact is, Jesus tied His promise of "greater works" to the coming of the Holy Spirit.

In John 14:12, Jesus said, "And greater works than these he will do." For what reason? Here's the key: *"Because I go to My Father."*

This is a common phrase and a common teaching. John 7:39 states: "But this He spoke concerning the Spirit, whom those believing in Him would receive; for the Holy Spirit was not yet given, because Jesus was not yet glorified." He had not yet left.

In John 16:7 Jesus said, "Nevertheless I tell you the truth. It is to your advantage that I go away; for if I do not go away, the Helper will not come to you; but if I depart, I will send Him to you."

These greater works Jesus promised were dependent upon Jesus' physically leaving this world and going back to heaven. Those things could not happen, He told them, until He went to His Father and sent the Holy Spirit down to take His place.

After Jesus had spoken these words to His disciples, He went to the garden that night where He was captured, taken to trial, and brutally crucified. He rose from the grave on the first day of the week and appeared to the believers over a period of forty days. He then ascended back to His Father, and ten days after His return to heaven, the Holy Spirit was poured out at Pentecost, and the third person of the Trinity came upon them in power. Then Peter and the other disciples stood in front of the very mob and the very rulers who had crucified Jesus and proclaimed His resurrection and offer of salvation. Three thousand people experienced the miracle of regeneration in one day.

Someone has said that more people believed on the Day of Pentecost than had believed in the entire three and a half years Jesus walked on this earth. I believe that is true.

Amazing as our Lord's words in John 14:12 may be, it is literally true that a believer today may accomplish greater works on earth than our Lord Himself acomplished. I would like to suggest to you three ways that our works are "greater."

WE HAVE A GREATER MESSAGE

The great works Jesus did while He pitched His tent among us dealt with the material. The greater works that He promised deal with the spiritual.

In Luke 10:17, the disciples had just returned from their first preaching mission:

> Then the seventy returned with joy, saying, "Lord, even the demons are subject to us in Your name."

In other words, they were thrilled that they had been able to cast out demons. But Jesus said to them,

> "Behold, I give you the authority to trample on serpents and scorpions, and over all the power of the enemy, and nothing shall by any means hurt you. Nevertheless do not rejoice in this, that the spirits are subject to you, but rather rejoice because your names are written in heaven." (Luke 10:19–20)

Did you hear what Jesus said? They had been cheering and laughing and high-fiving because they were able to order some evil spirits around. Jesus said, "That's okay, but don't get so excited about *that*. What you really need to get excited about is that your names are written down in heaven."

What was Jesus saying? The spiritual is far more important than the material. The eternal is infinitely more important than the temporal.

You and I have difficulty understanding that. One of the reasons we do not have greater works going on in our lives is because we, as believers, do not understand the priority of the spiritual over the material. We have a much greater message because conversion is the greatest miracle we could ever be associated with.

A friend of mine told me about a group of short-term missionaries who recently held evangelistic meetings in Africa. During those meetings, these believers reported, a blind man miraculously received his sight. When the believers came back to report to the sending churches, that was just about all they could talk about. A man's sight restored—what a miracle! Yet during those same meetings, many embraced Jesus Christ as Savior and found eternal salvation. Many stepped out of spiritual blindness into the light of God's kingdom. But that news always seemed to receive second billing to "the miracle."

If we could only view these things as God does! The message of reconciliation meets the basic needs of every man and woman, every boy and girl, and it meets those needs *permanently*. In miracles, only God's power and goodness are revealed, but in conversion, God's grace is revealed—something that causes even the angels to look over the ramparts of heaven in wonder (see 1 Peter 1:12).

The message of the saving grace of God is the greater message because it was the message that extended to the Gentiles and rolled outward across the world like a mighty tsunami wave. The death, burial, and resurrection of Jesus Christ have given to us in this generation the greatest message that has ever been communicated to any people. Anywhere. At any time. Period.

It is called the eternal gospel, the Good News.

You and I can show compassion and reach out to help people with their hurts. We can minister to them in their sorrow. We can assist them in dealing with terrible addictions or dysfunctional family situations. But if, in the process, we do not give to them Jesus Christ and salvation, we have only postponed the inevitable. We have not helped them!

In years past, when the "social gospel" was popular, many Christians became excited about meeting people in their social, physical needs. There are many versions of the social gospel out there today, and certainly we need to do good to those in need. And yes, it is true that if we meet the physical needs of "the least of these" brothers and sisters, we have ministered to the King Himself. But if we do all these things and we leave them without the permanent message of salvation, we have not changed them.

Our message is greater because it is for eternity.

WE HAVE A GREATER MINISTRY

Not only is the message greater, but we literally do have a greater ministry. The works Jesus did while He walked the dusty paths of Palestine were localized in scope. If you were up on a space shuttle flight, you could look down at the great curve of the earth and, if the shuttle was in the right orbital position and weather permitted, you might strain your eyes and see a tiny strip of land at the edge of a great continental shelf.

Israel.

During his lifetime, the Son of God was confined in His influence to a comparatively small section of that thin slice of Middle East real estate. That was His ministry. If you've ever been to Israel, you know it's not a very big place. It's a postage stamp.

Martin Luther said, "For Christ took but a little corner for Himself to preach and to work miracles, and but a little time; whereas the apostles and their followers have spread themselves through the whole world." Jesus committed the gospel to a small group of eleven men in order that they might carry it to the ends of the earth. At that time, the whole world, with the exception of a few in Israel, was lost in the darkness and despair of unbelief—"without hope and without God in the world." And yet in just a little more than three hundred years, Christianity closed nearly all the temples of the heathen Roman empire and numbered its converts by the millions.

These were the greater works, and down through the centuries, He still carries on this ministry through the believers in the body of Christ. Today, our words are carried across the entire globe. I do not pastor in a little corner of Palestine. When I preach, I speak in a large city. But not only that, what I say is recorded, and it will be on television in the whole community the following Sunday. And these words, somewhere down the road, will get into the mix of a radio ministry that is on many radio stations, and they will go all over the United States.

Jesus never did that.

Could He have done it? Yes, He could have. But He has chosen, rather, to give the opportunity to us—to you and me—to do the greater works.

My son David, who is a computer whiz, was showing me something amazing a few days ago. Many people want to listen to our radio program but find that it's not being broadcast at a time when they can listen. Now that is no longer a problem. You just crank up your computer, push a few buttons, my face swims up on the screen, and you can program the day's message to be heard at any time you wish, right through your computer.

I was at the Billy Graham Training Center right before Dr. Graham decided to communicate to the most people he had ever communicated to in his life. The number was in the billions. They had a satellite hookup that took his image and his words literally across the world.

We have a greater ministry, just as Jesus said we would.

Our dreams will always be greater than our memories because this world is exploding in its ability to communicate. Back in 1962—some thirty years before the advent of the Internet—Marshall McLuhan wrote, "The new electronic interdependence recreates the world in the image of a global village." Unfortunately, Christians are sometimes the last people to take advantage of this technology.

I remember when television first came out. Many Christians shunned it, believing it was run by the prince of the power of the air. The evil one certainly had his influence in that medium (and still does), but why not use television as a means to proclaim the Good News? Why not use radio? Why not use print?

Why not use the Internet? Why not use any means at hand to take the message of the gospel and spread it throughout the whole world? The farther the better. The faster the better. The sooner the better. Until He comes!

What Jesus was saying to His disciples was this: "While I was on this earth, I was localized, I could only touch individual men and women in My travels and speak to a few local audiences. But believe Me, after I am gone and the Holy Spirit comes to fill and empower My sons and daughters, then My ministry will be as far spread as Christians are." So wherever there is a Christian, there is Christ. Wherever there is a believer, there is ministry.

We have a greater message and we have a greater ministry. But there is something else.

WE CAN DO GREATER MIRACLES

I can almost hear some of my readers speaking out loud as they read this: "Now, wait a minute. I've been tracking with you to this point, Jeremiah, but this one's a little bit scary. What in the world do you mean?"

Let me suggest to you that the Lord Jesus, while He was on this earth, never saw a conversion like that of Saul of Tarsus. He never saw a revival like the Great Awakenings that have shaken our world. The miracle of regeneration is indeed a grade A miracle. It is the greatest miracle there is. Do you believe that?

Dr. Henry Morris, a member of the church I pastor and a distinguished creation scientist, has a way of stating things in scientific terms. Ponder for a moment Dr. Morris's unique description of conversion:

> A person who is a closed system spiritually, utterly inadequate and self-centered, suddenly becomes an open system, integrated, and with his life centered in the omnipotent Creator. He who was spiritually deteriorating day after day, as a matter of fact "already dead while he liveth," through the power of the Holy Spirit, now the God of hope fills him with joy and peace. He abounds in hope through the power of the Holy Spirit, and he becomes quickened together with Jesus Christ. His life was a chaos, and now is a cosmos, with order, meaning, and goal. He is born again, a miracle of grace, a living testimony to the great Power of creation, who also is the God of salvation.[2]

Wow! That's what happens when a person receives Jesus Christ as Savior and Lord. That's what happened to *you* when you said yes to Him. You were a closed system, and you became an open system. You were chaos, and now you are cosmos.

You can tell people about that. Just look them in the eyes and say, "Did you know I once was a chaos, but now I'm a cosmos?" That ought to at least get their attention!

What are we talking about? We're talking about the miracle of regeneration. The longer God gives me the opportunity to preach and teach, the more over-whelmed and amazed I am at how God, by His grace, works in human hearts. He can take a person who is going totally in the wrong direction and—in a moment of time, through an encounter with Jesus Christ—radically change that person and set him on the road to glory with holy happiness and joy in his heart.

Jesus Christ is the only one who can do that. And that is the miracle He has called us to perform as we spread throughout our neighborhoods, our nation, and our world as ambassadors of the gospel of Jesus Christ.

How do we go about doing the greater works? If you read this passage of Scripture in context, you won't have any doubt about what this is all about. Look again at John 14:12:

> "Truly, truly, I say to you, he who believes in Me, the works that I do shall he do also; and greater works than these shall he do; because I go to the Father. And whatever you ask in My name, that will I do, that the Father may be glorified in the Son. If you ask Me anything in My name, I will do it." (John 14:12–14, NASB)

THE POWER BEHIND THE GREATER WORKS

The greater works are accomplished by prayer.

I am so excited about the future of Shadow Mountain Community Church, the church I pastor. Here's why: I know that our dreams are greater than our memories, because all the wonderful things God has done in the past years—in our facilities, in our schools, in our multiplied outreach opportunities—have been accomplished through the agency of a few people who have faithfully prayed every day for these ministries.

Not long ago, the Lord gave us a vision to raise up a whole corps of people who would pray around the clock, twenty-four hours a day, for the ministries of our church. And my thought is this: if God has done what He has done with a few people praying, and if the secret to the greater works is in the power of prayer, what should be expected when God's people consistently and regularly and throughout the whole day and night get on their knees and bring this ministry before God in prayer?

I promise you, our dreams are greater than our memories.

It is exciting to me to understand what begins to happen as we pray. It's not that we pray in order that *we* might do the work. Take another look at the verse: "And whatever you ask in My name, that will I do." If you ask anything in His name, *He* will do it.

That is no small distinction! Sometimes Christians get weary because we forget. We think God wants us to do His work for Him. That will make you tired very, very quickly. You can't do it! I can't do it! Our legs are too short to run with God! What Jesus is saying is this: when we pray, God is going to do His work through us, and we will be channels for His work.

I remember hearing about a preacher who said he could build a great church even if there was no God. I'm not sure that's a compliment. Sometimes we do commendable, praiseworthy things in the energy of our flesh. But when God begins to do the work *through* us, it is an entirely different proposition altogether. Incredible things begin to happen. Dreams take shape that are greater than our memories.

THE PRIORITIES OF THE GREATER WORKS

A long time ago a pastor of the Moody Church in Chicago made this comment: "Never undertake more Christian work than can be covered in continual prayer." Good counsel! I have a feeling that many of us are over our limit. I have a feeling that many churches are well over their limit. Oh, how we need to grasp the priority of prayer! I have no idea what is going to happen in and through my ministry because I'm not going to do it. God's going to do it.

As we pray, God will show us what He is doing, we will get under the spout, and He will pour His work down through us. The reason I'm excited about it is because I know God's vision for you and for me, for my church and for your church, for my family and your family, for my city and your city, is much greater than ours would ever be. I'm energized just thinking about what God is going to do.

So often in the past I have concentrated on this goal and that goal. I'm really into goals and objectives and plans—both in my personal life and as the pastor of a church. But I believe that people should not concentrate so much on the goal as on the *power*. And as we pray, we may discover that what we thought were great and lofty goals are pale and puny alongside *His* goals for our life and ministry.

Let us ask God to make us faithful as people of prayer, and let us pray that God will do His work through us. Then, whatever God wants to do, let's be open to it!

I have no idea what God is up to in your life and mine, but as He works through His mighty Spirit, we are about to find out! I promise you, it will not be on anybody's chart. You are not going to find a framed copy of it hanging on the wall of some office. God is going to do it in His own way—in startling, unexpected ways—through us as we trust Him and as we pray.

Our prayers are greater than our past, and our dreams are greater than our memories.

Just as Jesus said they would be.

Chapter Two

THE ATTRIBUTES
OF THE SPIRIT

DISCOVERING THE
FORGOTTEN GOD

A woman was trying to teach her Sunday school class the doctrine of the Trinity. That's quite a challenging subject to tackle with adults, let alone primary children. But she happened to be a very creative lady, and she felt sure she could come up with a visual aid to help them grasp this difficult concept.

She decided on a pretzel.

Why a pretzel? Well, she reasoned, it's made up of one strand of dough but is so intricately interwoven that it possesses three distinct holes. So she brought a pretzel on Sunday morning, held it up in front of her class, and pointed to the hole at the top. A dozen sets of little eyes followed her.

"Children," she said, "this is like God the Father."

No one challenged that comparison. If the teacher said God the Father was like a hole in a pretzel, she must know something about it. "Just think of this first hole as the heavenly Father," she told them. After letting that sink in for a moment, she pointed to the second opening. "This is like God the Son. Think of this second hole as our Lord Jesus. Then here, this hole down at the bottom, is like God the Holy Ghost. And just as this pretzel is made up of one piece, yet there are three separate holes, so the Trinity is one God with three separate persons."

It wasn't a bad illustration in a pinch. But had it made the desired impact? She asked the children to repeat what she had taught them: "God the Father, God the Son, God the Holy Ghost." When she was all done, she asked one of the children, a little boy, if he could stand up and repeat what he had learned. Rather reluctantly, he shuffled to the front of the class. Holding up the pretzel, he went through this miniature catechism—just as he remembered it.

"This hole here on top is God," he said. "I mean, God the Father. And then this hole right here is Jesus. And this," he concluded triumphantly, "is the Holy Smoke!"

Well, two for three isn't so bad, is it? His answer reminds me of one of my favorite stories, about a little girl who'd never been to a Baptist church before or observed what they did there. She was especially interested in the way they baptized people...thoroughly.

When she went home, she thought she would try that. Her mother heard the water running in the bathtub upstairs and went up to investigate. Her little girl had all her doll babies lined up next to the tub. She was going to do what she saw in church and make sure her little brood was thoroughly baptized. Her mother stood at the door watching.

The little girl took the first doll, put it in the water, looked up at the ceiling, and solemnly repeated these words: "I baptize you in the name of the Father, the Son, and in the hole you go."

Children aren't the only ones who feel confused about the Holy Spirit. Often when people try to describe the person and ministry of the Spirit, they become mystical, vague, tentative—and maybe a little uncomfortable. The way you view the Holy Spirit is very likely colored by your tradition, the teachings and attitudes you've grown up with.

In this book you hold in your hands, I would like to do more than just dispel confusion, important as that may be. I have a great desire in my heart to see the church of Jesus Christ embrace the wonderful, life-transforming truths about this mighty third person of the Trinity—this forgotten God, the Holy Spirit.

I'm convinced that we have put the church at a great disadvantage because of our unwillingness to proclaim these all-important truths.

The forgotten God needs to be remembered.

WITHOUT HIM, WE HAVE NOTHING

One day it hit me all at once that just about everything we count important to us in doctrine and practice is rooted in some aspect of the ministry of the Holy Spirit.

As I searched the Scriptures, I encountered an amazing series of "can'ts" relating to His touch on our lives. Consider this...

You can't be saved without the Holy Spirit

In John 3, Jesus entertained a night visitor. In my mind's eye, I picture the Lord and Nicodemus standing together at the edge of a rooftop, under a sky blazing with stars. The cooling night wind whispers in the leaves of the olive trees, and Jesus turns to His distinguished guest with a statement that must have seemed utterly shocking.

"Most assuredly, I say to you, unless one is born again, he cannot see the kingdom of God.... Unless one is born of water and the Spirit, he cannot enter the kingdom of God" (John 3:3, 5).

Jesus told Nicodemus that one of the indispensable ingredients for salvation was the Holy Spirit. (I personally believe the reference to water is a reference to the Word of God. We'll look into that more carefully a little bit later.) But don't miss the crucial truth here: There are two important aspects regarding salvation, the Word of God and the Spirit of God. Nobody finds salvation without the Spirit of God.

You can't have assurance without the Holy Spirit

In Romans 8:16, Paul told the Romans, "The Spirit Himself bears witness with our spirit that we are children of God."

Wherever I travel across this country, people ask me, "How can I have assurance of salvation? How can I know that I really belong to Christ?" There are many Scriptures to which we can point, but the bottom line is this: if you have the Holy Spirit living within you, that Spirit testifies with your spirit that you are a child of God. It is the inward witness of your faith.

Most of us have had the experience of saying to people, "I don't know exactly how to explain it, but I *know* I'm a Christian."

"Well, how do you know?"

"I just know inside."

We know inside because the Spirit of God is there, witnessing to our assurance. Somewhere within us, a voice whispers, *"You are Mine. You are not your own. You belong to Me."*

You can't become holy without the Holy Spirit

The book of Galatians tells us that the characteristics of holiness are ninefold. "The fruit of the Spirit is love, joy, peace, longsuffering, kindness, goodness, faithfulness, gentleness, self-control" (Galatians 5:22–23).

It isn't your fruit; it is the fruit of the *Spirit*. It isn't something you go out and try to do. You can't sit in a chair and try to work yourself up to peace or love or patience or goodness. It grows within you—a natural product of the Holy Spirit living within you. He produces these qualities in your life.

You can't understand the Bible without the Holy Spirit

Does that surprise you? Years ago, I remember hearing Campus Crusade founder Bill Bright teaching on the Holy Spirit. In his message, he told about a man to whom he'd been witnessing. One of this man's problems with the Christian faith was that he'd tried again and again to read the Bible but couldn't make any sense of it.

Then the man received Jesus Christ and came back to visit Dr. Bright a week later. He had an amazing story to tell. During that week's time, he said, it was as though somebody had rewritten his Bible. Suddenly the Scripture came alive to him. Understanding broke into his thoughts like quick lightning strikes.

How had it happened? The Teacher had taken up residence within him. What had once been obscure and confusing now pulsated with meaning, encouragement, and hope.

I read about a man who carried a tiny little folder in his Bible case. Inside the folder was a microfilm reproduction of the entire Bible. All 1,245 pages and 773,746 words were printed in a space just a little more than one square inch. But the man couldn't make out one word of it! Holding it up to the light or putting it against a dark background wouldn't help. Only with the aid of a high-powered microscope could it be read. This need for an outside source of help to read a microfilm reproduction of the Scriptures reminds me of the difficulty people outside of Christ have in understanding the Bible.

Listen to what Paul said to the Corinthians: "The natural man does not receive the things of the Spirit of God, for they are foolishness to him; nor can he know them, because they are spiritually discerned" (1 Corinthians 2:14).

Just prior to this verse, Paul wrote, "Now we have received, not the spirit of the world, but the Spirit who is from God, that we might know the things that have been freely given to us by God" (1 Corinthians 2:12). That means that Christians, who have the Spirit of God living within them, have an inward interpreter who helps them to understand what the Bible means.

A companion.

A tutor.

A private instructor.

He illuminates our minds. The scales fall off our eyes, and all of a sudden, the Spirit of God makes it possible for us to understand God's truth.

You can't understand the Bible without the Holy Spirit. What's more…

You can't pray without the Holy Spirit

Ephesians 6:18 (NIV) instructs us to "pray in the Spirit on all occasions with all kinds of prayers and requests." Romans 8:26 says, "Likewise the Spirit also helps in our weaknesses. For we do not know what we should pray for as we ought, but the Spirit Himself makes intercession for us with groanings which cannot be uttered."

Yes, we know that all things work together for good to those who love God (Romans 8:28). But within that same context we are told that we don't even know how we ought to pray. What was Paul saying? He was telling us that although we can be sure of the *ultimate,* there will often be times when we don't know what to make of the *immediate.*

We know that all things work together, but sometimes on the road to the "all things" we find ourselves so confused or filled with pain that we don't even know how to pray.

I heard a story about a pastor who frequently visited a woman who was dying from cancer. One day she told him, "I'm so often racked with pain that it's hard for me to gather my thoughts to pray. Even when I rally a little from the influence of the medication, my mind is still so dull I can't concentrate for any length of time."

He looked at her a moment and said, "Well, you can groan, can't you?"

"Oh yes," she replied, "my days are spent doing that."

"Well, never mind that you can't formulate prayers," the pastor told her. "The Holy Spirit translates your groans into eloquent petitions and presents them to the Father!"

Can you remember moments in your life when your heart was so heavy or your thoughts seemed so confused that you couldn't even find words to speak to God? Sometimes, even though we're on our knees in an attitude of prayer, we can only manage to sigh or groan or whisper the Lord's name. And in those moments, according to Paul, the indwelling Holy Spirit takes our sighs and our groans and brings those prayers to God. He understands the inward turmoil in our life. He is the searcher of our hearts, and He knows us better than we know ourselves.

Have you ever asked someone to pray for you because of a crushing heaviness you felt in your life, but didn't even know how to word your request? Sometimes what we feel inside seems so hard to explain. Sometimes we're embarrassed to admit to an old problem or habit that has been with us for years. But we don't have to explain anything to the Spirit of God. We don't have to search for words. He knows very well what plagues us and burdens us and worries us and presses in our spirit. And He spreads those very things out before the Father's throne.

You can't serve God without the Holy Spirit

The Bible says that when you're saved you not only get the Giver, you get the gift! You receive the Spirit of God, but you also receive the gift of the Spirit. Every Christian, at the moment of belief, is immediately endowed with a special gift of ministry. You will find those gifts listed in Romans 12, in Ephesians 4, and in 1 Corinthians 12.

Paul writes:

> There are different kinds of service, but the same Lord. There are different kinds of working, but the same God works all of them in all men. Now to each one the manifestation of the Spirit is given for the common good. (1 Corinthians 12:5–7, NIV)

In other words, every believer has a gift of the Spirit. We are to exercise that gift so that everyone else profits. I exercise my gift, and it helps you. You exercise your gift, and it helps me. And all of us using our giftedness help the whole body to grow.

But you can't do that without the Spirit of God. The whole concept of service is based on the spiritual filling of the believer. No wonder so many of God's people are running around with their tongues hanging out trying to figure out how to survive! Do you know what we're trying to do? We're trying to accomplish a supernatural task in the energy of our own weak flesh. It's insanity, but we do it all the time! We run like crazy trying to keep up with everything, trying to dot every i and cross every t, and we fall into bed at night totally exhausted. There is no human way for us to do the work of God in the energy of the flesh. If the Spirit of God doesn't fill us with His power, we're attempting the impossible.

Please read these next words very carefully: The Christian life isn't hard; the Christian life is *impossible*. And unless the Spirit of God indwells us, we can't serve.

You can't witness without the Holy Spirit

Remember how the disciples waited in the upper room? They were waiting because they were *told* to wait. Jesus had said: "But you shall receive power when the Holy Spirit has come upon you; and you shall be witnesses" (Acts 1:8).

I would hate to measure all the damage done in the church throughout the years by people who tried to witness in the energy of the flesh without the Holy Spirit. I could chronicle a few of those disasters if you'd like the sad details. We literally drive people away from God by our own self-effort, however well-intentioned. Our presentation may be pleasant, our statements may be doctrinally sound, and our logic may be seamless. But unless we move and speak in the power of the Holy Spirit, our words will ring hollow. We will have nothing to share.

When some people make up their mind to witness, it's as though they were on some sort of quota system. Every Thursday night they set out to gather so many scalps in the neighborhood. I'm not saying we shouldn't have goals, but I am telling you that attempting to win people to Jesus Christ without the empowering of God's Spirit is an impossible task.

Carl Lawrence relates the eyewitness account of two young Chinese ladies in their early twenties who came to faith in an underground church in China. Just a week or so later, the pair reported that God had called them to go minister on Hainan Island off the southern coast of China—thousands of miles away.

Other believers cautioned them to get some training before they went, but they felt compelled by the Spirit to go right away and just trust God to lead them. The elders of the house church finally agreed to give them their blessing and sent them out.

Two years later the young women came home and reported to the church. They reluctantly got up and apologized for their "unfruitful work." It seemed they had won *only* three thousand people to Christ and started *only* thirty house churches. The astonished leaders asked what method they had used. All the women could reply was, "Every morning we just read God's Word and prayed, asking the Holy Spirit to teach us what to do. Whatever God's Word spoke to us, that is what we did. We only obeyed."

The Holy Spirit is the very center and the energy of all witnessing.

I could give you many more "can'ts." These represent just a few core thoughts. We have an indwelling source of power in the person of the Holy Spirit, who empowers us to live the Christian life. Without Him, we're about as useful to God's kingdom as an unplugged toaster.

DON'T BE IGNORANT ABOUT THE HOLY SPIRIT

J. Vernon McGee used to love to quote verses that began like this: "Be not ignorant, brethren...." The venerable old expositor used to say that the largest denomination in the world was the "Ignorant Brethren."

The Bible tells us again and again not to be ignorant:

We're not to be ignorant concerning God's righteousness. (Romans 10:3)
We're not to be ignorant about the future of Israel. (Romans 11:25)
We're not to be ignorant regarding spiritual gifts. (1 Corinthians 12:1)
We're not to be ignorant about the destiny of believers who have died. (1 Thessalonians 4:13)

Sometimes we're asked questions like the one found in 1 Corinthians 6:19: "Do you not know that your body is the temple of the Holy Spirit?"

In essence, Paul was saying to the Corinthian believers, "Don't you know? Haven't you heard? Hasn't it sunk in yet? Are you ignorant that the Holy Spirit dwells in you?"

The book of Acts takes us through a time of transition from Old Testament thinking into the concepts of the church, the body of Christ. In Acts 19:1–2 (NIV), Paul came upon some Ephesian disciples in desperate need of instruction.

While Apollos was at Corinth, Paul took the road through the interior and arrived at Ephesus. There he found some disciples and asked them, "Did you receive the Holy Spirit when you believed?" They answered, "No, we have not even heard that there is a Holy Spirit."

When I read those verses recently, they hit me with a whole new meaning. It occurred to me that those words could be written over a large section of the church: *We haven't even heard that there is a Holy Spirit.* There's nothing wrong with not knowing...unless you have a chance to know and don't try to know! But the Bible has been given to us so we *can* know, and the whole Book is filled with truth—both in picture in the Old Testament, and in actual practice in the New—of the Holy Spirit's ministry in the believer's life. There is no reason to be ignorant!

DON'T BE INDIFFERENT TOWARD THE HOLY SPIRIT

Some people aren't necessarily ignorant, they're just indifferent.

"Don't talk to me about the Holy Spirit. I haven't got time for that kind of stuff. Just give me the basics. I'm a meat 'n' potatoes Christian. I don't want any exotic vegetables or salads or fancy desserts. The teaching on the Holy Spirit is out there on the edge somewhere. People are always arguing about it, and I don't want anything to do with it. It's too controversial."

Some time ago I heard about a woman who came home one evening and rushed breathlessly through her front door. "I've got it!" she hollered at her husband. "I've got it!"

The man of the house peered over the top of his sports pages. "What did you get?"

"I got the Holy Spirit."

"Martha," he said, "you left the motor running in the car, and gas is now at a buck-forty-five a gallon." That was his Spirit-filled response to his Spirit-filled wife. His thought was, "Don't tell me about the Holy Spirit. The real issue is the idling car engine and the price of gas." That's the way a lot of people feel about the Holy Spirit. They just don't want to be bothered.

DON'T TAKE THE TEACHINGS TO EXCESS

When we hear that the pastor is going to talk about the Holy Spirit, some of us get a little nervous. Why? Because most likely we've run into people who have a problem with overindulgence on that subject. They get wild and crazy. They go on and on about their experiences. While we may be a little apathetic toward teaching on the Holy Spirit, they're out in the ozone somewhere. And you say, "The Holy Spirit! Man, I don't want any of that! That's weird stuff."

No, it isn't.

It's sad when people take important truths like these to unbiblical excess. It has the effect of driving us away from the very teaching that will give us the greatest joy and fulfillment in our lives! The Holy Spirit was given to us to help us grow into Christlikeness. He belongs to *all* of us.

THE ATTRIBUTES OF THE HOLY SPIRIT

Who is He? Who is this mysterious "third person" of the Trinity? First of all...

The Holy Spirit is a person

Now, when I say that, you might reply, "I thought you said He was a spirit."

I did say that. He is a person, and He is a spirit.

"Wait a minute," you reply. "You can't be a person *and* a spirit."

Oh yes, you can! Think about it. Perhaps you've recently lost a loved one to death. What do you say about that person? You say, "he died" or "she died." But that person didn't die. That person's *body* died. The individual who lived in that body went on into eternity, either into the presence of the Lord or away from His presence. If that person knew the Lord, and you know the Lord, you will be reunited one day. Why? Because the person isn't the shell that the person lives in. The person is the individual within the shell.

When the body goes into the grave, the *person* goes to be with the Lord. That is why Christians have great hope at a time of death. That man didn't die. That dear woman didn't die. That boy or girl or little baby didn't die. He or she simply retired their old house and went to be with God. That is our hope. That is what sustains us when sorrow threatens to crush us. Paul says that we do not "sorrow as others who have no hope" (1 Thessalonians 4:13).

When my father-in-law passed on, my wife, Donna, and I went to the funeral home with Donna's mother to view his remains. Before we walked into the viewing room, I felt the need to remind this dear lady of something she already knew. "Annie," I said, "we just have to remember that *Bernard isn't in there.* He's not in that room. He's not in that coffin. He's already with God. What we'll be looking at in there is just the empty house where he used to live."

We believe that a person lives and goes on even after death. Therefore we know that a person is a spirit being. The Bible says, "God is Spirit, and those who worship Him must worship in spirit and truth" (John 4:24).

Some people think the Spirit of God is an "influence." They refer to Him as an "It," as though He were some vague, impersonal force—like the earth's electromagnetic field. No, the Holy Spirit is a *person*. Psychologists and sociologists tell us that the attributes of personality are threefold. A person must have intellect, emotion, and will. That's why animals aren't "persons." You may think your cat has a great personality, but I need to tell you that under the normal, true, psychological definition, your cat doesn't have a personality. All right? I'm sorry if that comes as a shock to you. You may think I'm just after cats. (And you may be right!)

Let me tell you how we know the Holy Spirit has personality.

The Holy Spirit possesses intellect

First Corinthians 2:11(NIV) says, "For who among men knows the thoughts of a man except the man's spirit within him? In the same way no one knows the thoughts of God except the Spirit of God."

The Spirit of God *knows*. Therefore, He has intellect.

The Holy Spirit possesses emotion

Listen to Romans 15:30: "Now I beg you, brethren, through the Lord Jesus Christ, and through the love of the Spirit, that you strive together with me in your prayers to God for me."

The Holy Spirit *loves*. Therefore, He has emotion.

The Holy Spirit possesses will

He has volition. Notice what it says in 1 Corinthians 12:11: "But one and the same Spirit works all these things, distributing to each one individually as He wills."

Just stop and think for a moment. The Holy Spirit is a person because He thinks, He feels, and He wills. Those are the building blocks of personality. The Holy Spirit is a person. But there is something that's even more important than that.

THE HOLY SPIRIT IS GOD

He is the third member of the Trinity, the triune God, one God in three persons. A lot of people don't treat the Holy Spirit like He is God. They treat Him as though He was almost God...but not quite.

An important passage in Acts 5 illustrates His deity in a startling way. Ananias and his wife had conceived a plot concerning some funds they had accumulated. When they were questioned about their story, they had agreed to "fudge" on the truth.

> But Peter said, "Ananias, why has Satan filled your heart to lie to the
> Holy Spirit and keep back part of the price of the land for yourself?...
> You have not lied to men but to God." (Acts 5:3, 4)

Peter called Him the Holy Spirit at the top of the passage, and he called Him God at the bottom of the passage. Ananias lied to the Holy Spirit. The Holy Spirit is God. (And Ananias was in big trouble!)

The Holy Spirit is clearly linked with the Trinity in Scripture. In Matthew 28:19 we are told, "Go therefore and make disciples of all the nations, baptizing them in the name of the Father and of the Son and of the Holy Spirit." We are to bring those three persons of the Trinity together in the baptismal formula, because all three are God. The Holy Spirit is associated—on equal footing—with the other two members of the Trinity.

In Paul's benediction to the church at Corinth, he said, "The grace of the Lord Jesus Christ, and the love of God, and the communion of the Holy Spirit be with you all. Amen" (2 Corinthians 13:14). What a ringing statement of the triune God!

The Holy Spirit is God because He is actually called God. He is God because He is associated with God in the Trinity. And thirdly, He is God because He does the actions of God. Everything God does, the Holy Spirit does.

God creates. The Holy Spirit creates.

God performs miracles. The Holy Spirit performs miracles.

How did Jesus get into this world? The angel told Joseph, "Joseph, son of David, do not be afraid to take Mary as your wife; for that which has been conceived in her is of the Holy Spirit" (Matthew 1:20, NASB). So the virgin conception is of the Holy Spirit.

Finally, the Holy Spirit has all the attributes of God. He is omnipotent, He is omniscient, He is omnipresent, He is holy, He is wisdom, He is love. Everything you say about God, you can say about the Holy Spirit.

I want you to know who it is I'm talking about! He is a person, and He is God. And we had better treat Him that way when we talk about Him. We had better treat Him with reverence. We had better understand that the One who indwells us is *God* living within us.

THE ADVANTAGES OF THE HOLY SPIRIT

So we have all of this biblical teaching on the person of the Holy Spirit. But why should we care? Why should we devote all these pages to talking about Him? There must be some better topic to discuss.

If this book were on the family, many people would respond because everybody needs help with their families. There are whole shelves of books in Christian bookstores about how to be a great dad, how to be a loving mom, how to relate together as father to daughter, mother to son, husband to wife, and on and on. Yes, but...what will help the family more than anything else is to have a father and mother and children who are filled with the Holy Spirit, who understand more and more what it means to be controlled by the Spirit of God. That would change families! That would revolutionize family life.

When it comes to our human relationships, we're quick to put Band-Aids on the sore places, aren't we? We're forever fixing this and fixing that. We're always looking at the external and trying to respond to the most immediate and pressing problems. Maybe one of the reasons why we have to keep doing that all the time is because we're only addressing the symptoms and never get to the source of the problem.

What is that source? We need wisdom beyond our own wisdom. We need power beyond our own power. We need insights and perspective and balance and persevering love beyond our own insights, perspective, balance, and love. What we really need is God living inside us, guiding us, counseling us, and pointing out the way we should walk.

What we need is the Holy Spirit.

Let me describe just a few advantages of having this wonderful resident within us.

He permanently enters us

You don't have to ask, plead, or beg the Holy Spirit to come into your life. You don't even have to wait, as the disciples once "tarried" in the upper room. He permanently enters into our lives the very instant we believe.

The Holy Spirit isn't the second blessing; He is part of the *first* blessing—the great blessing of salvation. He comes to take residence within you the moment you receive Jesus as Savior and Lord. John 14:17 describes Him as "the Spirit of truth, whom the world cannot receive, because it neither sees Him nor knows Him; but you know Him, for He dwells with you and will be in you."

What a pregnant truth that is!

This is what Jesus was saying to the disciples before He went back to heaven and before the Day of Pentecost. Watch carefully how Jesus spoke about the old and new ways of relating to the Holy Spirit. He said first of all, "He dwells WITH you." That describes the Spirit's ministry to believers *before* Pentecost. But then Jesus added, "And He will be IN you." That was the ministry He would have in their lives *after* Pentecost.

"The Spirit has been with you all this time," Jesus was saying, "but not many days from now, He will be *in* you."

No wonder Paul said to the Corinthians, "Do you not know that your body is the temple of the Holy Spirit?" (1 Corinthians 6:19). Why was He telling them that? Because the Corinthians were doing things with their bodies that were an embarrassment to the Holy Spirit. They were living lives divorced from the awareness of His holy presence within them.

Perhaps you've found yourselves at certain crossroads recently where you didn't know whether you should go to a certain place or participate in a certain activity because you are a Christian. The fact is, where you go, the Holy Spirit goes with you. So before you go, you'd better ask Him if He *wants* to go. And whatever He tells you, you do it.

Many Christians don't even think about that. They just drag the Holy Spirit everywhere into all kinds of things that are dishonoring to His first name, which is *Holy.*

The Holy Spirit permanently indwells you. If you grasp that concept, it could have a life-changing impact on you. He is there. He is in you. He will never leave you.

He powerfully equips us

Acts 1:8 reminds us that we receive *power* when the Holy Spirit enters our lives.

One of the terrible things we do in the church—whether through guilt, or through secular methods of motivation, or through business techniques that we pull right out of the world—is to try to do the work of God in the energy of the flesh and with the world's methods. We don't teach people about being powerfully equipped with the Holy Spirit. We secularize the church by taking business administration principles, baptizing them, and putting them into the church.

What do we end up with? Form without power. Empty instruction. A framework that is as dead as old bones. I've had a hand in that sorry operation myself at different points in my life. You probably have, too. Out of ignorance, or maybe just out of our strong desire to make things happen, we undertake to do something that belongs to God, neglecting to use His methods or seek His empowerment. The end result will always be the same; we'll be left with a sense of frustration and failure and fatigue. It comes with the package.

But oh, what a wonderful thing it is to step back from our busy and sometimes frantic activities now and then and say, "God, by Your Holy Spirit, You just take this and powerfully equip us. Enable us by Your power, or we won't accomplish a blessed thing."

He personally encourages us

The Holy Spirit's other name is Comforter. That is my favorite name for the Holy Spirit. The word *comforter* is a Greek word, *paraclete,* and it is the same word that is translated "encourage."

The Holy Spirit is my Encourager. He comes and puts His arm around me when I am discouraged, and He encourages me.

Yes, there are times when this pastor loses his perspective a little and becomes discouraged. I may have actually slipped into depression once or twice (not recently, thank the Lord). It's the same with anyone in leadership; sometimes you feel as though there is hardly anywhere to turn. You just have to get alone with your Bible, get down on your knees in prayer...and then the Spirit of God comes to bring encouragement to your heart. I've had that experience time and again. It is almost (almost!) worth experiencing the dark and heavy times, because the encouragement of God's Spirit is so sweet. I praise God that the Holy Spirit is my Comforter and Encourager and Helper.

One thing for sure...the world certainly isn't out to bring encouragement to our lives. Have you noticed that? You go to church on Sunday for spiritual nurture because if you don't come together with God's people, you just won't make it through the week! Between Monday and Saturday the whole system is set up to beat you up and beat you down.

Evangelist Miles McPherson recently spoke to my son's college football team. Miles takes no prisoners. When he gives the gospel, he just gives it straight. He tells people if they don't believe, they're going to hell. And in a chapel service, the night before a big game, he asked those who wanted to receive Jesus Christ to raise their hands. About 60 percent of the guys on the team responded to that invitation.

The next day, they played the big game and lost by a single point. The coaches blamed the loss on the religious chapel. The following week they announced the beginning of Sunday morning practices. The kids would no longer be allowed to attend church.

That's the world in action. Is that natural? No, that isn't natural. It is *unnatural* in the sense that it doesn't belong to the kingdom of God. It belongs to the kingdom of this world. So what do you do when things like that start to gang up on you? You've got to encourage yourself by the Holy Spirit. You've got to have the Holy Spirit within you to help you because if you don't, you'll end up discouraged.

In the troubling days before David sat on the throne of Israel, when he was still being chased from pillar to post by Saul and his troops, the young man came to a day that was one of the darkest of all. While David and his men were away from their home base, a band of raiding Amalekites swept into the camp and carried away all of the men's wives, sons, and daughters.

In a move so typical of human nature, the men blamed David, the guy in charge, for their loss. And David knew very well that his soldiers were angry enough to pick up rocks and stone him to death. What would you do?

Here's what David did:

> Then David was greatly distressed, for the people spoke of stoning him, because the soul of all the people was grieved, every man for his sons and his daughters. But David strengthened himself in the LORD his God. (1 Samuel 30:6)

David went with an empty bucket to the Well that will never go dry. You and I have such a Well. We have a resource for the very darkest of days. It is a resource that many of us don't know very much about, and I'm excited for the opportunity to open Scripture with you and tell you more about that Holy Spirit who lives within you. God gave Him to you, and the Bible says He is the seal of your redemption.

He not only wants to be the resident in your life, He wants to be the president of your life. When you get saved, He becomes the resident. But there is a time when all of us get tired of trying to accomplish this Christian life business in our own way and in our own strength, and we elect Him *president* of our life. When that happens, the joy of His presence fills us as never before.

How did Paul put it?

> May the God of hope fill you with all joy and peace as you trust in him,
> so that you may overflow with hope by the power of the Holy Spirit.
> (Romans 15:13, NIV)

In Europe some years ago, a young man and a young lady were walking together along a river, discussing a mutual acquaintance. The young man said, "Mary has what I call a radiant personality."

"That's right," his friend agreed. "But how do you account for it?"

Just then they came to a wide vista on the path, with a long view of the river flowing along in the sunlight. Pointing to the opposite bank, the young man said, "See that impressive old castle over there? When I was a small boy I loved to sit right here in the evenings and look at it. I knew what was going on inside by the number of lights that were burning. If only a few people were home, just a faint glimmer filtered through the windows. But when company came, many lamps were lit and the place became a thing of beauty. One time when a member of the royal family visited, the entire castle was illuminated! I've never seen such brilliance."

Then, turning to his companion, he said, "I think that's the only way I'm able to explain Mary's personality. She's entertaining a Royal Guest!"

In the pages that follow, we're going to explore God's Word and learn more and more about this tenant, this Royal Guest who has set up housekeeping in the very center of our lives. If you are even half as encouraged and excited as I am to open up these doors of truth, you will find it is well worth the journey.

The forgotten God will never again slip from your memory.

Chapter Three

BORN OF THE SPIRIT

THE TRUTH ABOUT SECOND BIRTHDAYS

*H*ow far back does your memory reach? When you *s-t-r-e-t-c-h* your mind backward as far as you possibly can, through the dim and misty swirl of images and snapshots and emotions, what's the earliest picture that comes up on the screen?

Many older people who can't remember your name (that you just told them) or tell you what they had for lunch yesterday have crystal clear memories from when they were very small. They can describe certain childhood days in great detail: sights, sounds, conversations, smells, feelings. If you had the time and patience to listen, they could recreate it for you as though it happened yesterday.

How about you? Can you remember your first day of school? Kindergarten? The nursery at church? Anything before that? Can you remember being in the crib? Can you remember sitting in a high chair? Some people can! What's the earliest birthday you can remember? Most likely, you don't remember the day you were born. But you can still be fairly certain you *were* born (otherwise, what are you doing here?).

Can you remember the day you were born again?

Can you remember when you were born of the Spirit?

What does that mean, you ask? Good question. It's the logical place to begin any discussion of the Holy Spirit. That is the first time we have any knowledge of the Spirit's working in our hearts. Before we talk about being filled with the Spirit or walking with the Spirit, it only makes sense to talk about being born of the Spirit. After all, you have to be born before you can walk or talk or feed yourself.

Our Lord Himself introduces the subject in the first eight verses of the third chapter in the gospel of John. Under the cover of darkness, Jesus was having an intimate conversation with one of Israel's foremost teachers, a Pharisee named Nicodemus. Most likely, Nicodemus came at night because he didn't want to be observed speaking to this strange young rabbi from Nazareth. It wasn't "politically correct" to be seen with Jesus. And yet...there was something about Him that drew this Jewish leader—something about His words that touched Nicodemus's heart.

I imagine this teacher to have been middle-aged to older when this conversation took place. I can close my eyes and see him stroking his long gray beard in great perplexity. He had come to discuss points of theology.

But all Jesus seemed to want to talk about was birthdays!

> Nicodemus...came to Jesus by night and said to Him, "Rabbi, we know that You are a teacher come from God; for no one can do these signs that You do unless God is with him."
>
> Jesus answered and said to him, "Most assuredly, I say to you, unless one is born again, he cannot see the kingdom of God."
>
> Nicodemus said to Him, "How can a man be born when he is old? Can he enter a second time into his mother's womb and be born?"
>
> Jesus answered, "Most assuredly, I say to you, unless one is born of water and the Spirit, he cannot enter the kingdom of God. That which is born of the flesh is flesh, and that which is born of the Spirit is spirit. Do not marvel that I said to you, 'You must be born again.' The wind blows where it wishes, and you hear the sound of it, but cannot tell where it comes from and where it goes. So is everyone who is born of the Spirit." (John 3:1–8)

Nicodemus was undoubtedly a very bright man. He was a respected scholar who had studied the Scriptures for most of his life. But in this conversation, he was lost at sea. *Born again? Born of the Spirit?* What was this young Teacher talking about?

According to Jesus, everyone needs to have two birthdays. We all get one, right? When we're young we like everybody to remember it. Then when we get older, we're hoping everyone forgets it! (Funny how that works.) But the truth is, the second birthday is just as important as the first. The first is for time, the second is for eternity.

But as it happens, this second birthday is one most people know very little about. And it is a birthday that is frequently confused with religion or good works or twelve steps or self-improvement plans. But if you read the Scripture carefully, you will discover that the new birth is nothing less than a *miracle*. It is an extremely important, supernatural work that takes place within the heart of a person when he or she comes into a relationship with God.

The Bible calls that being born anew, being born again.

That term, "born again," has come on some hard times. I remember when it was something of a sacred term. But now it has moved into common jargon. We hear of "born again" baseball careers or "born again" political campaigns. But however the world cares to use or abuse those words, the expression itself is a very strong biblical term. It is a term from which we get the spiritual concept of "regeneration."

I'm sure you remember, from the teaching you hear at Christmastime, that the birth of Jesus was a miraculous birth. But did you ever think of it as a picture of the spiritual birth every one of us needs to undergo if we're to know God? It's true. In Luke 1:35, we read:

> And the angel answered and said to [Mary], "The Holy Spirit will come upon you, and the power of the Highest will overshadow you; therefore, also, that Holy One who is to be born will be called the Son of God." (Luke 1:35)

Christian faith believes this truth, that Jesus Christ was born of a mother without a father, that He was born of the virgin Mary, and that the conception that took place within her womb was from the Holy Spirit. The Holy Spirit came upon her, and she was with child.

I suggest to you that the same imperceptible, invisible work takes place every time a man or woman or little one comes to faith in Christ. In a mysterious, invisible way, the Holy Spirit comes to work upon the heart, and from the inside out, there is a spiritual regeneration.

A miracle.

A new birth.

A second birthday.

Now, some are going to say, "Well, Pastor Jeremiah, I go to church all the time, I've worked hard, given my money, and done lots of good things." Yes, but in this discussion, I'm not talking about the outside of your life, *what you do;* I am talking about the inside of your life, *what you are.* I'm not talking about those external things that might give someone reason to believe you're "a good person."

What I am saying is this: we need to make very, very certain we understand these words Jesus spoke to Nicodemus that balmy night in Palestine some two thousand years ago. Why? Because our eternal salvation is tied to these words!

There is only one way into the kingdom of God, and that is through receiving Jesus Christ as personal Savior. When we do receive Him, the Spirit of God is the One who causes us to be "born again."

We don't give that miracle anything close to the credit it deserves. When it comes to witnessing to my faith in the Lord Jesus, I don't feel the pressure to try to manipulate or push people into a relationship with God. Why? Because it wouldn't work. I have no power to do that at all. All I can do is to make the message plain and trust the Word of God, as it is applied by the Spirit of God, to do its work within the heart of an individual.

I can't create children for God. But I can sometimes be in the birthing room to witness the miracle!

WHY THE NEW BIRTH IS ALL-IMPORTANT

There are some very good reasons why that second birthday is so very important. I would like to suggest a couple of them to you.

Without a new birth, you're living in the wrong family

You say, "Pastor Jeremiah, I'm in God's family. Don't you believe in the fatherhood of God and the brotherhood of man?"

Well…it depends on what you mean by those words. Yes, I do believe God is a Father, and I believe that we who are Christians are brothers. But I also believe there is another family that people don't talk very much about. On one occasion, Jesus spoke to some religious people and bluntly told them that they were of their father the devil. (See John 8:42–44.)

It is an awesome thing to hold a precious, innocent little child in your hands. But we need to understand that when children are born into the world they aren't—by their first birth—born into God's family. They are born into the family of the world. They have to experience a *second* birth to get into the family of God. I don't know how to say this nicely, but if you haven't had a second birth, you aren't in God's family.

The Bible says the new birth is essential to becoming a part of the family of God. Jesus made that clear in John 3:6, when He said, "That which is born of the flesh is flesh, and that which is born of the Spirit is spirit." In other words, whatever is born of the flesh can *only* be flesh. It can't be anything else. There has to be a spiritual birth in order for the Spirit of God to live within a person and for that individual to become a part of the family of God.

Romans 8:8 tells us that "those who are in the flesh cannot please God." If you are in the flesh, if you haven't been born in the Spirit, all you can ever do is what the flesh can do. What can the flesh do?

It can make itself look good.

It can posture.

It can speak fine-sounding words.

It can do good deeds.

It can dress up on Sunday and go to church.

It can do all manner of outward things in order to be recognized, lauded, and appreciated. *But it can't do anything to get into the family of God.* The only way you can get into the family of God is through a spiritual birth.

Jeremiah 17:9 tells us that the flesh can't be trusted. "The heart is deceitful above all things, and desperately wicked." In the Hebrew language, that small phrase, "desperately wicked," could well read, "incurably wicked."

Humankind has a heart disease beyond cure! Science could never find a remedy for this ailment if they searched ten thousand years. We hear, of course, about how our society continually labors to find cures for humanity's maladies. We're trying to cure the political system. We're trying to cure our educational system. We're trying to cure sociological problems in our culture. We're trying through the United Nations to cure the world of wars and massacres. We've been at it for many years, but the cures don't work because the basic problem is incurable! The only cure for a sin-diseased human heart is to be born a second time into a different family.

One of the wonderful things about getting into that family is that you get everything that goes with being a part of it. I love this promise from 2 Peter 1:3–4 (NIV):

His divine power has given us everything we need for life and godliness through our knowledge of him who called us by his own glory and goodness. Through these he has given us his very great and precious promises, so that through them you may participate in the divine nature and escape the corruption in the world caused by evil desires.

The Bible says that when we receive the new birth, we receive a new nature, and that nature is from God. Without that new birth, you are outside of God's family.

Without the new birth, you are condemned as a sinner

You say, "That's awfully harsh. That's condemning and judgmental. I don't like the sound of that."

I'm not sure I like the sound of it either, but it happens to be the truth; I didn't make it up. It is right from the Word of God. The Bible says that without the new birth we are lost and we are condemned. It doesn't say we're going to be condemned; it says we *are* condemned. That is our status before God.

Consider John 3:18: "He who believes in Him is not condemned; but he who does not believe is condemned already, because he has not believed in the name of the only begotten Son of God." That's pretty clear, isn't it? The Bible says that until we believe in Jesus Christ, it isn't a matter of "someday" we're going to be condemned. We are *already* condemned. And the only way we can get out from under that condemnation is through Jesus Christ.

Oh, what a terrible predicament I'm in! Who will free me from my slavery to this deadly lower nature? Thank God! It has been done by Jesus Christ our Lord. He has set me free. (Romans 7:24–25, TLB)

In these days of increased capital punishment, there have been many condemned men—and women—who have sat in their holding cells on death row, waiting their last summons. On that final day and in that final hour of their lives, their last hope is for a call from the governor. They hope against hope to hear that phone ring and to hear the governor's voice on the other end of the line say, "I have decided to commute your sentence." It doesn't happen very often, but it *could*.

Please allow me to give you the good news. Even though humanity stands rightfully condemned before a holy God, the phone is ringing. Your pardon is assured. But you have to pick up the phone and answer it. You have to receive that pardon.

The first verse of Romans 8 states: "There is therefore now *no condemnation* to those who are in Christ Jesus." After you experience spiritual birth, after you are born into God's family, you are no longer condemned. Until you have that new birth, you are condemned already. That is the clear and simple teaching of the Bible.

A condemned man on death row can really only hope to have his death sentence commuted to life imprisonment. But in Jesus Christ, our sentence was not just commuted, it was paid in full. Somebody already died in our place, paying the debt we could never pay. The list of our charges and offenses was nailed above His cross (Colossians 2:13–14). And more than that, we're not only pardoned, we have become part of God's family.

Can you imagine that governor getting on the phone and saying something like this to a condemned young man on the other end of the line?

"Son, I have good news for you. Yes—take a minute to catch your breath. Listen now—your death sentence has been commuted. And not only that, but by the authority vested in my office, I offer you today a full and complete pardon. You are a free man. Wait—there's more. Not only am I setting you free, I've made arrangements to adopt you into my own family. We have a room waiting for you in the governor's mansion and you'll always have a place at our table. Welcome home, son."

I don't know about you, but I'd call that amazing grace! Here is how Paul put it:

Now, therefore, you are no longer strangers and foreigners, but fellow citizens with the saints and members of the household of God. (Ephesians 2:19)

The apostle John marveled over the same astounding truth:

See how very much our heavenly Father loves us, for he allows us to be called his children—think of it—and we really are! (1 John 3:1, TLB)

The beautiful thing about the new birth is that when you are born into this family of God, you immediately come into possession of everything God wants you to have. Everything—all that you need—is a part of the new birth.

Let me give you an illustration. We've been traveling around a little bit these last few days, and we've had our new grandson and his parents with us. I love that little boy. He's so tiny I can hold him in one hand. I can't describe the love that's in my heart for our grandson, David Todd Jeremiah. I was thinking about this the other day. We were traveling in an airplane together, and David Todd was there, and next to him was his father, my son, David Michael Jeremiah.

As I looked at David Todd, I said to my wife, Donna, "Is it possible that our children were ever that little?" Was there really a time when I could hold David Michael in one hand? They grow up so fast you forget that at one time they could have ever been that tiny.

As I was looking from David Todd to David Michael, a thought struck me. Everything that David Michael is was once part of a package as small as David Todd. Everything that David Michael became was in that package that was David Michael when he was born. And everything that I am as a believer was a part of what God gave me when I was born into His forever family. On that wonderful second birthday, I had all of the genes, all of the characteristics, all of the potential, all of the wonderful promises that are mine. As I grow up in Christ, I develop those, and I become in reality all that I was in potential when I was a little baby.

Sometimes people get exasperated with immaturity in God's people, and as pastors, we do that, too. But there's nothing wrong with immaturity in a baby Christian! What do you *expect* from a baby? Perfect manners? Perfect diction? Perfect understanding? Perfect cooperation? Of course not! You expect them to be immature. You expect them to act like babies. They'll talk gibberish and flail around and make messes, and there's nothing wrong with that. But if they grow to be forty or fifty years in the faith and they're still talking gibberish, flailing around, and making messes, there is something wrong with that.

When you are born into the family of God, you arrive with everything God wants you to be and everything you will be. It just continues to grow and mature, as a physical child grows and matures.

The new birth is essential for you to become what God wants you to become. You can't be in the family of God, you can't have a relationship with God, and you can't avoid condemnation unless you are born of the Spirit.

THE EXPERIENCE OF THE NEW BIRTH

How does one become born again?

"Well," someone might reply, "you've got to try. You've got to work hard at it."

Really? How hard did you work when you were being born as a baby? I don't think you worked very hard at all. It was your *mother* who labored. You were just along for the ride! (You might remember that, come Mother's Day.)

No, you can't be born again through your own effort. Listen to Ephesians 2:5–6: "Even when we were dead in trespasses, [He] made us alive together with Christ (by grace you have been saved), and raised us up together, and made us sit together in the heavenly places in Christ Jesus."

The new birth has to happen to you from a force outside of you. *God* has to do this in you. You can't do it of yourself. There is no such thing in the universe as do-it-yourself salvation. In fact, in the first letter of John in the New Testament you'll find the phrase "born of God" seven times. That is what the second birth is. It is to be born of God.

> To all who received him, to those who believed in his name, he gave the right to become children of God—children born not of natural descent, nor of human decision or a husband's will, but born of God. (John 1:12–13, NIV)

The new birth is God-birth. It is you being born of God through His Spirit, filling the vacuum that exists in every human heart outside of Christ. God never intended for His creatures to be one-dimensional; God never intended man and woman to be just flesh. God wanted His prize creation, humankind, to be fully dimensional, and that includes the spiritual dimension. So He put within us this vacuum that can only be filled by Himself. And what do we do? We spend our whole lives trying to stuff everything we can into that vacuum, until, at last, out of frustration, we finally come to realize the only thing that fits there is God Himself. And when we invite Christ to come into our life, we become a fully dimensional creature of God.

Perhaps you have experienced that yourself recently; you can talk with vivid color about the difference that Christ has made in your life.

The new birth is something that can only take place through the agency of almighty God. You can't, of your own volition, of your own strength, of your own efforts, bring about the new birth. It doesn't matter what church you attend. You might be Baptist, Presbyterian, charismatic, Pentecostal, Catholic, or whatever you call yourself, but if that is all you've got, you're still one-dimensional. Until the Holy Spirit comes to live within you because you have invited Christ to be your Savior, you haven't been born again.

The good news about being born again is something I've reveled in as often as I've thought about it. If you are born twice, you only have to die once, but if you have only been born once, you've got to die twice. It works like this: if you have been born physically and spiritually, the only death you have to worry about is physical death—and you might even beat that rap if the Rapture comes!

But if you've only had one birthday, if you haven't been born again into the family of God, you not only have to die physically, but after you die physically, you have to face the second death—which means eternal separation from God. That's spiritual death. That's what Scripture calls the second death.

Physical death is the separation of the soul from the body, and spiritual death is the separation of the soul from God. You don't want to mess with the second death, I promise you. And the way you escape the second death is to be born twice.

THE EXPLANATION OF THE NEW BIRTH

How does it happen? How can it be?

That's the same question Nicodemus had! He was trying to put it all together in physical terms, and it wasn't working for him. Can a man get back into his mother's womb to be born a second time? Let's hope not—for everyone's sake! Jesus, in essence, told Nicodemus that the new birth was a mystery. As I've pictured these two men talking, on a flat rooftop out under the stars, it's easy to visualize a night breeze rustling the leaves of a nearby tree as Jesus spoke.

"It's like the wind," Jesus told him, gesturing to the dark shapes of the trees.

"The wind blows where it wishes, and you hear the sound of it, but cannot tell where it comes from and where it goes. So is everyone who is born of the Spirit." (John 3:8)

There is a little play on words here in this Scripture. The word for *Spirit* and the word for *wind* are the same word in the Greek language. *Pneuma.* We get our term pneumatic brakes from that word...*air* brakes.

"Do you feel that wind?" Jesus was saying. "Can you hear it whisper in the leaves? Can you feel it tug at your hair and your robe? Sure you do. But what do you *see*, Nicodemus? You can't see the wind at all. It's invisible. You can only see what the wind does. You can see that it has an effect. You know that it is coming from this direction and going that direction. But you can't see the wind."

Well, guess what? You can't see the Spirit, either. But you can see what the Spirit does! You know where the Spirit comes from and where He is going and the impact that He has upon one's life.

Jesus didn't try to explain the action of the Spirit much beyond that, so how would I explain Him? Yet at the same time, I think there are some things we need to know about this new birth—truths important to our hearts today.

TWO AGENTS IN THE NEW BIRTH

This new birth is the result of two agents acting together.

Listen to what Jesus said: "Unless one is born of water and the Spirit, he cannot enter the kingdom of God" (John 3:5).

As for the second part, we don't have any doubt about the fact of who the *Spirit* is. The Bible says, "If any man has not the Spirit of Christ, he is none of His." It says, "No man can call Jesus Lord except by the Spirit." You can't get saved without the Holy Spirit. You may think you are getting to Christ without the Holy Spirit, but the Holy Spirit is doing His work in your heart. You just don't see it, so it isn't difficult to understand that Jesus is talking about the Holy Spirit in John 3:5.

Some people have taken the reference to water in this verse to mean you have to be baptized in order to be saved. But that isn't what Jesus meant at all. What, then is the "water" Jesus speaks of here? Look at some verses with me, and let's see if we can end up on the same page together.

Psalm 119:9 says: "How can a young man cleanse his way? By taking heed according to Your word."

In Ephesians 5:25–26 (NASB), Paul states that "Christ also loved the church and gave Himself up for her; that He might sanctify her, having cleansed her by the washing of water with the word."

The Word of God has a washing, cleansing action...like water.

James 1:18 associates the Word of God with the new birth. "Of His own will He brought us forth by the word of truth." In other words, we were brought into existence spiritually by the Word of God.

First Peter 1:23 adds this: "Having been born again, not of corruptible seed but incorruptible, through the word of God which lives and abides forever."

The water is the Word! So what Jesus said to Nicodemus was, "Nicodemus, you can't be born again unless you are born of the Spirit and of the Word."

It works like this. The Word of God is preached or read or heard, and then the Spirit of God takes the Word of God and strikes fire in the heart of a person, and they become a Christian.

Not long ago somebody asked me, "Why do you just keep on preaching the Bible, Jeremiah? Don't you know any other book? Don't you get tired of preaching the same old book?" Here's my answer: I'm hoping to live to be about a hundred and fifty, but even if I do, I'll only just be getting started in the Word of God!

I am continually awed and amazed at how God takes His Word and uses it to bring people to faith in Jesus Christ.

Someone else asked me, "What's your evangelism program at your church?"

Well, we try to encourage people, teach people, and reach out to people, but we have a continual stream of people coming to Christ in this church, and there is only one explanation for it: We have a steady diet of the Word of God. It is the Word of God that is continually bringing men and women to faith in Jesus Christ.

If you don't use the Word of God to communicate spiritual truth, you take the Holy Spirit out of His environment. The only way the Holy Spirit can work in the heart of a person is if the Word of God is present. If you take the Holy Spirit out of His arena, then you've got nothing! But when the Word of God is preached, the Spirit of God uses that Word to bring about conversion in the heart of a person.

I just keep preaching the Word of God. I'm never going to quit preaching the Word of God. In Nashville, Tennessee, a man came up to me and said, "I'm a long-haul trucker, and I got saved listening to you on the radio. I started listening to you once when I was flipping the dial around. Then I started listening every day—and one day it just all made sense to me. I pulled my rig off at a rest stop and gave my heart to Jesus Christ."

What brought this man to conviction of sin and salvation? It was just the

Word of God. I couldn't do it; I'd never seen the guy before in my life. He didn't find the new birth through listening to David Jeremiah fill airtime on the radio with chatter. No, through the medium of radio, he heard the Word of God, and his life was transformed!

If I told you all the experiences like that that we've cataloged—just from preaching the Word of God—you would understand as I understand that the most powerful thing I can ever do is to teach the Word of God. God blesses His Word, and it is impossible for anybody to be saved without the Spirit of God and the Word of God. You have to be born of the water and of the Spirit.

EXAMPLES OF THE NEW BIRTH

Take a minute and think of your best candidate for the following category: Least Likely to Become a Christian.

Who would it be? An ayatollah in Iran? A Mormon bishop in a dark suit? That crusty old agnostic professor you had in college? A profane army drill instructor? An alcoholic relative, who scoffs at the name of Jesus?

If you had asked that question of the believers in the early chapters of Acts, Saul of Tarsus would have made every list, just ahead of Caiaphas the high priest, Herod Antipas, and nudging out Tiberius Caesar in Rome.

In Acts 9, Dr. Luke, the author of the book of Acts, relates Christ's confrontation with this unlikely candidate for grace. Saul was a religious fanatic who thought he was gaining points with God by persecuting, jailing, and brutally exterminating Christians. It was his passion. He chased Christians down in Jerusalem, and he was willing to travel to distant cities to carry out his campaign of terror.

On his way to Damascus to pursue yet another group of believers, he suddenly came face to face with the risen Christ and fell to the ground. He had a miraculous experience with almighty God because the Spirit of God and the Word of God came together, and he was born anew. He got up off his face, and after his blindness went away—you know the rest of the story—he became the greatest influence for the gospel of Jesus Christ who ever lived, apart from Christ Himself.

How do you explain that? How do you explain the greatest enemy of Christianity becoming its greatest advocate and apologist? He had a miraculous inside-out experience. He was born again spiritually, and through that new birth, his life was transformed. Yet this conversion seemed so remarkable and unbelievable to the disciples in Jerusalem that they remained afraid of this former enemy for a time. Even those who had walked with Jesus Christ had trouble believing such a man could be so totally, radically, dramatically changed.

I could go through the New Testament, but I could also go through more recent history as well, and tell you about the people I know. I might even put *you* on my list. You might well say of yourself, "I wasn't running toward God; I'd been running away from Him for years. But somehow, the Spirit of God and the Word of God came together in my life and I found salvation. I was born into the family of God. My life has been totally changed!"

Only eternity will allow us enough time to hear all the stories of the glorious life changes that have taken place as men and women and boys and girls all over the world have experienced regeneration through the new birth into God's family.

I'm not talking about personal reformation.

I'm not talking about cleaning up your act.

I'm not talking about turning over a new leaf.

I'm not talking about trying to do better.

I'm not talking about going to some religion class or catechism or spiritual seminar.

I'm talking about a grade A miracle. I'm talking about being born into a new family, whether you are fourteen, forty-four, or eighty-four.

It isn't completely different from physical birth. The baby doesn't conceive itself...it is accomplished through the mother and the father. The baby doesn't birth itself...it is done through the mother's labor. Though there is a process that leads up to the birth, there is a moment in time—and I noticed at the hospital how they write down the exact time—when the baby is *born*. They think it is very important to note the day and the time.

It was three o'clock in the morning when our grandson, David Todd Jeremiah, came. I remember the time very clearly.

People come to me and say, "Pastor Jeremiah, I'm born again."

I say, "Good! *When* were you born again?"

They respond, "I don't know. I guess I've always been born again."

Now, wait a minute. What if someone asked you how old you are? Would you tell them, "I don't know. I guess I've always been born"? I don't think so! You're not that old.

We don't have any problem understanding that physical birth begins at a point in time, do we? There's a process leading up to the time of physical birth, and sometimes it's a very hard process. In the human realm, it is nine months. But there is a point in time when the birth takes place. The doctor or nurse looks up at the clock and writes that time down. And I am convinced by the Word of God that there is also a point in time when we pass out of spiritual death into life, and we are born anew.

You say, "I know that has happened to me, but I don't know what day it was. I didn't write it down."

You don't need to worry. God took notice of it! And just as your physical birth was recorded in the hospital where you were born, so your spiritual birth was recorded in heaven in a book called the Lamb's Book of Life. You just need to know there was a specific day and hour when it occurred. It's a far different thing to say, "I don't know when it happened because I don't remember writing it down" than it is to say, "I've always been a Christian."

You can't "always" have been born again. You were born again at a point in time when the Spirit of God and the Word of God came together in your heart and you embraced Jesus Christ in faith.

Has that happened to you? Have you been born again?

Can you look back at a time in your life and say, "Pastor Jeremiah, that's when it happened. I don't remember exactly what month it was, but it was back in that period of time, and I heard the Word of God and asked Christ to come into my life."

If you can't remember or if you aren't sure, that's all right, too. You can take care of it today! You can make this your debut, your birthday party, your day when you declare, "I am a Christian, and if I wasn't sure about it before, I'm sure about it today because I'm going to put my faith in Christ."

Yes! *Why not?*

It's a beautiful day for a birthday!

Chapter Four

THE BAPTISM
OF THE SPIRIT
WHERE LIFE IN CHRIST BEGINS

*T*he French word for "shoe" is *sabot*.
That fact, I suppose, might help you if you happened to be shopping in Paris.

But there's something else about that word that might affect you a little more directly at some point in your life. The practice of throwing a wooden shoe into machinery to stop it and to spoil the work was referred to by the French as *sabotage*.

It's amazing how much havoc a single tossed shoe—wooden, canvas, or otherwise—can create in a finely tuned operation. Maybe you've had the experience of having someone sabotage something you'd been planning on or working toward. But it may not have been a piece of discarded footwear that wrecked your hopes or dreams. It may have been a few destructive words launched at a sensitive moment. A distortion here, an exaggeration there.

Sabotage of that sort goes on even within the church. Somebody throws a theological shoe into the works, and it causes spiritual havoc and paralysis in the ministry.

It has always been Satan's desire to sabotage the work of God. Did you know that? Wherever and whenever he can, he wants to throw a shoe into the works. Christians feel the intensity of his attacks because we represent God to the world. Every Christian ought to be prepared for whatever it is that the enemy of our soul is up to.

Back in the 1930s, the French built the massive Maginot Line between France and Germany to hold off future attacks by Hitler's Nazi army. Not such a bad idea, I suppose. But when the attack came, it was by air, and it was by way of Holland and Belgium where there was no line. France had been aware of her enemy and even prepared for an attack, but her preparation was inadequate. She didn't sufficiently know her adversary, so the attack caught the nation unprepared, and France fell to Hitler's blitzkrieg.

Most Christians are aware of Satan's desire to destroy the work of God. But few of us ever stop to evaluate his power or consider his methods and "devices," as Scripture puts it. We get taken off guard.

If I were Satan, my first attack would be on the supply line of the Christian, which is the Word of God. And in fact, since the beginning of time, this has been Satan's target. Every single problem in the church of Jesus Christ can be traced to this particular issue. When people get unhooked from the Word of God, they begin to be destroyed by the enemy. They're vulnerable to sabotage!

There is only one way any of us can grow and be upheld in our walk with the Lord, and that is through ingesting the meat of God's Word.

Satan has had two different strategies to take the Word of God away from us. In years past he has used liberal scholars to cast doubt upon the Word. For generations the church has withstood barrage after barrage from those who have sought to dilute, undermine, compromise, and discredit the Bible. And the church *has* withstood these attacks. Through the years we have proven beyond any doubt that what we have in our hands is indeed the infallible, inspired, inerrant Word of God.

I don't fear that line of attack upon God's people today. If we want to know the truth, we can know it. The evidence is before us. We stand convinced that God's Word is true, and we're not going to be sabotaged by disbelieving His Word.

But Satan has more than one *sabot*. He isn't just given to one approach. If he can't take the Word of God away from us by undermining its authority, he will take us away from the Word of God by giving us another basis of authority. Satan has developed just such a substitute, and it seems to have a great attraction for many people.

It's called "experience."

People become so wrapped up in their spiritual experience that they no longer look to the Word of God for their authority. Their experience becomes the determining force in their lives.

Two groups, then, are vying for our minds—but with the same end in view.

The liberals would take the Bible away from us, and those who hold to the experiential view would take us away from the Bible. Whenever experience is placed on the same level as Scripture, the experience group will always overrule biblical interpretation.

A lady once said to me, "You always come back to the Word of God. Well, I don't care what the Word of God says. I've received more from my experience than I ever got from the Bible, and I'm going to go with my feelings." Dangerous decision! When you go with your feelings, you're on a trip that ends on a dead-end street.

I want to remind you that what I'm stating in this chapter is not "what I feel." I want to walk with you through the Word of God and show you what the Bible says about a very controversial issue that often comes up among believers.

HAVE YOU RECEIVED THE BAPTISM?

If you've been around Christian circles long enough, you've probably had someone ask you, "Have you received the Baptism yet?"

Baptism? What baptism? Water baptism?

"No," they reply, "there's something more than that. I mean the baptism of the Holy Spirit. Have you gotten it yet?"

How shall we answer that question?

It really doesn't make any difference whether you're charismatic, Presbyterian, or Nazarene. It doesn't make any difference what your background is. The only thing that really matters is, *What does the Word of God say?* That ought to be our standard. If it isn't, we're in a heap of trouble, because then it's just my opinion versus someone else's opinion.

Life is too short to get tangled up in strong opinions, don't you agree? Let's see what God's Word says, and draw our conclusions from there. In the next few pages, we're going to search the Scriptures together. I pray that God will use this brief chapter not only to instruct us, but to strengthen our hearts and remind us again what a wonderful thing God has done for us in His gift of eternal salvation.

Through the faithful teaching of God's Word and through our understanding of Scripture, we can know what God is up to when we read about the baptism of the Holy Spirit.

First of all, let me remind you that I'm not on the attack in this issue. I don't have a chip on my shoulder. I don't have any desire to put anyone down. What

I would like to do is what Secret Service agents do when they're learning how to detect counterfeit money. Those who teach people how to recognize bogus bills never have the trainees study counterfeit currency. They always have them study the originals. They make their agents so aware of every nuance of the original bill that they can spot the funny money right away.

In the same way, you and I don't need to invest a lot of time and emotional energy attacking what other people believe. We just need to make sure we know what *we* believe, and when we know that, we'll be able to tell when something isn't in sync.

BAPTISM OF THE SPIRIT DECLARED

You might be surprised to learn that the whole doctrine of the baptism of the Holy Spirit rests upon just eleven passages in the New Testament. These verses fall into categories.

Prophetic passages

These are verses that speak about the baptism of the Holy Spirit as something still in the future. All of these Scriptures are in the Gospels except for one, which is in the first chapter of Acts.

In Matthew 3:11, John the Baptist says, "I indeed baptize you with water unto repentance, but He who is coming after me is mightier than I, whose sandals I am not worthy to carry." Who is that? The Lord Jesus Christ. "He will baptize you with the Holy Spirit and fire." That same wording is basically repeated in Mark 1:8 and Luke 3:16.

In John 1:33, John the Baptist speaks again: "I did not know Him, but He who sent me to baptize with water said to me, 'Upon whom you see the Spirit descending, and remaining on Him, *this is He who baptizes with the Holy Spirit.*'" The Spirit descended on Jesus Christ that day in the Jordan River. And this same Jesus, John tells us, is the One who will baptize with the Holy Spirit.

In Acts 1:5 there is another reference to the baptism of the Holy Spirit. From the perspective of this verse, too, the event is still future—but not very far in the future! Notice what it says: "For John truly baptized with water, *but you shall be baptized with the Holy Spirit not many days from now.*"

All of these passages were spoken by John the Baptist or by Jesus Christ, with this prophecy: On a coming day, Jesus Christ will baptize His people with the Holy

Spirit. That prophecy was fulfilled. If you read Acts 2, you discover that when the Day of Pentecost had fully come, the house where the believers were praying was shaken, and they began to speak in languages they hadn't learned so that everyone who came to that meeting heard the gospel in his own language. Then Peter preached his great sermon and thousands rushed into the kingdom of Christ.

The Bible says the Spirit of God came down, and the church was baptized by the Spirit into the body of Christ. That was the birthday of the church. The church was born in Acts 2, and the birthday gift from God in heaven was the Spirit of God Himself, who came at that moment to live within the heart of every single person who was in the church.

Pentecostal passage

Only one passage fits in this category, and it is Acts 11:16.

> "Then I remembered the word of the Lord, how He said, 'John indeed baptized with water, but you shall be baptized with the Holy Spirit.'"

In the verse prior to this one, Peter says that the Spirit baptism is what took place "at the beginning" on the Day of Pentecost. Peter looks *back* at that event and states that what happened that day was indeed the baptism of the Holy Spirit.

Perhaps we can look at it this way:

Gospels	Acts 1:5	Acts 1:8	Acts 2	Acts 11:16
Future Event	Future Event	Future Event	Birthday of Church; Baptism of the Holy Spirit	Past Event

Purpose passages

The prophetic passages tell us it is *going* to happen.

The Pentecostal passage tells us it *has* happened.

The purpose passages tell us *what it means* to be baptized by the Holy Spirit. These verses bring us right into the heart of the teaching.

Romans 6:3–4 says, "Or do you not know that as many of us as were baptized into Christ Jesus were baptized into His death? Therefore we were buried with Him through baptism into death, that just as Christ was raised from the dead by the glory of the Father, even so we also should walk in newness of life." We were baptized into Jesus Christ by the Holy Spirit.

Colossians 2:12 tells us: "[You were] buried with Him in baptism, in which you also were raised with Him through faith in the working of God, who raised Him from the dead."

Galatians 3:26–28 is very important to this subject: "For you are all sons of God through faith in Christ Jesus. For as many of you as were baptized into Christ have put on Christ. There is neither Jew nor Greek, there is neither slave nor free, there is neither male nor female; for you are all one in Christ Jesus."

On the Day of Pentecost, God Almighty began a whole new work that took individuals from diverse backgrounds, races, and regions and made them *one*. One in Jesus Christ. What a mighty work! What could have accomplished such a thing? It was the baptism of the Holy Spirit.

Ephesians 4:5 says there is one Lord, there is one faith, and there is one baptism. That, too, is a reference to Spirit baptism.

But (as we will soon see) the key passage in all of Scripture on this subject is 1 Corinthians 12:13.

> For by one Spirit we were all baptized into one body—whether Jews or Greeks, whether slaves or free—and have all been made to drink into one Spirit.

THE BAPTISM OF THE SPIRIT DEFINED

Let me give you a definition of the baptism of the Holy Spirit. Ready?

The baptism of the Holy Spirit is the imperceptible work of God by which the believing sinner is placed by the Holy Spirit into the body of Christ at the very moment of his conversion.

If you are saved, you received the baptism, because the baptism is what happens at the moment of your conversion when the Holy Spirit places you in the body of Christ. *When you received salvation, you got all of the Spirit there is for you to get.* The real question is this: Does the Spirit have all of you?

Over a hundred years ago, a group of pastors had gathered to make plans for a citywide evangelistic campaign. One of the men suggested that the well-known evangelist D. L. Moody be considered as a possible speaker. The pastors discussed the suggestion and several spoke favorably about Moody. But one young preacher who wasn't in favor of inviting the evangelist stood up and said with a note of sarcasm, "From the way some of you talk, you'd think Mr. Moody had a monopoly on the Holy Spirit."

The room became quiet. Then another pastor spoke up.

"No," he mused, "Mr. Moody doesn't have a monopoly on the Holy Spirit. But the Holy Spirit does have a monopoly on Mr. Moody!"

The fact is, you have all of the Holy Spirit that you will ever need. He came to live within you at the instant of your salvation. The very process of the Spirit of God placing you in the body of Christ is the baptism of the Holy Spirit. Nothing more, nothing less. And if we don't understand that, we'll find ourselves looking and looking for something we already have.

An absentminded friend of mine frequently searches high and low for his glasses—only to find them resting on his nose! What a terrible thing to go through one's life always searching for something that you already possess. It would be like being saved and then pleading with God to give you eternal life. You already have it. Why would you ask Him to do that?

I want you to get this straight. The baptism of the Holy Spirit is the wonderful, original equipment of every single believer, because we were all, at salvation, placed into the body of Christ.

Now, having said that, I want you to note some points that will help you understand what this major life event is all about.

The baptism of the Holy Spirit is a unique work of God

The baptism of the Spirit is unique to this church age in which you and I are living. Did you know that the Holy Spirit didn't baptize people in the Old Testament? He came upon people individually, but He did not baptize them into the body of Christ. Not until the Day of Pentecost did the Holy Spirit perform this major work. This was a special gift from God to His church. How privileged we are to be living in this age of history! Peter tells us that the Old Testament prophets longed to see and better understand these days in which you and I are living (see 1 Peter 1:10–12). How ungrateful we are to take our wonderful position and privileges for granted!

Remember that when Jesus was getting ready to go back to heaven He said, "I have to go back to heaven, because if I don't go back, the Holy Spirit can't come to you. It's *better* for you that I go away so that He can come!"

And so...at the very moment determined in eternity past...He came.

With a rush. With fire. With a sound like a mighty wind. With great power.

It is unique that the Holy Spirit came only at the Day of Pentecost. The Holy Spirit may have been available for all those people who lived up until Acts 2, but He did not baptize them into the body. Yet ever since that day, it has been the experience of every single person who has trusted in Jesus Christ that when they get Christ, they get the Spirit of God to live within them. Praise His name!

The baptism of the Holy Spirit is a universal work of God

If anyone is a believer in Jesus Christ, he has received the baptism of the Holy Spirit. He doesn't have to wait for it, long for it, seek for it, pray for it, plead for it, agonize over it, or stay awake through the night worrying about it. If he's a Christian, *he has been baptized* by the Holy Spirit. Again, please understand that this isn't simply my studied opinion. Please don't ever tell someone, "This is what David Jeremiah says." Who am I? I'm just an echo. All I do is repeat what I have studied in the Word of God.

What does the Word say? "For by one Spirit we were all baptized into one body—whether Jews or Greeks, whether slaves or free—and have all been made to drink into one Spirit" (1 Corinthians 12:13).

It doesn't matter what your tradition might say.

It doesn't matter what your denomination might say.

It doesn't matter what your mom or dad or Aunt Harriet might say.

It doesn't matter what the preacher on TV might say.

The only thing that matters is this: Did you put your trust in Jesus Christ? If you did, you have been baptized into the family of God. As my friend Jim Cymbala says, "God only has one family." He doesn't have two or three. He has just one. If you are a Christian you are in that family, and the process by which you were placed in that family is what the Word of God calls the baptism of the Holy Spirit.

Some people believe you have to be really "spiritual" to be baptized by the Holy Spirit. They believe that the baptism is reserved for some special, higher-echelon class of believers. Not so! Remember where our key verse is located: in the book of 1 Corinthians. Have you read that book recently? It isn't a book about superspiritual people at all. Far from it!

Some time ago, a friend of mine started a Christian bookshop and called it The Corinthian Bookstore. Why would anybody start a bookstore and call it *that*? I called my friend on the phone and asked, "Brother, have you read Corinthians lately? Just whom are you planning on catering to?"

The book of 1 Corinthians is all about factions, about fleshly carnality, about unyielding pride, about bitter battles in secular courts, about falling down before idols, about forgetting the purpose of the Lord's Table, about failing to comprehend the truth of the Resurrection. One whole chapter, chapter 5, tackles the problem of incest and the church's refusal to deal with it.

The book of 1 Corinthians is about carnal Christianity—people who aren't even close to living the way God intended. Yet in a letter to that very group of believers, Paul wrote that we are *all* baptized by the Spirit into the body of Christ. Every single, undeserving one of us.

This unique baptism of almighty God isn't about how spiritual you are. It's about how gracious *He* is! God has included *all of us* in the baptism of the Holy Spirit. We are in the body of Jesus Christ, and we are in it forever.

The baptism of the Holy Spirit is an unrepeated work of God

It is unrepeated in this sense: you only get it once, and you never need it again. Now, you may question me at that point. Perhaps you've been taught that you had to get saved and then keep yourself saved, and if you didn't keep yourself saved, you had to get saved all over again. If you believe that, then yes, you would have to have the baptism twice, or three times, or a thousand times, or however many times it was necessary. But if you've ever read the book of Romans, worked your way through the eighth chapter, and *still* believe that, I don't know what else to say to you. If our salvation depended upon us, then yes, we could lose it. But since salvation depends on God, *there is no way.*

God doesn't give us imperfect gifts. He has given us eternal life, and we shall never perish. Since that is true, when you get the gift of eternal life you also get the baptism of the Holy Spirit, and you never get it again. You don't *need* it again because you already have it! You should not expect the baptism of the Holy Spirit except at the moment of salvation. There isn't one command in all of the New Testament to seek for the baptism of the Holy Spirit. Why would there be? It isn't something you seek for. It's something that God does for you.

There isn't one instruction in Scripture on how to get the baptism of the Holy Spirit. Though you search the New Testament from beginning to end, you'll never find it. You don't need to be instructed on how to get something that has been done for you.

The baptism of the Holy Spirit is unrepeated.

God doesn't stutter.

The baptism of the Holy Spirit is an unemotional work of God

You may have been hoping for a mighty surge of emotion. You might have been wishing for some great spiritual high in your life you could tell your grandkids about. But the only emotion you have when you get the baptism is the emotion you had when you got saved. And that moment may or may not have impacted your emotions.

Some are deeply, profoundly moved in that instant when they step from darkness into light. Many others feel nothing at all—or only the quiet assurance about the rightness of their decision.

I've learned that our response to salvation usually runs along the lines of our personality. If we're emotional people, we'll have an emotional response. If we're more cerebral people, we'll understand it, accept it, feel grateful for it, but not necessarily be emotional about it.

When you got saved, several things happened to you that very moment. How many of them did you *feel*? Did you walk into your workplace the next day and say, "You know what? I felt adopted yesterday" or "I felt sanctified" or "I felt sealed"? You see, these are doctrinal things. These are truths about what God does for us at the moment of our salvation. We spend the rest of our lives studying His Word and learning about them.

What a wonderful realization! The moment you were saved, you were baptized into the body of Christ. It was unemotional except for the emotion you expressed at the time you received salvation.

The baptism of the Holy Spirit is a unifying work of God

Here's the part I really like.

The most significant result of the baptism of the Holy Spirit is the fact that it unites in the church all those who have put their trust in Jesus Christ. Before

Pentecost, before Acts 2, it was impossible for Jewish and Gentile and Samaritan believers to get along together. They didn't have any unity. They had no *basis* for unity. But the Bible tells us that now, through the gift of God's Holy Spirit, Jew and Gentile, bond and free, male and female, are all united in one organism called the body of Christ.

The church is God's great idea. He didn't want us to be separated. He doesn't want us dividing and subdividing ourselves, drawing lines and erecting walls. The great passion and heart's desire of Jesus Christ in John 17 was that redeemed men and women would be ONE. Someone has said that when we get to heaven, nobody is going to ask us if we're Methodists or Baptists or Lutherans. All tags will come off. If you go to hell, they'll burn off! So it isn't going to make any difference either way. Tags are unimportant. We make them so important down here!

No, I'm not saying we should give up our distinctives. But you'd better not let those "distinctives" or "traditions"—however timeworn and chiseled into granite—destroy the fellowship of brother with brother and sister with sister! The Lord of the church takes oneness very, very seriously. He died a horrible death to make it possible.

Now what is it that makes us one? It is the baptism of the Holy Spirit. We were all baptized into the body of Christ. This is an amazing truth. Yet we've let this mighty doctrine drift so far from its biblical moorings in recent years that we've lost the *wonder* of it. The wonder of the baptism is that out of every tongue and tribe, out of every nation, and out of every country, God has brought together people who have put their trust in Him. And He has made them all part of His one body, the body of Christ, which is going to be forever in heaven, glorifying God.

That's truly awesome. What an amazing, gracious God!

In France during World War II, a young soldier had been killed in battle and some GIs took his body to a local cemetery. When they got to the cemetery the priest said, "Sorry, boys, you can't bury your friend here if he isn't a Catholic."

The soldiers were discouraged by the rebuff, but they didn't give up. They decided to give their buddy the best burial they could manage just *outside* the cemetery. They dug a grave right outside the fence and laid their friend to rest. The next morning, however, when they went to pay their last respects at the grave before their unit moved on, they couldn't find it. After looking for nearly an hour, they asked the priest about it.

"Well," he said quietly, "for the first part of the night, I stayed awake, sorry for what I had told you. And the second part of the night I spent moving the fence."

That is exactly what Jesus did! He moved the fence and included every believer in God's promises. For every believer who received Christ by faith, apart from the works of the law, He opened a common ground for all people to come to know God. This means there is no reason for Christians not to love each other. Christ has removed all human distinctions. In the one new man there is a new quality of existence. There has never been anything in all the world like the body of Christ. He moved the fence to include us all and make us one.

I have traveled and preached in many places. It's such an exciting experience to go to a place I've never been before and meet people I've never seen—and may never see again until heaven. I usually have no clue what church they come from or what their background might be, but we come together around the Word of God and our love for Christ, and we are immediately just like a family. Who can explain that instantaneous bond we feel for one another?

You won't find the same dynamic among any other group. Two Republicans or two Democrats meeting in a café in some European country won't experience it. Neither will any grouping of unionists, libertarians, carpenters, plumbers, podiatrists, Shriners, environmentalists, agnostics, or atheists. There isn't anything like that fellowship in all the world. That is the body of Christ in truth, and the baptism of the Holy Spirit is what makes it happen.

THE BAPTISM OF THE HOLY SPIRIT DISTINGUISHED

Many Christians confuse the baptism of the Spirit with the *filling* of the Holy Spirit. These are not synonymous terms. The filling of the Holy Spirit and the baptism of the Holy Spirit are totally different theological truths. Don't get them mixed up.

Perhaps the following chart will help you distinguish the difference between these two important works of the Holy Spirit.

THE BAPTISM OF THE HOLY SPIRIT	THE FILLING OF THE HOLY SPIRIT
Happens once	Can happen many times
Past event	Present reality
For all believers	For obedient believers
Never commanded	Commanded
Positional truth	Experiential and practical
Places the believer in the body of Christ	Enables the believer to live for Christ
Holy Spirit resident in the life	Holy Spirit is president of the life
Brings into union	Brings about communion
Identification with Christ	Fellowship with Christ
Instantaneous act of God at salvation	Repeated experience when a believer is fully yielded
Finished work	Improves the product
Greek grammar in 1 Corinthians 12:13	Greek grammar in Ephesians 5:18
Aorist tense: once for all action of the Holy Spirit	Present tense: continuous ministry of the Holy Spirit
Single act of placing into body of Christ	Diverse ministry in helping believers to serve the body of Christ

Please understand that the baptism of the Holy Spirit is your original equipment. It comes "standard" with salvation...it isn't "optional." If you are a Christian, you have been baptized by the Spirit.

So the next time somebody says, "Have you received the baptism?" just smile and reply, "Oh, yes. I've had it ever since I was saved. I received the baptism of the Holy Spirit as a birthday gift from my heavenly Father the moment I was born again."

Secondly, there seems to be some confusion about the baptism and the *indwelling* of the Spirit. The baptism of the Holy Spirit places the believer in the body of Christ. The indwelling of the Holy Spirit just says He's still there, living in perpetual residency within you. Though baptism and indwelling occur at the same moment, baptism is a once-for-all action and is related to union with Christ. Indwelling is a continuous work of the Spirit of God and is focused on His presence in the believer. So don't confuse the baptism and the indwelling.

Some say there is a relationship between the baptism of the Holy Spirit and speaking in tongues. I don't know how many people have asked me about that.

For many years now, it's been a "shoe in the machinery," causing strife, dissension, and untold confusion.

One fact in Scripture is very clear: the baptism of the Holy Spirit does *not* produce tongues-speaking. Paul said in 1 Corinthians 14:5 that not everyone spoke in tongues. But you just read with me in 1 Corinthians 12:13 that *everyone* had been baptized by the Holy Spirit. Not once in either letter to the church at Corinth did Paul exhort those who had not spoken in tongues to seek to do so. It isn't a necessary sign of the baptism of the Holy Spirit. If it were, then every single Christian would have to speak in tongues because every single Christian has been baptized in the Holy Spirit. We would all have to speak in tongues, and if we didn't, we wouldn't be saved.

Yet that is the very misconception that is so often taught: if you haven't spoken in tongues, you're told, you haven't received the baptism. Friend, that teaching is plain wrong. It is simply untrue. The Bible teaches no relationship between the baptism of the Holy Spirit and speaking in tongues.

What I want you to understand more than anything else is that the baptism of the Holy Spirit isn't the "second blessing." It is the *first* blessing. So many people are looking for the second blessing and can't enjoy the first one.

The *filling* of the Spirit is the second blessing and the twentieth blessing and the one hundredth blessing!

The *baptism* of the Holy Spirit isn't the second work of grace; it is rather what God has accomplished by placing you in the body of Christ. You are in His family. You are a believer. He has made you new and unique, and He has given you a whole new sphere of existence.

When we have baptisms at the church where I pastor, it is a picture of what the Spirit does. Just as the individual is totally immersed in the water, so you were totally immersed into the body of Christ at the moment of salvation. You became one with Him, and you were uniquely changed.

Have you ever watched a movie or television drama where someone is placed in the witness protection program? Somebody who has agreed to witness for the prosecution is told, "If you bring testimony against this guy in the Mafia (or whoever it might be), we'll take it upon ourselves to protect you from harm."

Here's the way it's supposed to work: The witness is taken out of his environment and placed in a totally new environment. He is given a new name, a new house, a new job, and a new identity. Yes, he still has the same voice. He still has the same body and the same personal characteristics. But his whole identity has been changed. He has been placed in an entirely new environment.

That's what happened to you when you received salvation. That is God's witness protection program. He picked you up out of where you were, and He set you down in a whole new environment, under His protection.

That new environment is called the body of Jesus Christ.

So yes, if you know Jesus Christ as Savior, you most certainly do have "The Baptism." You have it! And you have it forever.

Let Satan throw his shoes around however he will.

It really doesn't matter, as long as *your* feet are standing on solid ground.

Chapter Five

THE FILLING
OF THE SPIRIT

A NEW POWER WITHIN

henever I think of a "new power within," I flash back to an incident from my youth that made a great impression on me. We lived in a neighborhood in Dayton, Ohio. I was a paperboy at the time, and my paper route went up and down Woodman Avenue and into some subdivisions along that road.

Living in one of the subdivisions was a very mean man. Mean in every sense of the word. He did everything he could to terrorize the kids who lived in his neighborhood, and if you happened to be a paperboy there, you delivered papers on that street as fast as you could and got out of there.

One Halloween, some of my buddies and I decided it was time to get even with this guy. We cooked up some elaborate tricks, because we knew Mr. Nasty wouldn't be giving out any treats! (I won't tell you the trick we attempted, because I don't want to contribute to anyone's delinquency.)

When my friends and I got to his door that night to spring our gag, however, it became immediately apparent that somebody had already been there before us with the same idea. Old Mr. Nasty was primed and ready. As we rang the doorbell, ready to play our joke, he suddenly ran around from *behind* the house, screaming at the top of his lungs, and firing tin cans at us like missiles. Mr. Nasty may have been old, but he was also fast! He was almost on top of us before we knew what was happening.

I have never been so afraid in all my life. You have to understand, it was dark…it was Halloween…we were doing something we knew we shouldn't be doing. And the old man's yelling could have awakened the dead. I took off from that front porch like a cat with a mousetrap on its tail. I tore down the cul-de-sac, raced across Woodman Drive, and leaped clean over a high fence I could not jump again if I tried for a hundred years.

There was a new power within David Jeremiah that night—a power unlike anything I'd experienced before! After that incident, I knew the meaning of "wings on your feet." I *soared* over that fence, hit the ground in full stride, and sprinted through a cornfield as fast as my Converse All-Stars could carry me.

The next day I found myself back at the scene of the crime, delivering my papers.

And I saw the fence.

I remember standing there in awe, straddling my bike and thinking, *How in the world did I ever jump over that fence? Man, I should go out for track.* Oh, the wonders of adrenaline! Filled with fear, I had discovered strength I never knew I possessed.

Have you ever been filled with fear? It isn't much fun, but perhaps you, too, tapped into that hidden reserve. Mothers filled with fear have been known to lift a car off a child pinned beneath its wheels. You find a source of strength and speed beyond anything you have experienced.

What then does the Bible mean when it says we're to be filled with the Spirit? And why in the world is it important for us to even think about it? Is it some mysterious doctrine that belongs to the mystics? Does it have anything to do with real life? Does it have anything to do with Monday mornings…or that stack of dirty laundry…or paper routes…or the daily commute?

WHY DO WE NEED TO BE FILLED?

Most of us would agree that the standards for Christianity are high. So high, in fact, they simply aren't attainable through normal means. If you've ever had the experience of trying to live the Christian life in the energy of your own discipline and resolve and physical strength, you will understand what a wearing, wearying process that can be.

You look at the standards of Scripture and think to yourself, *There's no way.* The high-jump bar is far higher than you could ever clear—even with springs strapped to your feet!

Scripture says, "Be completely humble and gentle" (Ephesians 4:2, NIV).
How could I attain to that?

Scripture says, "Rejoice always, pray without ceasing, in everything give thanks" (1 Thessalonians 5:16–18). *Who can live like that?*

Scripture says, "Take captive every thought to make it obedient to Christ" (2 Corinthians 10:5, NIV). *Every thought? How in the world could I do that?*

Scripture says, "Do good to those who hate you, and pray for those who spitefully use you and persecute you" (Matthew 5:44). *Even on the freeway, Lord?*

These standards, and many more I could mention, are just...well, impossible. If we don't have a power that is beyond us as human beings, we can't live the Christian life. We'll never jump that fence.

But that isn't all. Not only do the high standards of the Christian life cry out against us, but we also have an enemy who will do all he possibly can to make sure we *don't* succeed. Satan and his army of fallen angels will do everything they can and use every strategy at their disposal to undercut us. So not only is the fence too high, we have vicious dogs snapping at our ankles as we're preparing ourselves to jump!

How does Scripture describe it?

Let us strip off everything that hinders us, *as well as the sin which dogs our feet.* (Hebrews 12:1, Phillips)

What do we conclude? If there isn't something resident within a believer that makes it possible for him to live at the "next level," then he can't possibly succeed as a Christian. His life will be one of absolute failure, experiencing defeat over and over again.

When we accept Jesus Christ as our Savior, as we've already learned, the Holy Spirit comes to live within us. We call that the indwelling of the Spirit. We're also brought into the body of Christ, which is called the baptism of the Spirit. The Holy Spirit becomes resident within our hearts. He indwells us from then on—forever.

But unfortunately, when the Holy Spirit comes to live within us, He doesn't always get control of us. Sometimes we push Him off into a closet in some dark, unused wing of our soul, while He is living within us. Yes, He is an occupant, but He has no access to the TV room, or the master bedroom, or the kitchen, or the garage. He is resident in our life, but He isn't president of our life.

Only as a Christian comes to the place in his experience where he understands the vital importance of giving control of his life over to the Holy Spirit and being filled or controlled by the Spirit, will he be able to live his life with a sense of victory every day.

It is my experience (and I don't think mine alone), that the average church is filled with three different kinds of people. First, there are those who come to church but don't know the Lord at all. The Holy Spirit doesn't live within them, so they can't be filled with Him.

Second, there are other people who come to church who are Christians, and the Holy Spirit lives within them, but they've never given Him control of their life. They're believers, but they don't live a very Christlike life. They live on a carnal level.

Then third, there are those who have consciously and knowingly given over their lives to the Spirit's control. They live every day with the knowledge that there is power within them, the third person of the Trinity, who controls their life and destiny.

I don't know at which level you find yourself today, but I will tell you this: if you don't come to the place where the Spirit of God controls your life, your days as a believer will be marked by discouragement and defeat.

I love that old joke about the man who bought a new chain saw from a local hardware dealer, took it home, and cut a cord of wood.

The dealer happened to be in the area just as the man was finishing up and stopped to chat.

"How do you like that new saw?" the dealer asked.

"Oh, it's all right I guess," the man replied, mopping his brow with a big red hankie. "Though to tell ya the truth, it ain't much of an improvement over my old saw."

The store owner frowned. "Really? That doesn't seem right. This is the latest model. Let me see that thing." He picked it up, pulled on the starter cord, and the big saw roared to life.

The new saw owner was visibly startled. "What's that *noise?*" he yelled.

If we're trying to live the Christian life outside the power of the Holy Spirit, we're in for a long, weary time of it!

THE COMMAND

In the Bible, we're told to be filled with the Holy Spirit. Scripture doesn't speak of this filling as a "helpful add-on to life" or "something to shoot for in the next five years."

No, it is nothing less than a *command.*

> And do not be drunk with wine, in which is dissipation; but be filled with the Spirit. (Ephesians 5:18)

There are four things to notice about this command. Stick with me through these four observations, and you'll get the full flavor of what God had in mind—perhaps a better taste than you've ever had before.

First of all, this command is in the *imperative mood.* By that I mean, it isn't optional. The text says, "Be filled!" It isn't something you have to ponder for days and weeks. It isn't one of those nice-sounding-but-far-away goals out there on the hazy horizon of our Christian life. No, the Word of God says that every believer, no matter who we are, no matter how long we've been saved, is commanded to be filled and controlled by the Holy Spirit.

Second, it is in the *plural* rather than the singular form. Why is that important? Because it's another reminder that the command is given to ALL of us. These aren't special instructions for supersaints or spiritual giants. This isn't some private word for pastors or elders or deacons. This is a command given to everybody.

Third, it's in the *passive voice*—which means the object has something acting upon it from the outside. In other words, we don't fill ourselves. The filling comes from an outside source. We are to put ourselves in a position where the Spirit of God can control us.

Fourth, it's in the *present tense.* Unlike the baptism of the Holy Spirit, which happens only once in a believer's life, the filling of the Holy Spirit is a *repeated* event. In essence, the text says, "Be BEING filled with the Holy Spirit." Continually give over control of your life to Him.

More and more as I grow in the Lord, I understand that being filled with the Holy Spirit is an ongoing process. Sometimes, as I read and study the Word of God, the Spirit of God will reveal to me some area of my life or ministry that isn't under His control. And as He brings that issue to mind, I will have to yield that over to Him. We should never imagine that being filled is a once-for-all deal that you can nail down at some Bible camp when you throw a chunk of wood in the bonfire. Being filled is a continuous thing, every day seeking that the Lord would control our lives by His precious Holy Spirit.

Now, what are the conditions for this gracious act of God's Spirit?

DESIRE TO BE FILLED

Being filled with the Spirit of God begins with desire.

As a good football coach might tell his embattled troops at halftime, "Guys, you gotta want it."

Many people will take notes on a sermon and promptly file them in the back of their Bible. They won't really think very much about the message after that, because the general mentality in the evangelical world goes something like this: *We don't want to be lost, but we don't want to be so Spirit-filled that we can't enjoy the mediocrity of a middle-of-the-road position.*

Ouch! Does that hit close to the mark?

They say, "We're in the church, but we're not going to get fanatical about it. We come on Sunday because it's the respectable thing to do. But we want to leave as many options open to ourselves as we can, for if we were to be filled with the Spirit, there might be some things He wants us to do that we really wouldn't want to do. Or, conversely, there may be some things the Spirit of God tells us *not* to do that we really enjoy." So, we're in this twilight zone of being in the faith—but not walking according to the Spirit of God.

If you don't get over that careless attitude, you will never be filled with the Spirit.

Why? Because being filled with the Spirit starts with a holy hunger in your heart to walk at a different level than where you're currently walking. Catch the passion in the following passage. Can you feel the words vibrate in the air of that hot afternoon in Jerusalem?

On the last day, that great day of the feast, Jesus stood and cried out, saying, "If anyone thirsts, let him come to Me and drink. He who believes in Me, as the Scripture has said, out of his heart will flow rivers of living water." But this He spoke concerning the Spirit, whom those believing in Him would receive; for the Holy Spirit was not yet given, because Jesus was not yet glorified. (John 7:37–39)

If anyone thirsts!

Does that describe you? Are you thirsty—maybe a little desperate—for a closer walk with God? Do you ever find yourself crying out with the psalmist, "My soul thirsts for God, for the living God. When shall I come and appear before God?" (Psalm 42:2).

Jesus said that when the Holy Spirit controls you, you will have a hunger and a thirst to know God and grow in Him. Out of this acute, life-defining thirst comes the Spirit-controlled life.

Matthew 5:6 tells us that we're blessed—or happy—when we hunger and thirst after righteousness.

Could I stop for a moment here and ask you a personal question? Just between you and me, with no one else listening in...are you happy with the way things are in your life? Some people have told me, "Pastor, I wish I would get to the place in my Christian life where I could just be happy."

Jesus says you will be happy when you hunger and thirst after righteousness.

If you are a Christian walking according to the Word of God, there will always be a desire for something a little more than what you've achieved and what you've learned from God and from His Word. I'm not talking about dissatisfaction, but rather the realization that as God controls you there will be greater power and victory in your own life.

I've been a pastor for thirty years, and I can tell you there isn't a day that passes when I don't have within my heart this desire: *God, help me to do better. Show me something better. Show me how to walk with You in a way that pleases You more.* There needs to be the desire—the thirst—to be filled with the Spirit of God. That's where it begins.

DENOUNCE SIN IN YOUR LIFE

Confession of sin is critical, but denunciation is a step beyond confession.

I might confess to a problem with impure thoughts, but what good does that do if I go out and buy a *Playboy* magazine this afternoon? Paul explained it like this:

Since we have these promises, dear friends, let us purify ourselves from everything that contaminates body and spirit, perfecting holiness out of reverence for God. (2 Corinthians 7:1, NIV)

When we come to be filled with the Spirit, we have to cleanse our hearts through the shed blood of the Lord Jesus Christ. We have to say, "God, if there is any sin in my life, if there's something I'm doing that isn't pleasing to You, put Your finger on it. Show me what it is, and Lord, I will denounce it. I will confess it, and I will turn from it."

You can't be filled with the Holy Spirit while you're harboring your own little pet sins. Maybe it's a place to which you go, a relationship in which you're involved, the types of entertainment you indulge in, or a habit you've clung to for years—something that you know violates God's standards. You will never be filled with the Spirit of God until you denounce it, confess it, and forsake it. The *Holy* Spirit isn't just a title, that's who He is, and He doesn't enjoy living in an unclean environment. If there is known, unconfessed sin in your life, the Holy Spirit will not take control. The very fact of your sin is evidence that He *isn't* in control.

I don't ever have to wait very long when I ask the Lord to show me what's wrong in my life. This is one prayer He seems to answer every time! (Have you noticed that?) I pray from my heart, "Lord, show me if there's something I'm doing that isn't pleasing to You." And sometimes the answer comes before I've even finished my prayer.

"Oh...*that,* Lord?"

"Yes, David, that."

You may be afraid to ask that question because you don't want to know the answer! Nevertheless, if you want to be filled with the Spirit, it has to start with confession and denunciation. You have to come to the place where you say, "I want God's Spirit to so control my life that nothing will get in the way of His doing that."

DEDICATING YOURSELF FULLY TO CHRIST

To be filled with the Spirit is to yield to His control. Those are basically the same two concepts. If God's Spirit is going to control me, then I have to be willing to say, "Okay, Lord, I want You to take control of my life."

Romans 12:1 and 2 have been recited over and over again—and for good reason! They are absolutely key to the Spirit-controlled life. Listen to this J. B. Phillips paraphrase:

With eyes wide open to the mercies of God, I beg you, my brothers, as an act of intelligent worship, to give him your bodies, as a living sacrifice, consecrated to him and acceptable by him. Don't let the world around you squeeze you into its own mold, but let God remold your minds from within, so that you may prove in practice that the plan of God for you is good, meets all his demands and moves toward the goal of true maturity.

Here it is: Number one, I want to be filled—*desire*. Number two, I want to get rid of the sin in my life—*denounce*. And three, I want to give control to God—*dedicate*.

We say, "All right, Lord, You know what I want and my life is clean now. I have confessed my sin. Now I'm just going to give You control. In my business...in my home...in my free time...in every part of me. Lord, You've got it all. No strings attached. No clauses. No reservations. I submit myself to You."

From everything I've read or heard, Dr. Lewis Sperry Chafer, the founder of Dallas Seminary, was quite a unique individual. I remember reading that on one occasion in Dallas, he was asked to speak at a banquet. There were a lot of preliminaries, a lot of music, and a lot of announcements along with various presentations and endless acknowledgments. By the time Dr. Chafer stepped to the podium, the unfortunate audience had already been in session for over three hours.

Dr. Chafer immediately endeared himself to everyone when he stepped to the microphone and said, "I had prepared a somewhat lengthy message, but the hour is late, and I will not detain you. Therefore, I am going to present just the three-point outline of the message and let the Holy Spirit speak to us out of that outline.

"My subject," he went on, "is 'The Reasonableness of Fully Surrendering Our Lives to God.' Reason number one: He is all-wise and knows better than anyone else what is best for my life. Reason number two: He is almighty and has the power to accomplish that which is best for me. Reason number three: He loves me more than anyone else in the world loves me. Conclusion: therefore the most logical thing the Christian can do is to surrender his life completely to God. What more can I say? What more need I say?"

With that, he sat down. That was his message.

He could have talked for an hour and it wouldn't have been any more powerful than that. What a simple, potent message!

God knows you better than anybody else knows you. He loves you more than anybody else loves you. He is more powerful than anyone else could ever be. He can accomplish in you what no one else can do. So why *wouldn't* you want to give your life over to Him?

You have to desire to be filled. You have to denounce sin in your life. And you have to dedicate yourself completely to the Lord.

We know the Bible says that we should take those steps, but sometimes things enter into our lives that interrupt that process. There are two verses in the Scriptures that are very short but also very graphic and powerful.

The first one is 1 Thessalonians 5:19: "Do not quench the Spirit."

Do you know what it means to quench the Holy Spirit? What do you do when you quench your thirst? You drink some water and the thirst is put away. When you quench a fire, you put it out—you smother it. How do you quench the Spirit of God? *You quench the Holy Spirit by not doing something He tells you to do.* When you walk in the Spirit and are filled with the Spirit, you don't want to quench Him. When He tells you to do something, you do it.

The other verse, Ephesians 4:30, says: "And do not grieve the Holy Spirit of God."

You grieve the Holy Spirit by doing something He tells you not to do. If you're going to walk in the Spirit, if you're going to be filled with the Spirit, the last thing you want to do is quench Him or grieve Him. You want to walk in daily fellowship with Him.

DEPEND DAILY ON THE SPIRIT

Galatians 5:16 says, "Walk in the Spirit, and you shall not fulfill the lust of the flesh." What does it mean to walk in the Spirit? When I walk, if I don't put my weight on the next leg, I will fall. So I step, and I depend...step and depend...step and depend...and I just keep moving and depending, one step after another. Walking in the Spirit is trusting in the Lord God every moment. Every day you get up and say, "Lord God, You are in control of my life, and I'm going to depend on You today. Show me what to do."

Let's sum it up. I want to be filled with the Holy Spirit. How does it start? First, I need to desire it.

Second, I need to denounce sin in my life. "Lord, I'm not playing games with You anymore. I'm not going to keep trying to hold the world by one hand and You by the other."

Third, I need to dedicate myself completely to the Lord. "Lord, You have every part of me. I might not be much, Lord, but You've got all I am."

Fourth, I need to depend on Him every day. I need to walk by means of the Spirit.

If you follow the command to be filled with the Holy Spirit, and you meet the conditions to be filled with the Holy Spirit, what will the consequences be?

THE CONSEQUENCES OF BEING FILLED

The Bible teaches that the results of being filled with the Spirit of God will be seen in the normal and natural relationships of life, not in some great mystic experience.

Many times we would like it to be a mystic experience, because it isn't quite so hard as wrestling every day with nasty reality. But if you are Spirit-filled, here are several things that the Word of God says will be true about you. Things will be different about your life. So much different, in fact, that people will notice something has changed. They will realize that there is a new controller in the control tower.

A different way of speaking

A Spirit-filled person, according to Colossians 3:16, will speak to others in psalms and hymns and spiritual songs. "Speaking" is a participle that defines what happens when we're filled. It's outward directed; we're speaking to others. We're touching other lives through our love, our fellowship, and our care and concern. When you are filled with the Spirit of God, it will affect your relationships.

A different way of singing

In the same context, Scripture says you will be singing and making melody in your heart. When we come together and lift up our voices in praise, we worship God. When I hear a body of God's people praising Him together, my heart just overflows. And that's the way it will be for you. When you are filled with the Spirit of God, it will make you a person of worship and joy.

The church, the body of Jesus Christ, is the only singing religious group in the world. Did you know that? We've had people coming out of various cults who have received Christ in our church. And when I ask them what was it that caused them to come to Christ, they frequently say to me, "Pastor, it was the joy.

We didn't have any joy where I came from."

My friend, when you are Spirit-filled, you have joy in your heart, and you worship God.

One of the first things people ought to recognize in a Spirit-filled, Spirit-controlled church is the elation and gladness people experience in worshiping the Lord and singing praise to His name. It isn't rote. It isn't mechanical. It isn't tedious. It isn't old hat. In fact, it is barely containable!

The psalmist wrote:

It is good to give thanks to the LORD,
And to sing praises to Your name, O Most High;
To declare Your lovingkindness in the morning,
And Your faithfulness every night....
For You, LORD, have made me glad through Your work;
I will triumph in the works of Your hands.
(Psalm 92:1–2, 4)

A different way of giving thanks

Giving thanks in everything! Spirit-filled men and women simply do not fall into the category of "grumblers," "whiners," or "complainers." You'd better be careful when you start complaining and griping, because you just might give yourself away!

When you are filled with the Spirit of God, your life will be characterized by a spirit of gratitude. I'm so glad to be worshiping God with other believers that I don't care if the music is loud or soft, fast or slow, new choruses or old hymns. I'm so delighted to be with God's people that I don't care if I'm in a padded pew or folding chair—or the rocky floor of a catacomb, for that matter. I'm so in love with God I just want to be in His presence in the company of His saints, and I praise Him for that privilege. That is a mark of the Spirit-filled Christian.

You show me a person who always has an agenda, who is always on somebody for something, and I will probably see a person who is not Spirit-filled. Yes, that individual may be a Christian, but not a Spirit-filled one! Spirit-filled believers are marked by a spirit of humble gratitude. You can't miss it!

Are you a thankful person? I think I've always had gratitude in my heart, but since I came back from my life-threatening battle with cancer, I hardly have a day when I don't just look up into the face of the Lord and say, "Lord, thank You for *today*. Thank You for letting me live."

One of my good friends recently died of cancer. Kip Jordon, the president of Word Publishing, was diagnosed with cancer just after I was. I told my wife the other day, "I almost feel guilty. Kip was a good man. He had a young family. We both had cancer. Yet here I am, still alive."

Lord, I'm so thankful. God, thank You for letting me live. Thank You for letting me be with my family, for letting me pastor a great church, and for allowing me to write a book about Your wonderful Holy Spirit. Praise Your name!

Do you have a spirit of gratitude? Does God have to take us through a tough time to make us thankful for all that we possess from Him? Do we take each day as an opportunity to give thanks to the Lord? Oh, how we need that perspective.

If you are filled with the Spirit of God, it will affect how you speak. It will affect how you sing. It will affect your very countenance. People will be able to tell by looking into your face whether you're a grateful, thankful person or not.

Have you ever been in the presence of a bitter old man or bitter old lady? I'll tell you something, you want to leave their company as soon as you possibly can! You find yourself looking over your shoulder for the back door. The passing years have made them more and more disillusioned, cynical, and unhappy. You can see it in the very lines of their face.

At the same time, there is nothing more delightful than being in the presence of an older saint of God who has walked with Jesus Christ and been filled with His Spirit for years and years. There is a fragrance when you walk into the room. There is a softness about their features and a sparkle in their eyes. After talking to such a man or woman for a while, you're reluctant to leave. You've caught a little glimpse of Jesus.

You and I are in the process of becoming one or the other…a bitter, unhappy old man or lady, or a delightful elder in the faith who blesses everyone he or she touches. Which path are you on today?

A different way of submitting

None of us like this one. Here's what the Scripture says: "Giving thanks to the Father, submitting to one another in the fear of God."

The Bible says that a Spirit-filled person isn't someone who's always looking to be first or get on top. The characteristic of a Spirit-filled individual is that it's all right if somebody else takes the lead. He doesn't always have to be first. She doesn't have to grab the spotlight. In Scripture, the Lord leaves little doubt as to what He's talking about. He states that there are four different relationships that this spirit of submission will affect.

First of all, wives are to submit to their husbands. You may not like that, but there's no way to read it out of the text. Ephesians 5:22 says, "Wives, submit to your own husbands, as to the Lord."

The word *submit* in verse 22 isn't found in the original text but is carried over from verse 21. The idea is that in submitting to one another, the first example is the wife: "Wives...to your own husbands."

There is an old story about a guy who heard his preacher preach on this topic and got a tad carried away with applying it under his own roof. He went home, sat his wife down in the living room, and said, "Woman, I've got to talk to you. I am the *boss,* and you are *nothing.* Got that?"

"Big deal!" she snorted. "Boss over nothing!"

Submission wasn't the topic of the day in that home.

I'm just saying that when a wife is Spirit-filled, and she is blessed with a Spirit-filled husband, there will never be an argument about submission. There will be a sense *between them* of how the family is supposed to run according to the plan of God, and they will move forward in a gracious and godly way.

I have a very submissive wife—a wonderful, wonderful example of what the Bible says. I don't require her to submit to me. She submits because she is a Spirit-filled woman.

The Bible also says that children are to submit to their parents. Beyond that, Scripture speaks of servants submitting to their masters, and masters to Christ.

A different way of serving

You can't really serve the Lord as a Christian unless the Spirit of God is filling you. Have you ever seen somebody serve the Lord in the flesh? It's devastating! And the sad truth is, every one of us has attempted that in the past. There is no success in such sorry endeavors—and there is certainly no joy!

The Bible speaks of John the Baptist as Spirit-filled. Listen to what Luke 1:15 says: "For he will be great in the sight of the Lord, and shall drink neither wine nor strong drink. He will also be filled with the Holy Spirit, even from his mother's womb." John the Baptist was a Spirit-filled servant.

The apostle Peter was filled with the Spirit. Listen to Acts 4:8: "Then Peter, filled with the Holy Spirit, said to them, 'Rulers of the people and elders of Israel...'" He spoke in the power of the Holy Spirit, not the power of Peter!

Did you know the deacons are to be filled with the Holy Spirit? In Acts 6:3, the apostles were looking for special servants within the body, and these were their instructions: "Therefore, brethren, seek out from among you seven men of good reputation, full of the Holy Spirit and wisdom, whom we may appoint over this business."

In John 7 it says that when the Spirit of God fills us, the result is that out of our heart will flow rivers of living water.

The publishing house that released this book is located in picturesque Sisters, Oregon. Just a few miles away from their offices, the beautiful Metolius River springs right out of a mountainside—a full-blown river. Downstream just a ways, fly fishermen cast their lines over this rushing, ice cold, crystal clear river.

Jesus said that will be the effect of those who are filled with the Spirit. You serve God out of the *overflow* of your life. You are so filled with the Spirit of God, He just flows out of you into other people. Have you ever been around somebody like that? I can think of four or five people I've known in my life. You get close to these people, and you find yourself wishing some of the outflow of their lives would spill over on you! These gentle spirits are overflowing with the love of God, and the joy of God, and thanksgiving and gratitude. Oh, God, help us to be like that, filled with Your Spirit.

It will also involve you in Christlike living. Galatians 5 lists for us the delightful, refreshing fruit of the Spirit: love, joy, peace, longsuffering, kindness, goodness, faithfulness, gentleness, and self-control. What are those things? The very character of Jesus Christ. How do you live with the fruit of the Spirit in your life? When you give your life to the Holy Spirit, you say, "Lord, control me. Just take control of my life."

Finally, you will be a victor in warfare. The Spirit-filled life gives you and me victory over temptation. Luke 4:1–13 describes our Lord's temptation in the wilderness, and how the Holy Spirit filled Him and gave Him victory over Satan. Yes, Jesus was and is the Lord God incarnate, but He went into battle Spirit-filled.

Every week—and probably every day—we are hit by temptations. If you let the Spirit of God control your life, do you know what will happen when you face that temptation? He will immediately set off an alarm within you. A light will blink on your spiritual instrument panel. Something will tell you *this isn't right.*

I may begin moving in a particular direction, and on the outside, everything looks fine. But suddenly I will hear the still small voice in my heart saying, "Jeremiah, you don't want to get involved in that. That's going to get you in trouble. You'd better back off, now!" Without even understanding the issues, I will listen, and I will obey. And maybe two weeks later I'll find out that if I had continued in that direction, it would have brought spiritual defeat. Then I'll find myself praying, *Lord, thank You so much for steering me away from that.*

Have you ever had that experience? The Spirit of God wants to lead and guide and direct us. And He will do it if we will put Him in the driver's seat, if we will put Him on the chair of authority within our heart.

I want to ask just as simply as I can: Are you filled with the Spirit? Have you given the control of your life over to the Spirit of God, or are you still hanging on to it, saying, "This is mine! This is my life. I am going to run this myself"? That's the message of the world we live in. Whatever your mind can conceive, you can achieve, they say. But God says, "You let Me have a shot at your life. You give Me control of your life, and you'll learn the true meaning of adventure."

The Spirit-filled believer is going to have the most exciting, most adventuresome, most thrilling life of anybody on the face of God's earth. You have to take that by faith, you have to believe that, and you have to walk into each day and each experience with your arms wide open, saying, "Okay, God, here I am. You take me and control me by Your Spirit. I will do whatever You say. I will read Your Word to get instruction. I will pray. Lord, here I am. Fill me with Your Spirit!"

Fear might help you leap over a fence in the night. Adrenaline might enable you to sprint through a cornfield in Olympic time. But only God's Spirit can enable you to walk right through the middle of each day with confidence!

Chapter Six

THE ILLUMINATION
OF THE SPIRIT

PENETRATING LIGHT
IN A DARK WORLD

It is these things we talk about, not using the expressions
of human intellect but those which the Holy Spirit teaches us,
explaining spiritual things to those who are spiritual.
But the unspiritual man simply cannot accept
the matters which the Spirit deals with—
they just don't make sense to him, for, after all,
you must be spiritual to see spiritual things.
The spiritual man, on the other hand,
has an insight into the meaning of everything,
though his insight may baffle the man of the world.
1 CORINTHIANS 2:13–15, PHILLIPS

Have you ever been lost in the dark? I have a friend who visited Bucharest, Romania, just months after the fall of that nation's insane dictator, Nicolae Ceausescu. Bullet holes scarred the walls of many buildings in that dreary capital city. Even with the tyrant deposed, it was still a nation filled with fear. It was also a nation filled with darkness, because commodities such as lightbulbs were simply unavailable in the country at that time.

My friend was staying for a week in an apartment in one of those massive, cement, Soviet-style apartment complexes. He got out of a taxicab after a meeting on the first night and tried to remember where his apartment was.

But everything was pitch dark. No streetlights. No lights in windows. Just black, hulking blocks of buildings—and a feeling of oppressive evil in the air. He got into an elevator in what he hoped was the right building. The elevator had no lights. The door shut, encasing him in a box of utter blackness. Was anyone else in the elevator? He didn't know. He felt for where the panel might be, found some buttons, and pushed one he hoped would take him to the third floor. The doors opened to yet another level of deepest night.

An attack of panic began to clutch at his throat as he groped his way along an outside hallway. Was that the elevator doors he heard—opening again? Was he being followed? He stared in vain at the doorways, trying to make out an apartment number. Finally, he had to walk up to a door and try to *feel* the numbers.

He finally got through the right door to the right apartment and, shaking with relief, vowed to pay much closer attention to instructions in the future. Before they had left home, the group leader had specifically told everyone to bring a small penlight or flashlight on this journey. What a difference a bright, cheery little light would have meant! In that thoroughly dark place, it would have cut through the gloom like a searchlight.

And so it is in this dark world of ours. Without the illumination of God's Word, we have to feel our way along, guessing at dangers, guessing at direction, hoping against hope that we will find our way and won't stumble into trouble or disaster.

But our Father has not left His children alone in the dark. The Holy Spirit is the One who shines His light on the pages of God's Word, so that we can find wisdom and direction in a fallen world. In this chapter we will discover that we can't really even understand the Bible without the Holy Spirit. Why? Because spiritual truth in the Bible can only be seen through spiritual eyes.

In presenting God's Word to us, the Holy Spirit has a complex ministry of grace. First of all, He was involved in the inspiration of the written Word of God. He tenderly oversaw the whole process, utilizing the personalities of individual writers, but so directing them that the resulting text is precisely what He wanted to say.

But He's also involved in a day-by-day ministry we call the *illumination* of the Holy Spirit. Illumination, of course, is the word for light. To illumine a dark room, you flip on the light switch. To illumine a thought or idea means to shine the light of understanding on it.

The Bible tells us that without the Spirit of God shining on our hearts, we can never comprehend what the Bible says. There are a number of reasons for that. If you are an unbeliever, for instance, you simply will never be able to understand Scripture. You can read it. You can memorize it. You can diagram its sentences. You can take apart its Hebrew and Greek word by word. *But it will never come alive.* The light will never come on because you don't have the spiritual equipment to study it.

"Well, David," you say, "that's just your opinion."

No, that's the Word of God. Look with me at Paul's graphic description of those who don't know the Lord:

> But even if our gospel is veiled, it is veiled to those who are perishing, whose minds the god of this age has blinded, who do not believe, lest the light of the gospel of the glory of Christ, who is the image of God, should shine on them. (2 Corinthians 4:3–4)

The Bible says that before you invite Christ into your life you have spiritual scales on your eyes and can't understand Scripture. You can read it for all you're worth, but it's just a bunch of words. It doesn't make any sense. You might as well be a Lithuanian trying to read a Portuguese phone book.

In 1 Corinthians 2:14 we're told that the "natural man" (that's the person who doesn't know the Lord), "does not receive the things of the Spirit of God." Why doesn't he? Read on. "For they are foolishness to him; nor can he know them, because they are spiritually discerned."

If I were to go up and down the aisles of the church where I pastor and ask for testimonies, I would have no trouble finding people who were perplexed and confused by the Bible before they were saved. Many of them would say, "You know, Pastor Jeremiah, before I invited Christ into my life, I tried to read that book, and it made no sense to me. In fact, it seemed like foolishness. I couldn't understand why people would study the Bible and get so excited about it, because to me it was just so much gibberish."

But when the Spirit of God comes to live within you, He opens the Word of God so you can begin to understand it. He directs His light on its pages. He highlights verses that apply to your situation. He whispers meanings and insights into your mind. Sometimes those insights come as a quiet word of assurance in the night—like the soft glow of a night-light. At other times they come like thunderbolts, suddenly lighting up the sky.

That's illumination.

It's the Spirit of God casting light on the Word and shining in our hearts, so that the Word begins to come up off the page and make sense in our lives.

But did you know that Christians can be blinded too? Immaturity or carnality can dim our spiritual vision. Even though you have the basic equipment to study the Word of God when the Spirit comes to live within you, you can put a shade on that light by not walking in faith.

Sometimes people say, "Well, I don't see why I need all this new truth. I don't need to know about this and that. After all, I'm saved, I'm going to heaven, and that's all I really care about. I don't really need to understand this stuff."

But we really do need to know and understand these things; God has given the Bible to us as a key to success in the Christian life. There's nothing else that will help us, and you never know what portion of Scripture (even Malachi!) the Holy Spirit might want to pick up and use as a tool to change your life.

There are many thousands of books published each year, of course, but the Bible is different. Solomon's words are still appropriate. In fact, more than ever. "Be warned," he said; "the writing of many books is endless, and excessive devotion to books is wearying to the body. The conclusion, when all has been heard, is: fear God and keep His commandments, because this applies to every person" (Ecclesiastes 12:12–13, NASB).

What Solomon was saying is that God's wisdom is different than the world's wisdom. Paul picks up on that thought in his letter to the Corinthians.

> We do, however, speak a message of wisdom among the mature, but not the wisdom of this age or of the rulers of this age, who are coming to nothing. No, we speak of God's secret wisdom, a wisdom that has been hidden and that God destined for our glory before time began. None of the rulers of this age understood it, for if they had, they would not have crucified the Lord of glory. (1 Corinthians 2:6–8, NIV)

Yes, there's a wisdom and a knowledge out there in the world that you can get your arms around—but it won't mean anything to your life. It's tragic to see people spend their lives pursuing "learning" and "education" and advanced degrees. Yet for all the good it's doing them in understanding eternal truths, they're just taking up time. It doesn't have any enduring value. Paul is writing about the wisdom of God that is concealed from the people of this age. The princes of this world, the rulers of this age—the aristocrats, the intellectuals—don't know His wisdom. Their money can't buy it. Their power can't demand it. Their influence can't obtain it.

They can't download it from the Internet.

They can't acquire it from the world's finest universities.

They can't discover it from some guru sitting in a hut in the Himalayas.

I've often said that a little old lady with no education at all who knows Jesus and has a Bible, has more eternal wisdom than a person with a Ph.D. who is the president of some prestigious university. Her wisdom will take her further than his knowledge will ever take him, because we're speaking about two different kinds of wisdom—the wisdom of the world and the wisdom of God.

If you want the wisdom of the world, you don't need the Holy Spirit. You can get that sort of content any way you want. As Solomon said, there are plenty of books out there. Universities and colleges and correspondence schools will be more than happy to relieve you of your time and money. *But if you want the wisdom of God, you must have the illuminating ministry of the Holy Spirit.*

First Corinthians 2:7–8 contains a very important concept: "But we speak the wisdom of God in a mystery, the hidden wisdom which God ordained before the ages for our glory."

Did you see that? The wisdom of God is a *mystery.*

Now, we're not speaking of an Agatha Christie novel here, where you're trying to figure out who did what to whom and when. A mystery in New Testament terms is information which is available, but unknown. For instance, the church of Jesus Christ is referred to in the New Testament as a "mystery." People didn't know about the church in the Old Testament. It was a mystery yet to be revealed. The Bible tells us that when we're trying to get into spiritual truth, we're dealing with God's mysteries, with His hidden wisdom, and with truth that the princes of this world don't know. They can't comprehend it; they will *never* comprehend it apart from the illumination of God's Spirit.

Whatever you do, my friend, don't go to someone who is not a Christian and ask for spiritual insight. She may be an impressive woman and have degrees as long as your arm. He may be a warm and caring man, or host a radio talk show broadcast in the nation's top fifteen markets. But if those individuals don't have the Lord, if they don't possess the indwelling Holy Spirit, they can't help you with your spiritual problem. They don't know the language. They don't have a clue.

Once in a while someone will tell me, "You know, Pastor, I was going through this problem and I went to see a secular psychologist and tried to explain my spiritual dilemma to him."

Give me a break! He doesn't know what you're talking about. I'm not saying that counselors are incompetent or insincere or without value. I'm just saying that if you want *spiritual* counsel from another individual, if you want the wisdom of God, you have to go to somebody who knows the Spirit of God. For that matter, the Spirit Himself will be your Counselor, if you give Him the opportunity.

What, then, are some of the facets of this phenomenon we call spiritual illumination?

SPIRITUAL DISCERNMENT

One of the last promises the Savior made to His disciples before His crucifixion concerned the ministry of the Holy Spirit. This is what He said:

> "I still have many things to say to you, but you cannot bear them now. However, when He, the Spirit of truth, has come, He will guide you into all truth; for He will not speak on His own authority, but whatever He hears He will speak; and He will tell you things to come. He will glorify Me, for He will take of what is Mine and declare it to you." (John 16:12–14)

Jesus said, "When I go back to heaven, I'm going to send you the Holy Spirit, and when He comes, He will live within you and will guide you into all truth. He won't speak His own words or pursue His own agenda. He will speak My words. And there's no one," said Jesus, "who knows God better than the Spirit of God."

Have you ever had anyone try to tell you "who you are"?

Drives me crazy. There are some folks who just insist on doing that—and seem to take pride in it. They'll say, "Ah, Pastor, I know what's in your heart. I know what you're thinking. I know what concerns you."

Oh no, they don't! They don't have a clue. For you to know what's in me, you've got to *be* in me. I don't care who you are; you can't know me unless you know my spirit.

And what Jesus is saying is this: when the Spirit of God comes, He will take what He knows of God—as God Himself—and will reveal those things to you through the Scriptures. You really can't know God, you can't know His Word, unless the Spirit of God is involved in the process.

First Corinthians 2:10 says this: "But God has revealed them to us through His Spirit. For the Spirit searches all things, yes, the deep things of God." If you want to know the deep things of God, the Spirit of God must be part of that transaction.

And guess what? He *wants* to reveal those deep things to you! He *wants* to give you discernment. He *wants* to give you the ability to understand the Word of God. James says that God gives us wisdom "liberally and without reproach" (James 1:5). The great desire of the Spirit's heart is to flood the light of Scripture into your mind and help you to know more and more and more about your heavenly Father and your Lord and Savior Jesus Christ. The Holy Spirit is like a lighthouse keeper who just loves to send that powerful beam out across the fog and the darkness.

But sometimes He doesn't need a great floodlight, does He? Sometimes it's more like the tiny beam from a penlight, suddenly illumining a word or phrase from Scripture. And you sit back in your chair and say, "Of course! I'd never thought of that before. That makes sense. Thank You, Lord."

The problem we have in many of our evangelical churches isn't a lack of information about the Bible. We've got copies of the Bible in just about every translation you could imagine. (Maybe you have one of those New English Standard Authorized International Revised Living Versions, thumb indexed.) Most churches can hardly have congregational readings of the Scripture, because it sounds like the Tower of Babel. Everybody is reading in his or her own translation.

And it's really more than a matter of "not understanding" what the Scriptures mean. Do you know where I think we lose it as evangelicals? Bible study is finding out what the Bible says, finding out what it means, and then finding out *what it means to you* and how you apply it in your life. That's where we're losing it.

People tell me, "Well, I think there are too many things in the Bible you can't understand." And I tell them that I agree with Mark Twain: It's not what I don't understand in the Bible that troubles me, it's what I *do* understand that gives me problems! There is enough and more than enough for us to apply to our lives as we give the Holy Spirit room to operate.

THE PARAMETERS OF DISCERNMENT

In general, the content of the Spirit's ministry is "all the truth." That's what it says in John 16:13.

That truth is the Bible, the written Word of God.

Sometimes people tell me, "Well, you know, the Spirit told me thus and so last night." Do you know what I answer? "Really? What *chapter* is that in? What's the verse? What's the reference? If the Spirit told you that, where is it in the Bible?" I say that because the ministry of the Holy Spirit is to take the Word of God, apply it to our hearts, and teach us what we need to know.

When we talk about spiritual illumination we're not talking about dreams, special messages, or "words of knowledge." What we're talking about is God's Word coming alive to us as the Spirit of God opens our understanding and applies the living Word of God to our hearts.

In other words, the parameters of spiritual discernment are between the covers of the Bible.

A couple came to me for counsel not too many years ago and described their lifestyle. They were living together without the benefit of marriage, and I immediately confronted them about that.

"Oh no, Pastor," they assured me. "You don't have to worry about that. We've prayed about this and God has given us real peace."

I told them, "I don't know what you got, but you didn't get it from God."

Because the Bible speaks very clearly in these matters, doesn't it? So if the Bible says it, don't come along and say the Spirit told you something else. That "something else" may have come from a spirit, but it wasn't God's Spirit. He will never contradict the written Word of God.

Spiritual discernment always deals with the content of the Bible. The Spirit will take the Word and help you understand it. Those are the parameters.

THE PROCESS OF ILLUMINATION

Now, how does this happen? There's a wonderful passage of Scripture in the little book of 1 John.

But you have an anointing from the Holy One, and you know all things. But the anointing which you have received from Him abides in you, and you do not need that anyone teach you; but as the same anointing teaches you concerning all things, and is true, and is not a lie, and just as it has taught you, you will abide in Him. (1 John 2:20, 27)

Did you know that every Christian has an "anointing"?

Sometimes, if someone really likes a particular sermon on a given Sunday, he or she will come up to me after the service and say, "Boy, that was anointed," or "You were anointed today, Pastor." Now, I know what they mean. It's meant as a compliment, and that's how I take it. But the real truth is that *every* believer has an anointing. If you're a Christian, you are anointed. John says this anointing is the Spirit-given capacity to know and understand God's truth.

John makes a statement in the above passage that confuses many people. He says, "You do not need that anyone teach you." I know of a few students who would like to make that their life verse. *Hey, we don't need teachers! Let's get rid of 'em all and we'll just have class and get on with it!*

We obviously know that isn't true. If that were the case, John wouldn't have written a whole book that is packed with teaching. If you "don't need teaching," why do that?

Here's what I think John means. He means you don't need teachers who approach life from a non-Christian perspective. You don't need teachings from outside the faith. You have the teaching of the Spirit of God; you don't have to go outside of that sphere to get information to know what to do. You don't need horoscopes. You don't need Ouija boards. You don't need psychic hot lines. You don't need talk radio. You don't need the daily advice column in the newspaper. I could go through a whole list of things people are doing today to find information about what to do with their lives.

John is saying, you have an anointing from the Spirit, and you don't need to travel out into the other "fringe" areas where people are trying to glean information. Why? Because you have the Spirit of the living God right inside you! When you've been walking with the Lord, and the Holy Spirit has sensitized your human spirit, you will begin to know and discern when something is right spiritually. Someone stands before a group and begins to teach, and a little alarm goes off in the back of your head. You may not even have a Bible in front of you to know what's wrong, but a little warning message keeps blinking in your spirit, and you say, *Something's not right here.*

What is that? That is spiritual discernment from the indwelling Spirit of God. I'm not saying that you and I should always be moving in the area of feelings or whims or intuition. I'm just saying that part of spiritual discernment is the inward witness of the Spirit, who tells you when something is right and rings true, and when something is wrong and you need to tread carefully. The Spirit takes the Word of God and ministers to your mind so that you're sensitive to things both good and bad as you seek to walk with the Lord.

I will sometimes hear people say there's a chapter and verse in the Bible for every situation in life. There isn't! I've been looking for some of them for years. What then do you have in the Word of God? You have principles and concepts and parameters—dynamic, living truth. And the Spirit of God will direct His powerful light onto those portions of the Bible that directly apply to your life situation. God will help you. I believe that with all my heart. The anointing of the Holy Spirit sensitizes your spirit so that you know the truth, and that truth will set you free to be God's person.

Is that happening in your life?

THE POWER OF DISCERNMENT

"But the Helper, the Holy Spirit, whom the Father will send in My name, He will teach you all things, and bring to your remembrance all things that I said to you." (John 14:26)

Amazing!

If you were a Christian when you were in high school or college (and maybe even if you weren't!), you probably got serious about prayer just before a big test. You may have prayed, "Oh, God, help me to remember the things I've studied." My prayer was a little different than that. I used to pray that He'd help me remember things I *never* studied. I didn't just want reminders, I wanted direct revelation!

Sometimes you will hear the Word of God preached in church and you'll walk out the door saying, "I guess I don't get it. That didn't touch me anywhere. I'm not even sure what he was talking about." You may not think about that message again for weeks—or even months. But if you keep coming back and interacting with the Word of God and nurturing your spiritual life, then little by little, you will obtain a body of information in your spirit that the Holy Spirit can use. In that moment when you need it, the Spirit of God will sensitize your conscience and bring something to the front of your mind that you can immediately apply. It might even be something from that sermon that had gone right over your head a few weeks before.

Most of the time when I suddenly find myself faced with a crisis in my life, I don't have the opportunity to say, "Um…could you come back in a week or so? I'd like to do some homework on this; then I'll figure out what we're supposed to do here." Sometimes you have to make decisions on the spur of the moment, don't you? You have to decide what you're going to do. You have to choose Response A or Response B, and putting it off isn't an option! How do you prepare yourself for those moments?

I don't know of any better answer I could give you than this: put the Word of God into your heart. Expose yourself to truth. Turn off the TV. Listen to tapes. Read God's Book. Read books that help you to understand God's Book. Fill your spiritual computer with truth and in the moment when you need it, the Holy Spirit will cause you to remember the things you've learned. In computer terms, He is the "Search Engine" who locates exactly what you need. It's His ministry. It's His specialty. It's His delight.

When that happens, friend, when the Holy Spirit brings that right answer to your heart in the moment of need, write it down so that you can remember it. Treasure that moment. Glory in it. It's a moment when God's Spirit intersected with your life.

The problem with many of us, however, is that we don't give the Spirit of God anything to work with. The Holy Spirit is doing a search in the computer, and there's nothing in the files! The screen's coming up blank. He's trying to find a Scripture He can use to apply to your life situation, and there's nothing there.

Don't do that to the Author of Scripture! Give Him something to work with. Put as much truth as you can into that computer of yours. Read the Word. Study the Word. Memorize the Word. Sing the Word. Pray the Word. You will never, never regret that investment. It will impact your life now and for years to come.

SPIRITUAL DEPENDENCE

You and I don't have to be timid as believers. Did you know that? We don't have to be afraid to speak. We don't have to always be looking over our shoulders.

What does the Bible say? "For God has not given us a spirit of timidity, but of power and love and discipline" (2 Timothy 1:7, NASB). Through the ministry of the Holy Spirit, we can face life in a different way than the average person. We can face crises and times of testing and not get blown off course.

All of us face crises, don't we? In the last few weeks, I've encountered more stresses in my ministry than I can remember in many years. These things have come upon me suddenly, like bolts of lightning out of a clear, tranquil sky. You think you're doing great, and everything is moving along nicely, then, *wham!* You have a train wreck. Plans get derailed. You don't know what to do.

How do you face those crises? You face them with the knowledge that God's mighty Spirit lives within you, closer than hands or feet, closer than breathing. You face them with the confidence that nothing catches God by surprise and that His Spirit will give you a kind of discernment and discipline and direction you would otherwise never have. Praise His name!

How do you explain that sort of discernment? I think it comes about as the Spirit of God helps you and me to see the whole picture instead of just the narrow focus of that moment. The more I live and the more I try to learn about God, the more I understand that this is what is going on. Isn't it true? He gives you *perspective.* He helps you to see your particular situation in light of the whole situation. He reminds you that today's setbacks will pass, and that much greater things are afoot.

Let me give you an illustration of this from the New Testament. Do you remember the story of Stephen? Here was a young man who loved the Lord yet died an unjust and violent death. He was stoned to death for boldly proclaiming Jesus Christ as Savior and Lord. He told people what they didn't want to hear, and because they had no answer for his arguments, they killed him. Now, I want to ask you a question. If you knew you were going to be martyred for your faith, what would be the thoughts going through your mind?

You'd be afraid, normally. (If you weren't, there's something wrong with you.) You'd probably be wondering about your friends, your family. And I'm sure all those thoughts went through Stephen's mind as well. But Stephen had a perspective on that moment that came because he was filled with the Holy Spirit. Listen to these ringing words:

But he, being full of the Holy Spirit, gazed into heaven and saw the glory of God, and Jesus standing at the right hand of God, and said, "Look! I see the heavens opened and the Son of Man standing at the right hand of God!" (Acts 7:55–56)

How did he see that? With death rushing upon him…with murderous hatred all around him…with sharp, heavy stones crashing into his body…*how did he see those things?*

He saw them through spiritual illumination. He saw them by the power of the Holy Spirit. He saw them through his spiritual eyes. The spiritual illumination of the moment gave him confidence and strength and ability to see beyond the tragedy of the loss of his physical life. He was enabled to see into that place where he would spend eternity. He saw God. He saw Christ. He saw heaven. And he died with a blessing on his lips rather than a curse for those who were taking his life.

I'm reminded of yet another situation, this time from the Old Testament.

A great army of enemy soldiers had surrounded the city where the prophet Elisha and his servant were staying. And that huge army was intent on only one purpose: to capture and eliminate that troublesome man of God, Elisha. When Elisha's servant went out in the morning to stretch and watch the sun coming up, he was shocked and overwhelmed by what he saw. The rising sun glinted off of tens of thousands of helmets, shields, and spears.

White with fear, he stumbled back into the little apartment with a message of anguish and despair.

> [Elisha's] servant said to him, "Alas, my master! What shall we do?" So he answered, "Do not fear, for those who are with us are more than those who are with them." And Elisha prayed, and said, "LORD, I pray, open his eyes that he may see." Then the LORD opened the eyes of the young man, and he saw. And behold, the mountain was full of horses and chariots of fire all around Elisha. (2 Kings 6:15–17)

For that moment, the Lord opened the young servant's eyes, and he saw what the prophet saw: spiritual resources beyond his imagination! Angelic armies. Chariots of fire.

Suddenly those enemy soldiers didn't look quite so intimidating. Suddenly the situation didn't seem quite so hopeless. Far from it! My friend, when you ask God to give you the illuminating power of the Spirit, He will do it. He will help you to see life in a different way. You will see life through spiritual eyes, not just with physical eyes. And the people around you will be amazed and won't understand how you can respond the way you do.

SPIRITUAL DIRECTION

When the Spirit of God comes to live within you, He not only gives you discernment into His Word and a sense of dependence on the Lord in times of crisis, He's also able to *direct* your life, to help you to know what to do. As you read the New Testament, and the book of Acts especially, you see that the apostles were Spirit-directed people.

Paul left no doubt whatsoever. In a strong, bold hand, he wrote: "For as many as are led by the Spirit of God, these are sons of God" (Romans 8:14). One of the marks that you are a Christian is that you are led by God's Spirit. You let the Spirit of God direct you.

Everyone who knows David Jeremiah knows that I didn't come into this world equipped with an internal compass. Let's be nice about it and just say I'm "directionally challenged." I know where I want to go, I just don't know where I *am* sometimes. Actually, my sense of direction is so faulty that when I'm not sure what to do, I deliberately do what I think is wrong—because I'm sure that's going to be right. If I come out of an elevator and every instinct in my body says "turn left," then I promptly turn right, and usually end up fine. (Thank God my wife has a good sense of direction, or I'd be in a lot of trouble.)

Oh, but there are times in life when even a good compass won't help you, aren't there? You might even have one of those expensive high-tech devices that take their readings from global positioning satellites. It doesn't matter how accurately you can locate yourself on a map, the fact is, life sometimes puts us in situations where we don't know where to turn. What do you do?

Turn to the Holy Spirit.

He is the One who helps us know where to go, where to turn, and what to do. He knows everything that's involved in where you are headed and gives you guidance so you make the right decisions.

Listen how Romans 9:1 underlines this wonderful truth. Paul wrote:

I tell the truth in Christ. I am not lying, my conscience also bearing me witness in the Holy Spirit.

I believe there is an inward witness within us that helps us to know what to do. I believe the Holy Spirit will direct us if we will give Him the opportunity to illuminate our path and show us where we should go.

Life is so complicated that I don't want to even try living it on my own, in my own wisdom. I don't want to be my own travel agent through life, writing up my own itinerary, arranging my own accommodations, and flying my own 737 to get there. I'd only mess everything up! There are too many options. Too many paths. Too many opportunities. Too many choices. Too many serious consequences if I make a wrong decision. What did that old bumper sticker say? *Life is fragile. Handle with prayer.* How I need the guiding hand of God's Spirit!

How does He guide? We'll get into this in more detail in a later chapter. But in a thumbnail sketch…He leads us through God's Word, through prayer, through circumstances, and through godly counsel. Through all of these means, God will help us and guide us to make right decisions. But it all starts with the illuminating ministry of the Holy Spirit. He is the One who floods our path with light.

Four thousand years ago, when David was hiding from his enemies in the depths of a limestone cave, he wrote these words: "When my spirit was overwhelmed within me, then You knew my path" (Psalm 142:3). It is the same for you and me today, whether we're walking in the sunlight or find ourselves in a cave of our own.

You see, the whole thing with the Holy Spirit's direction is that you can't be depending on your own wisdom and depending on His as well. In recent days, I've flown across the country with some friends in a private jet. I'd never had the opportunity to watch the inner workings of such a craft, but on this occasion I had the chance to sit right up in the cockpit, just behind the pilot.

On the way we flew into some stormy weather and found ourselves in the middle of some huge banks of clouds. For what seemed like an eternity (to me at least) you couldn't see *anything* out of the windshield. It didn't bother me that you couldn't see out of the side windows. But hey, don't we have to see where we're going? It was just incredible to me to watch the pilot and copilot. They never even bothered to look out the windows. They never even thought about that. They just watched the gauges. They kept their eyes on their instruments and got us through the storm and clouds.

Into the sunlight. Home again.

Sometimes as Christians you and I find ourselves wanting to watch our circumstances, don't we? We focus our eyes on the storm. We get worried about the clouds and the rain and the darkness. And when that happens, what we have to do is to home in on the ministry of the Holy Spirit and let Him be our guide. Sometimes you have to put blinders on. "Lord, help me not to look at the circumstances. Help me to hear and listen to what You are saying to me." And then we walk by the Spirit of God, and He directs our paths.

If you're the pilot of an airplane, you have to decide what you're going to do and how you're going to fly. Scripture says, "Trust in the LORD with all your heart, and lean not on your own understanding" (Proverbs 3:5). In other words, you can't be ambivalent about it. You can't say, "I'm not sure these instruments are right. So I'd better stick my head out the window of this jet and check this out." I wouldn't want to fly with a pilot like that! I'd be looking for a parachute. I want somebody who is instrument rated, someone with absolute confidence in those gauges and dials. That's my only hope of getting from where I am to where I want to go.

It's the same when you're following the lead of the Holy Spirit. You don't want to find yourself vacillating between what you think and what you know God says. You've got to get into instrument flight and let the Holy Spirit keep you on course.

I love David's prayer in Psalm 143: "Teach me to do your will, for you are my God; may your good Spirit lead me on level ground" (v. 10, NIV).

When you study the Word and ask the Holy Spirit to illuminate your mind, you get spiritual direction from the Word of God. When you ask the Holy Spirit to illuminate your heart, you get spiritual confidence to live your life no matter what's going on all around you. When you ask the Holy Spirit to illuminate your path, you get a sense of direction you would never have apart from Him.

If you don't know about the Holy Spirit…if you don't trust in the Spirit…if you don't walk by means of the Spirit…if you're not filled with the Spirit, life can be very, very unsettling. But when you put the Holy Spirit in control of your life, He has everything you need to make it through with victory and joy—no matter how dark and violent the storm.

When you finally break through the clouds of earth and touch down on heaven's long, golden runway, you'll know it wasn't your own skill that got you through that troubled flight.

It was that still, small voice in the control tower. He led you all the way.

Chapter Seven

WALKING IN THE SPIRIT

AN EVERYDAY DEPENDENCE UPON GOD

hen you're a pastor, you just never know what the next ring of your telephone or knock on your office door might bring. If you like routine and predictability, you'd best stay out of the ministry. You'd be better off selling insurance.

Years ago, when I was pastoring in the Midwest, a woman walked into my office with a request I will never forget. She walked up to my desk where I was working and handed me her Bible.

"I want you to take this," she said with a sigh.

"Why?" I asked her. "What for?"

"I'm turning it in," she replied. "I'm quitting."

It was like a policeman turning in his badge and quitting the force. She said, "You take this, Pastor. There's no way I can live this life. I'm giving you my Bible back, and I'm not going to do this anymore."

Have you ever felt like that? *This is just too much. This is more than I can do, more than I can accomplish. I'm overwhelmed. I'm tired. I'm discouraged with this Christian life stuff. No matter how hard I try, I never measure up.*

I can understand that response. I've felt that way myself at times. The demands of the Christian life are incredibly great. As we've already noted, it isn't just difficult, it isn't just challenging, it's *impossible*. You can't do it in your own strength. And if you try to do it, you will burn out.

There are a good number of burned-out Christians out there. Maybe you've met one recently. Maybe you saw one when you looked in the mirror this morning. Christians burn out by trying to accomplish something they were never supposed to accomplish in their own strength in the first place.

That's why the instruction from Paul to the Galatian believers is such an incredible concept. He says in Galatians 5:16, "I say then: Walk in the Spirit, and you shall not fulfill the lust of the flesh."

I know what *walking* means; I've been doing that since I was about sixteen months old. But what does it mean to walk *in the Spirit?* How do you do that?

To walk in the Spirit means to live every day in dependence upon God. It is unbroken fellowship and reliance on the Holy Spirit to do what He came to do, and what He alone *can* do. Sometimes we get the idea that the Christian life is a matter of grim determination. Maybe that's how you were taught at some point in your life. You get up in the morning, square your shoulders, tighten your belt, set your jaw, draw in three deep breaths, and determine in your heart to live for Jesus...even if it kills you.

It just might! As worthy as that goal might sound, it is not how the Lord intended us to live the Christian life. Keep that up for very long and you'll be wanting to turn in your Bible too. You'll be looking for the place to resign. The truth is, it's not an issue of determination at all, it is an issue of dependence. It isn't trying, it's trusting.

What a vast difference there is between determining and depending, and between trying and trusting! If I understand anything at all about the Word of God and about the ministry of the Holy Spirit in the life of the believer, the relationship is one of depending on Him to do His work in us and through us. It is not our trying to somehow manufacture all of the evidences of the Holy Spirit through our own energy and determination.

There are some major reasons why trying to live the Christian life in our own resolve and strength won't work. Instead of walking in the Spirit, we'll find ourselves staggering, lurching, wandering, or even tripping and falling. But if you and I could learn the secret woven into Galatians 5:16...what a difference it would make! We could begin enjoying a lifestyle that is more characterized by victory and joy and a sense of being in the center of where God wants us to be.

The Spirit-filled walk is the only option for Christians. There are at least three very significant reasons why this is true.

BECAUSE THE DEMANDS ARE SO GREAT

Watchman Nee once wrote a book called *The Normal Christian Life*. But the fact is, there's nothing "normal" about it. This past week I took a sharp pencil and a yellow pad and listed every New Testament instance of the simple little verb *walk*.

Did I say simple? You wouldn't believe all that Scripture has to say about a Christian's "walk." Let me give you a little sampling...

We're to walk in good works. Ephesians 2:10 says, "For we are His workmanship, created in Christ Jesus for good works, which God prepared beforehand that we should walk in them."

We're to walk properly. Romans 13:13 urges us to "walk properly, as in the day, not in revelry and drunkenness, not in licentiousness and lewdness, not in strife and envy."

We're to walk by faith. Second Corinthians 5:7 says: "For we walk by faith, not by sight." (How difficult is that? The whole world is built around what we see and hear and touch and taste and smell. But the Bible says that those are not to be the parameters of the believer's life. We are to walk by means of that which we can't discern with our five senses. And friend, that's not easy.)

We're to walk in love. Ephesians 5:2 tells us we must "walk in love, as Christ also has loved us and given Himself for us, an offering and a sacrifice to God for a sweet smelling aroma."

We're to walk as children of light. Ephesians 5:8 states: "For you were once darkness, but now you are light in the Lord. Walk as children of light."

We're to walk worthy of the Lord. Colossians 1:10 urges us to "walk worthy of the Lord, fully pleasing Him."

We're to walk as Jesus walked. First John 2:6 says, "He who says he abides in Him ought himself also to walk just as He walked."

We're to walk worthy of our vocation. Ephesians 4:1 tells us that we have been given a new vocation, a new assignment, as God's people. We're to walk, therefore, worthy of the calling by which we have been called.

Are you getting the picture here? This is no amble in the park. This is no stroll through the tulips. This is *power*-walking! Just let your eye scan those instructions listed above. Think about that list. Anybody want to resign? Anybody feel like going back to bed or taking a long nap? I do, sometimes. This isn't an easy thing we've been called upon to do. And that was just one little word in

Scripture! Yet the demands are very great. It would be easy to feel completely overwhelmed by them.

But (as if those things weren't enough!) there is another reason why the Spirit-filled walk is our only option.

BECAUSE OUR ENEMY IS DETERMINED

Not only is the walk itself difficult, but we have someone pursuing us and laying traps for us along the way! When I say that we have a determined enemy who is after us, I'm not being paranoid. I'm telling you the truth. He is real, and he *is* after us. His whole goal, his whole reason for existence, is to undermine God's people. He will go to any lengths to do that.

Who is this enemy? You know who he is. He's the devil, Satan, the adversary. Listen to Paul's chilling description of our situation in this paraphrase of Ephesians 6:12:

> For we are not fighting against people made of flesh and blood, but against persons without bodies—the evil rulers of the unseen world, those mighty satanic beings and great evil princes of darkness who rule this world; and against huge numbers of wicked spirits in the spirit world. (TLB)

This isn't a struggle against the kinds of enemies you face out in the secular world. This isn't an irate driver on the morning commute or an argument over the back fence. This is an ancient and powerful foe with vast resources and bitter hatred of Jesus Christ and all who belong to Him.

I become very concerned when I hear people joking or speaking flippantly about Satan. Scripture tells us that even the mighty archangel Michael did not dare to bring a slanderous accusation against the devil (Jude 1:9). I'm not saying that we should give him credit he doesn't need, but we must also bear in mind that he is a fierce, formidable enemy. No, we shouldn't overestimate his influence on our lives, but it's every bit as dangerous to *under*estimate him.

In 1 Peter 5:8 we're told that Satan is like a roaring lion, ever prowling, seeking whom he may devour. And many of God's people are being devoured. Have you noticed? He is devouring their influence, he is devouring their marriages, he is devouring their children, he is devouring their opportunities for ministry and service. They're being eaten alive by the enemy.

Revelation 12:9 tells us that he is "the great dragon…that serpent of old, called the Devil and Satan, who deceives the whole world." Does that tell you who he is? He's a dangerous and devious enemy, and his goal is to undermine and neutralize God's people.

Satan doesn't waste much time with people who aren't Christians. Why should he? He's already got them. They're already on his side of the ledger. They're already (whether they know it or not) doing his bidding. But once you become part of God's family, you can count on a new relationship with Satan. You're no longer in the "safe" column of his ledger. He puts you on his hit list, and he'll be after you the rest of your life.

Do you remember the conversation Jesus had with Peter shortly before He went to the cross? Jesus looked into His friend's eyes and said, "Simon, Simon, behold, Satan has demanded permission to sift you like wheat; but I have prayed for you, that your faith may not fail" (Luke 22:31–32, NASB).

That's what Satan wants to do. He wants to get his hands on our lives. He wants to shake us and sift us and unsettle us.

In 2 Corinthians 2:11, Paul tells us that Satan utilizes "schemes"—or "devices," as the King James puts it. That word *scheme* means the same thing as *strategy*. In other words, Paul is saying, we shouldn't be ignorant of Satan's strategies to undercut our lives and destroy us.

If you could sneak into Satan's office, wherever that might be (he's not in hell yet), and take a peek into his files, you might be surprised to find a file folder with your name on it. I'm not exaggerating. He keeps a file on you, and inside that file are all the strategies he's tried on you—the ones that have worked and the ones that have failed. He doesn't waste his time with the ones that don't work anymore. Instead, he uses variations on the strategies that have caused you to stumble in the past. As long as they keep working, he keeps using them.

Somewhere in that file cabinet there's a file labeled: *Jeremiah, David.* In this file, I wouldn't be surprised at all if there was a notation that reads something like this: *Subject may be prone to discouragement, especially if he becomes overly weary. This has worked several times before and seems a promising method of attack. Suggestion: Make sure he stays very busy, overcommitted, and physically tired. At all costs, keep him from extended times of Bible reading and prayer.*

So what is Satan's strategy for me? He looks for ways to discourage me, and if possible, cause me some depression. He will use whatever people, means, or circumstances it takes to achieve his goal.

It's the same for you. Maybe your file says, "Frequently tempted to gossip," or "quick temper," or "prone to coveting and jealousy," or "weak in the area of lust." Don't kid yourself, he knows very well where your vulnerabilities lie. It's all in his file. You've heard, perhaps, that God loves you and has a wonderful plan for your life. That's very good news, but it is also true that Satan hates you and has a plan and strategy to destroy your walk with Jesus Christ.

That's one big reason why you experience struggle and discouragement in your Christian experience. Sometimes I hear people say, "Well, if you're a Christian, you shouldn't have any struggles. You shouldn't ever feel discouraged. All is peace and joy and love and happiness."

I don't think so.

I personally think that description fits better with life *before* you found salvation in Christ. Do you know why? Because you only had one influence in your life at that time. There was no contest for your heart. There was no tug-of-war for your soul.

When I received Jesus Christ, that's when my problems *started.* When the Son of God entered my life, He set up a kingdom in my heart that was opposed to the kingdom already there. And suddenly there was warfare between these two kingdoms. I'm reminded of a little poem that often comes to mind.

Two natures beat within my breast,
The one is foul; the one is blest.
The one I love; the one I hate,
The one I *feed* will dominate.

Isn't that true? If you don't understand that a spiritual war rages within you, you will be the victim of that conflict, not the victor.

But there is yet another pressing reason why the Spirit-filled walk is the only option for our lives.

BECAUSE OUR FLESH IS DESTRUCTIVE

In Galatians 5:16 we read "Walk in the Spirit," and what's the rest of the verse? *"And you shall not fulfill the lust of the flesh."*

What does that mean? The word *flesh* in the New Testament is a term that goes beyond bones, blood, and muscle. It's a word—especially in Paul's writing—that speaks of life apart from God. The flesh is everything you are minus God. The flesh is everything you were before Christ became your Savior.

So Paul says if we walk by means of the Spirit we won't be walking in the flesh. We won't be walking like God wasn't a part of us. Did you know that you can be a Christian and act as though God isn't even in your life? For all intents and purposes, some Christians are practical atheists. They live their lives as if there is no God. Are they Christians? Yes, if they've trusted Christ. But somehow they've gotten away from walking with the Lord. They are walking in their old flesh nature.

The flesh has a great power over us. You don't lose your flesh when Christ comes to live within you! You will carry that same unredeemed flesh with you until you step into the new resurrection body that the Lord will fashion for you one day. Here on earth, however, you and I have to live with two natures, an old one and a new one. The old nature is by no means eradicated. If you think that it is, you've got some serious theological problems to wrestle with. Because every time something ugly, evil, or ungodly erupts in your mind or heart, where did it come from? It didn't come out of a vacuum. It came from the old nature that is still resident within you.

Yes, if you surrender to Jesus Christ and allow the indwelling Holy Spirit to take full control, He begins to rule and reign in your life. But never without conflict! His rule will not go uncontested. If you don't believe me, listen to the next verse:

> For the flesh sets its desire against the Spirit, and the Spirit against the flesh; for these are in opposition to one another, so that you may not do the things that you please. (Galatians 5:17, NASB)

What is Paul saying? He's saying that there is a war going on within you. Flesh against the Spirit. This is more than a matter of human "willpower." I'm reminded of the old farmer who was seen struggling with a balky mule. Finally someone asked, "Why, Sam, where's your willpower?"

"My willpower's all right," old Sam grunted, "but you oughta come out here and see this pesky animal's *won't* power."

Sometimes people ask me, "Why is the flesh so stubborn? Why does the flesh have such a powerful tug on God's people? Why does it seem to be so much more difficult for some than others?" Let me toss out several ideas for you to consider.

Physical age versus spiritual age

Sometimes the flesh has an impact on us because of the discrepancy between our physical age and our spiritual age. Let me explain.

When I was fifteen years old, I gave my heart to Jesus Christ and became a believer. For me then, the flesh had a fifteen-year head start. Maybe your flesh had a thirty-year head start or a fifty-year head start—or more!—before you said yes to Jesus Christ. Why are you having such a difficult time of it? Well, your flesh got into the race before the Spirit did. Your flesh was well into the contest before your new nature in Christ even stepped onto the track.

In other words, all of those tendencies and habits of the flesh—things you learned and practiced when you weren't a Christian—dug deep grooves in your mind and in your spirit. And when you become a believer, there isn't an automatic erasure of all those old habits and patterns.

Did you know that in parts of the western United States, you can still see the original wagon ruts from the Oregon Trail? Obviously no one has taken a wagon down the Oregon Trail for generations, but the ruts are still there. You can stand right between them and see where the old wagon trail wound its way through the hills and plains and valleys. Wagon after wagon rolled along that old highway, deeply scoring the earth and creating ruts that have remained for over a hundred years.

It's the same way with old habits and thought patterns. We may have chosen a new direction, but those old ruts are still there. The old beaten paths are still there, leading to the same places they have always led. If we're not careful our wheels have a tendency to slip back into those old ways, and we'll find ourselves going the way we used to go. In fact, everything in our flesh *pulls* at us to go down those old rutted trails.

During those years before you knew Christ, you may have frequented some places you would never frequent now. You may have indulged in some habits or behaviors you want nothing to do with anymore. You may have some images or experiences burned into your mind that you certainly wish were no longer there. You may be sitting in church and enjoying a glorious worship experience when some of those old images will suddenly pop back into your mind and heart. What is happening? Satan is using the flesh to distract you.

But there is still another reason why the tug of our flesh seems so strong sometimes.

The influence of our culture

Let me ask you, what message does our culture promote these days—the Spirit or the flesh? It's no contest! You have to really work at it if you're going to glean any true spiritual benefit out of today's culture. You've got to get up early on Sunday morning, get in your car, go try to find a place to park, and come in and sit down in a building so somebody can give you some influence from the Spirit. Isn't that right?

But when you're at home, all you have to do is flip on the television or grab a magazine, and what do you see? The culture *constantly* showcases the flesh. If you doubt that, just glance at the magazine covers as you're waiting in line for groceries. You'll probably see more flesh than you want to see! The message is everywhere—calling to you, winking at you, teasing you, seeking to bend your thoughts and play with your emotions. It pops up everywhere you turn. And the odds don't seem very even, do they?

So as a believer, we're tugged this way and that. We try to live a life dominated by the Spirit, and yet the calls and the enticements to our flesh surround us all day long. It's in the newspaper. It's on the radio. It's plastered across the billboards. It's in the commercials on even the "good" television programs. The believer begins to feel guilty for the way he gets pulled around. He feels defeated. Overwhelmed. And he doesn't know what to do. *It must be me!* he tells himself. *There must be something very, very wrong with me.*

If I didn't understand what that endless struggle within me was all about, I could become totally depressed and discouraged. I would feel like giving up. I would think there was no hope, no answer. (But there *is* an answer, so stay with me. We're not finished yet!)

The incompatibility of our lifestyle with the world's

Here's another reason why we feel the tug of the flesh so strongly. Once you become a Christian, you are immediately out of sync with the world. You say up and the world says down. You go left and the world veers right. You zig and the world immediately zags. Christians are always swimming against the current and walking into the wind. Have you noticed?

A. W. Tozer puts it this way: "The real Christian is an odd human being anyway. The Christian feels supreme love for one he's never seen. He talks every day with somebody he can't see. He expects to go to heaven on the virtue of somebody else. He empties himself in order to be full. He admits he is wrong so he can be declared right. He goes down in order to get up. He's strongest when he's weakest, richest when he's poorest, happiest when he feels the worst. He dies so he can live, he forsakes others to have, he gives away so that he can keep. He sees the invisible, hears the inaudible, and knows that which passeth knowledge."[1]

We're really into something, aren't we? The Christian life isn't compatible with the world in which you and I live. It will never "fit in." It's totally *other*. And the more you and I understand that fact, the closer we will walk with the Lord. I don't mean that you're out there being some sort of weird separatist person who holes up in a cabin in Montana and doesn't talk to neighbors. But the fact is, our lives truly are different. We have been fundamentally changed because of who Christ is and what He's done. That's another big reason why the spiritual part of you continues to struggle and war with the flesh part of you. As far as this world and this culture are concerned, you can never "go with the flow." Your goals and dreams and desires will always be incompatible with the goals, dreams, and desires of the very world in which you live.

But there is one final element I need to add here.

The irresponsibility of our lives

Many times we have conflicts with the flesh simply because we don't take the responsibility we should take to be in God's Word, to follow His instruction, and to be filled with the Spirit. And even when we do hear the Spirit speak or seek to nudge us in a certain direction, we close our ears.

What did Paul say? "Walk by the Spirit, and *you will not* carry out the desire of the flesh." It's as simple as that.

Now, if you want a good picture of what it's like to walk in the flesh, all you have to do is read on in the fifth chapter of Galatians, because it gives you a large-screen, full-color picture of what the flesh life is like. And friend, it isn't pretty.

The activities of the [flesh] are obvious. Here is a list: sexual immorality, impurity of mind, sensuality, worship of false gods, witchcraft, hatred, quarreling, jealousy, bad temper, rivalry, factions...envy, drunkenness, orgies and things like that. (Galatians 5:19–21, Phillips)

It's kind of like a little sketch of life...with God taken out of the middle.

Have I convinced you that we need help? The overwhelming testimony of the Bible is that the demands of the Christian life are great, the determination of the enemy is absolutely unwavering, and the destructive influence of the flesh is out to unravel everything we are or hope to be in Christ.

But listen to me...that's not the whole story! We have been given a power, we have been given a Person, we have been given an opportunity to live life on a completely different level as we learn to walk by means of the Spirit. When you walk by the Spirit, you learn how to depend on God every day for everything in every way all the time.

SPIRITUAL BREATHING

As a young pastor, I was exposed to the ministry of Campus Crusade founder Bill Bright. In his teaching about the filling of the Holy Spirit, Dr. Bright used a very simple word picture that has helped me for years. It went something like this.

If you ask the Spirit of God to control your life, He does! And life is better than it has ever been before. You experience a joy and a power and a perspective in your days that is beyond anything you've ever encountered before.

Along the way, however, sin enters the picture. It's like a black ink splotch on a white piece of linen writing paper. You do something that grieves or quenches this wonderful Holy Spirit who has been given to you. In a sense, you push Him off the throne of your life and allow the old flesh nature back in control. What do you experience then? Discouragement. Sadness. Struggle!

But that's where Dr. Bright's little word picture of "spiritual breathing" enters in. Think of normal physical breathing. What does it involve? Just two things, really: inhaling fresh air and exhaling bad air. It's what we do all day long, all night long. I can guarantee that if you're reading these words right now, you are engaged in the business of inhaling and exhaling.

Spiritual breathing is a similar process. It is exhaling the impure and inhaling the pure. It is rejecting the bad and embracing the good. It works like this: When you become aware of sin in your life, you deal with it at that very moment, wherever you are—in the car, at home, at the office, wherever. Let's say you just screamed at one of your kids. Now, little Johnny might have really pushed the limits—not to mention pushing your buttons. But you're supposed to be living in the Spirit, right? What do you do when you become aware of your sin? Well, you could spend the rest of the day justifying what you've done. After all, you've worked and slaved for those kids, and they ought to show a little more appreciation and consideration, right?

But in your heart, you know that you have sinned. You know that you have grieved the Holy Spirit of God. He has made you aware of this sin and wants you to immediately confess it and seek forgiveness. First John 1:9 says, "If we confess our sins, He is faithful and just to forgive us our sins and to cleanse us from all unrighteousness."

You say, "Lord, I agree with You that what I just did was wrong. I have sinned. I ask that You would forgive me for that sin." What have you done? You have just *exhaled* the impurity in your heart. Then you say, "Lord, I want You to be in control of my life once again. I want You to be the One who guides me in all that I do and think. Please fill me again with Your Holy Spirit." That's *inhaling!*

"Well," you say, "how often do I have to do that?"

As often as necessary.

"But," you protest, "I'd be praying all day long!"

Then pray all day long.

Let me tell you what will happen in your life as you begin to practice this principle. At first it will seem almost overwhelming to you. You'll be doing it every forty-five minutes, or every thirty minutes, or every five minutes! But the more you concentrate on confessing and forsaking sin and seeking the filling of the Spirit, the further apart those episodes of "spiritual breathing" will become. I believe this with all my heart. You may discover—to your joy—that you can live a whole day in the power of the Holy Spirit without having to exercise spiritual breathing. But, my friend, if you allow sin to remain in your heart and stop seeking the filling of the Spirit, you may wake up to discover you've been walking in the flesh a long, long time.

And that is a very dangerous way to live.

I read recently where two young women lost their lives in a fire that swept through their apartment as they slept. They probably died from smoke inhalation before the flames ever reached their bedrooms. The apartment manager was beside himself. The women's apartment had been equipped with a functional smoke detector. Why hadn't it gone off? Why weren't they warned?

Fire investigators concluded that the safety device had been deliberately deactivated for a party that had been held the night before. Someone had disconnected the unit to keep it from shrilling while meat broiled in the oven. But they forgot to reconnect it, so they had no warning of the fire that took their lives.

In the same way, quenching the voice of the Holy Spirit and continuing to walk in the flesh can be deadly to your spiritual health. The Spirit may be warning us about a course of action, but we no longer hear Him.

Christians can walk in the flesh for years because they refuse to deal with the sin in their life and reappropriate the fullness of the Spirit. Remember, the command in Ephesians 5:18 to "be filled with the Spirit" is in the present tense. It's telling us to "*keep on* being filled."

And so you walk along in the Spirit, consciously giving Him control of your life, and you stumble over something. What do you do? You immediately cry out to God. And does He hear you? Yes, He does.

Let's say you're driving along in your car and some guy in a dirty Ford Pinto cuts right in front of you, forcing you to jam on your brakes. A thought leaps to your mind. Words leap to your lips. And you feel yourself being controlled by anger and—yes—hatred. As soon as you're aware of it, you take it to the Lord. I've done this many times. I've said, "Lord, that wasn't right. Please forgive me for that thought. Forgive me for those bitter words. That's not who You are, Lord, that's who I am in my flesh. Lord, that thought isn't in keeping with Your holy character and Your desire for my life. Please forgive me. Now take control of my life, and help me to live this day for You." That ought to be a constant conversation with you and God throughout the day.

When that begins to happen in your life, it's an extremely encouraging thing. One day it will suddenly dawn on you that you and God have been on the same page for a long time. Glorious!

Maybe that's what happened to Enoch. Scripture says that "Enoch walked with God; then he was no more, because God took him away" (Genesis 5:24,

NIV). He walked with the Lord in close conversation for so many years that one day he and God just walked right off this earth and into heaven. I'm not sure Enoch even knew what happened until he looked around and realized that he and the Lord had walked right off the planet. What a way to go!

It's exciting to walk in the Holy Spirit. It's exhilarating to really sense that you are a "work in progress" and that the Spirit of the living God is reshaping and remolding your life from within. You find that you are becoming more and more sensitive to the Spirit's voice. You are becoming more and more careful about sin. When you do sin, the "interruption" in that walk with the Spirit feels so miserable that you want to put it behind you right away. Activities that never used to bother you begin to bother you. Attitudes in your heart that you never used to notice begin to seem obvious, and you want to put them away.

In short, the Holy Spirit is leaving His mark on your life...and that mark is holiness.

The average Christian who never gets hold of this lives a roller-coaster life. He never seems to develop any momentum toward godly living. He gets off the track a little bit, doesn't deal with it, and the next thing he knows, he's off a little bit more. Before long he's in a deep valley and wondering how in the world he ended up in such a place. Then a crisis enters his life and he cries out to God. Perhaps in those moments, God will seem far away. But that's not because *God* has moved!

The truth is, if you take care of the little problems, you'll never have to deal with the big ones. If you take care of the little interruptions in your relationship with the Holy Spirit, there'll never be a big, life-wrecking interruption. If you take care of the little foxes that spoil the grapes, you won't have to deal with a pack of wolves on your doorstep.

The Bible says that if you and I judge ourselves, we will not be judged. That means you and I need to be constantly asking God to help us walk by means of the Spirit. And what is the result of that? If you walk by means of the Spirit, you will not fulfill the lusts of the flesh. We have God's Word on that.

In Galatians 5:24–25 it says, "And those who are Christ's have crucified the flesh with its passions and desires. If we live in the Spirit, let us also walk in the Spirit." Here's the key. If we live in the Spirit, if we have the Spirit within us and He is our very life, let's *walk* that way. Let's really *live* that way. And God will honor that decision with victory all along the way.

Do you remember those great demands we spoke of at the beginning of the chapter? The Christian life is a demanding life. Right? Remember all those instructions on how we ought to walk? Well, how do you walk and meet those heavy demands? Let's wrap up this chapter by looking at three verses.

First, let's consider the words of Jesus. He told His disciples, "I am the vine, you are the branches. He who abides in Me, and I in him, bears much fruit." Now, how does the rest of this verse read? *"For without Me you can do nothing"* (John 15:5).

Do you know what nothing is? Nothing is a zero with the edges rubbed out. That's nothing. You can't do anything without God. If you try to keep those demands we spoke of at the beginning of the chapter, do you know what will happen? You'll fail. You'll burn out. You can't do it.

But here's the corollary...here is the verse that balances out John 15:5. Over in the book of Philippians, Paul writes, "I can do all things through Christ who strengthens me" (4:13). What you *can't* do to meet the demands of the Christian life in your flesh, you *can* do in the power of the Holy Spirit. He will equip and strengthen you to do it as you depend on Him and trust Him.

Picture being in the second seat on a tandem bicycle. The Holy Spirit is up front, steering and pedaling along strongly and easily. You're pedaling, too, but you know where the real power is coming from. And suddenly you find yourself gliding right up and over all of those long hills you never used to be able to climb on your own. The Holy Spirit is in control, and you get to go everywhere He wants to go. It's a tour through life that's better than anything you could have experienced solo.

"Well," you say, "what about this formidable enemy who's out to destroy me? What about this evil being who has laid all of those strategies to knock me off that bike and send me crashing into the ditch? Do you want some good truth about that? Listen to this! "Greater is He who is in you than he who is in the world" (1 John 4:4, NASB).

You're worried about Satan? Welcome to the club! But what does this verse say? Satan is no match for the Holy Spirit! The devil can't be the "opposite" of God, because he was originally created by God as Lucifer. He isn't the dark side of some impersonal force; he is a living creature who is subservient to the living God. Yes, the lion may roar and prowl, but greater is He, the Holy Spirit, who is in you than Satan, the one who is in the world. You already have the greater power, the greater person. Take great encouragement from that!

What about the destructive influence of the flesh? That's a question that brings us right back to where we began. "Walk in the Spirit, and you shall not fulfill the lust of the flesh."

Dwight L. Moody once demonstrated the principle like this. "Tell me," he said to his audience, "how I can get the air out of the tumbler I have in my hand?"

One man said, "Suck it out with a pump."

"Yes," the evangelist replied, "but that would create a vacuum and shatter it." Finally, after a number of suggestions, Moody picked up a pitcher and quietly filled the glass with water.

"There," he said. "All of the air is now removed." He then explained that victory for the child of God does not come by working hard to eliminate habits of the flesh, but rather by allowing the Holy Spirit to take full possession.

Yes, the demands of the Christian life are high, but Jesus is equal to the task.

Yes, the enemy is overwhelming, but the Spirit of God in you is greater than he is.

Yes, the flesh has incredible pull, but if you walk in the Spirit, you will not fulfill the lusts of the flesh.

There is victory in Jesus, praise His name!

Chapter Eight

THE FRUIT
OF THE SPIRIT

A GROWING EVIDENCE
OF HIS PRESENCE

But the fruit of the Spirit is love, joy, peace,
longsuffering, kindness, goodness, faithfulness,
gentleness, self-control. Against such there is no law.
And those who are Christ's have crucified
the flesh with its passions and desires.
If we live in the Spirit, let us also walk in the Spirit.

GALATIANS 5:22–25

uring World War II, a young teenager tried to enlist in the navy. Only fifteen but large for his years, he told the recruiting officer in Richmond, Virginia, that he was sixteen. The officer looked at him and shook his head.

"Sorry, son, you're not old enough."

Two months later, he returned. The recruiter didn't seem to remember him, so this time he listed his age as seventeen. Again the answer was, "Sorry, you're not old enough."

He waited a few weeks and returned again. This time, in reply to the recruiter's question, he said he was eighteen. The man looked at the teenager and smiled. "Young man," he said, "we would really like to have you in our navy. The only trouble is, you're aging so fast that I'm afraid we'd have to put you on pension before the war was over."

Wouldn't it be great if every believer had that kind of desire to mature in the faith? It's sad—and a little difficult to understand—how many Christians never seem to advance beyond "entry level" in their walk with the Lord. They have walked through the open door of salvation and stopped just inside the doorway.

Imagine an immigrant from "the old country" coming into New York harbor on a ship and then receiving the blessing and privileges of American citizenship. Then imagine that same individual setting up housekeeping and living out his years in a little shed behind the processing center on Ellis Island.

"What are you doing here?" someone might well ask this person.

"Well, my goal was to get to America. And here I am. I'm in America. This is good enough."

"But sir," someone might say, "you don't have to live this way. You're an American now. The country is wide open to you. There's a whole nation out there—tens of thousands of square miles—waiting for you. Endless opportunities! Towering mountains…great rivers…vibrant cities…beautiful forests…rich farmland…prairies wide as an ocean. Why content yourself with sleeping in the corner of this little shed when so much lies before you?"

It's the same for believers. There are untold resources and wonders waiting for us in our walk with Christ. Such awesome vistas. So much beauty and power. The Bible tells us that you and I have been "blessed…with every spiritual blessing in the heavenly places in Christ" (Ephesians 1:3). You cannot faithfully study the Scriptures without being challenged by the opportunities and excitement of growing into Christlikeness. The Word of God paints a strikingly beautiful portrait of what a Christlike person looks like, acts like, and feels like when they walk around in the world.

That's what we have in the fruit of the Spirit.

But don't miss the context of this powerful passage. Just before the listing of this radiant, attractive fruit of the Spirit, you have another list that isn't attractive at all. In fact, it's repulsive. What you have in Galatians 5 then are two opportunities, two options. You can live your life *that* way, or you can live your life *this* way. A person who isn't filled with the Spirit and exhibiting the fruit of the Spirit will ultimately begin to live his or her life after the categories of sin listed here among "the works of the flesh."

> Now the works of the flesh are evident, which are: adultery, fornication, uncleanness, licentiousness, idolatry, sorcery, hatred, contentions, jealousies, outbursts of wrath, selfish ambitions, dissensions, heresies, envy, murders, drunkenness, revelries, and the like.… (Galatians 5:19–21)

Paul paints this dark backdrop of life apart from the Holy Spirit so that we can really appreciate what happens when we let the Spirit of God control us and exhibit His qualities in our lives.

Fruit is something you can observe. It isn't concealed or secret. I've lived in Southern California nearly eighteen years now, yet as a Midwest boy, I still love to see an orange tree laden with oranges. (After you've eaten a tree-ripened orange, the store-bought kind will always taste like a weak imitation.)

Fruit isn't something hidden. You walk by the tree, and there it is. In the same way, if a person is walking in the Spirit of God, there will be visible, recognizable evidences in his or her life. How then is the beautiful fruit displayed? In a glass showcase? In a dusty museum? Is it like the plastic fruit people put on their coffee tables and dust every other week? No, the fruit of the Spirit is always displayed in the context of *relationships* with others. You don't bear fruit simply for yourself. You bear fruit in your life so that you might have the opportunity to touch the lives of others.

God, through the inspiration of the Holy Spirit, directed Paul to organize these characteristics in a very special way so that they literally describe every part of who we are in Christ. Let's imagine three tree branches with three pieces of fruit on each. In other words, there are three triads of characteristics or virtues.

On that first branch, three pieces of fruit describe our personal experience with God.

On the next branch, three pieces of fruit describe our personal relationships with others.

On the third branch, three pieces of fruit describe our personal development as people.

OUR PERSONAL EXPERIENCE WITH GOD

Being filled with the Spirit of God is no academic, intellectual exercise. Wherever the Spirit of God moves, there is an impact on *life*. Paul says that when you are filled with the Spirit of God, it will directly mark your own personal experience. Whatever your life may have been known for previously, your life in the Spirit will be characterized by love, joy, and peace.

The fruit of the Spirit is love

Men and women were created specifically to enjoy fellowship and relationship with God. It wasn't that God needed someone to hoe the corn or prune the apple trees in the Garden of Eden. God could have sent angels to do that, and you can bet they would have done a first-class job. Man and woman, beings with a free will, were created to enjoy companionship and a personal relationship with the Creator. God met them and walked with them every afternoon, "in the cool of the day."

There was conversation. There was sharing. There was love.

That fellowship was shattered in the garden by sin. And it was lost until Jesus Christ came and made fellowship possible again.

When Adam and Eve rebelled against God in the garden, love was broken— destroyed—in terms of God's original design and intentions. But when Christ came into the world and died on the cross, He brought back the possibility of real *agape* love, the very term Paul uses here in Galatians 5. I believe it could be said that love is the subject of this passage—love *is* the fruit of the Spirit—and everything that follows is a description of that love.

When you study the concept of *agape* love in the New Testament, you learn that it is the primary commandment God has given to us. Do you remember when the lawyer came to Jesus and said, "What is the greatest commandment?" And Jesus said in Matthew 22:37–39: "'You shall love the LORD your God with all your heart, with all your soul, and with all your mind'.... And the second is like it: 'You shall love your neighbor as yourself.'"

What is the greatest command? It is to love.

Not only is it the priority commandment, it's the perfect gift. In the book of 1 Corinthians, Paul teaches on the subject of spiritual gifts. But when he gets to the end of the twelfth chapter, after he has outlined all the different spiritual gifts that are possible, in the last verse of that chapter he says, "But I want to show you a more excellent way."

And what is that "more excellent way"? It is 1 Corinthians 13, the love chapter. It's the chapter that's all about God's *agape* love. Paul tells us that you can have all the spiritual gifts, but if you don't have love, you've missed everything, because the *agape* love of God is the perfect gift.

So, it's the priority commandment, it's the perfect gift, but I want you to note also that it's the permanent virtue. Read through 1 Corinthians 13 and what happens when you get clear to the end of it? In a summary statement the apostle says, "And now abide faith, hope, and love." What's the rest of it? "But the greatest of these is love."

It is the most awesome of all of the virtues. It is the most all-encompassing virtue that you can possess as a believer in Jesus Christ.

Finally, it's the proof of your faith. Did you know that? How do you know if someone is a Christian? Well, you might say, do they go to church every week? Do they give money to the church? Do they live upright lives in the community? Those are all important things, but Jesus gave us the one sure way you can tell whether or not a man or woman is truly a believer. By this very thing, Jesus said, all will know that you are My disciples. And what is that?

"If you have love one for another."

When we're controlled by the Spirit of God, when He is president of our lives, one of the things that will be evident is that we're people of love. If you get around folks who are cantankerous and angry and mean-spirited, they might be Christians, but they're not Spirit-controlled Christians. Because when the Spirit of God controls you, He makes you to be like Jesus Christ, the very embodiment of love.

When I was a young boy growing up in the church, my father was a pastor. Every once in a while we would have evangelistic meetings and bring in a chalk artist. Have you ever seen a chalk artist at work? You don't see them much anymore. With videos and all of the high-tech stuff available today, chalk artists have become out of fashion. But they were gifted people, and the Lord used them to touch many thousands of lives.

Typically, the artist would come into the church auditorium and prepare a canvas in the afternoon. In the evening service, he would do the remaining chalk work (usually while his wife was singing a solo). And then, when the time was right, he would turn on his black light with a dramatic flourish. And you would suddenly see things in that canvas that you had not seen to that point.

It was beautiful and extremely impressive to me as a boy. Every once in a while, I'd get my dad to ask for the chalk portrait when the artist was done. But I didn't know how to preserve a chalk painting, and by the time I got home with my prize, I'd have chalk all over my clothes. A day or two later, you couldn't even tell what the drawing was.

But I remember being impressed that these chalk evangelists would spend hours and hours during the day doing the initial artistry on the canvas. At night, during the evening service, they knew they would only have a few minutes to add finishing touches.

Love is like the preparation of the canvas for all of the other beautiful characteristics which we see in 1 Corinthians 13 and Galatians 5. Love is the backdrop, before all the other parts of the picture are chalked in. If you have God's self-giving love, the rest of these things will be true of you as well. If you don't have that kind of love, none of them will be true. The fruit of the Spirit is love.

Is that what you're all about? Would people describe you as a loving person? Maybe you should ask your spouse. Maybe you should ask the people you work with. Do you exhibit Spirit-filled love in your life?

The fruit of the Spirit is joy

Sherwood Wirt, a friend of mine who lives here in San Diego, wrote an excellent book recently with just one subject: joy. In introducing his subject he writes, "It seems that this book, known to us as the Sacred Scriptures, lists 542 references to joy, which would include gladness, delight, pleasure, laughter, merry, happy, exuberance, jubilation, merriment, rapture, bliss, elation. In other words, I made an incredible discovery. I discovered that the Bible is a book of joy."[1]

We ought to be joyous people. Our pastoral staff does conferences all over the country several times during the year. We take our whole staff, go into a place where we've never been before, and interact with as many people as we can. Again and again, I've heard the same response to our presence and ministry. "Boy, you guys sure have a lot of joy. You really have fun together."

Yes, we do! In fact...we don't let people work here unless they have joy. That's one of the ways we recruit. We take a person out to lunch and we tell him or her all the funniest stories we know. If they don't laugh, we don't hire 'em. Frankly, I don't want to work in a joyless environment. I don't want to spend my days with joyless people. Life's too short! The Spirit-controlled life is a life of joy.

Now, please be reminded that this joy isn't necessarily "happiness." Happiness has to do with *happenings*. And all of us face days when we feel some stress from the happenings of life—perhaps even great stress.

But joy...

That's something different, friend. That has to do with your relationship with Jesus Christ. It's centered in Him! It's centered in the One who does not change and cannot change. Jesus said in John 15:11, "These things I have spoken to you, that My joy may remain in you, and that your joy may be full." What kind of joy do we have as Christians? We have the joy of the Lord Jesus Christ. It's centered in Christ; it is complete and absolute.

Did you notice the last part of that verse I just quoted? The Bible says that our joy in Jesus Christ is FULL. Full joy. This is joy that tops off your tank. Have you ever been in a restaurant where the waiter fills your glass with orange juice to the point where the liquid almost bulges on top? And you say, "How am I supposed to drink this? If I even nudge this thing it will spill." By the way...what happens when people nudge *you*? What happens when people rub up against your life? What spills out of you? Do they get joy all over them?

In 1 Peter 1:8 we read these words:

And though you have not seen Him, you love Him, and though you do not see Him now, but believe in Him, you greatly rejoice with joy inexpressible and full of glory. (NASB)

Joy *inexpressible*. What is that? It's a joy you can't even put into words. It's joy that bubbles up from a well deeper than your understanding or intellect. If you tried to write about that joy, you'd have to throw down your pencil after a few sentences and say, "I just can't do it. No matter what I try to say about this, it falls short." Is that the kind of joy you possess in your life? Joy inexpressible and full of glory? Joy that's complete?

And not only is this joy centered in Jesus Christ, not only is it full and complete, but—listen to this—it is certain, in spite of circumstances.

You say, "Well, David, you grew up in a stable home, have a fine family, live in a nice house, and pastor a good church in a beautiful city where the sun shines most of the time. No wonder you have joy."

Yes, praise God, I have been *very* blessed. But let me tell you something. If you were sitting across the table from me right now, I could look you straight in the eyes and say these next words: I had joy in the midst of life-threatening cancer just as much as I have joy right now, after having been cancer-free for three years.

Was I happy about my illness? Was I pleased with the circumstances in which I found myself? Not at all! No more than you would have been. But that has nothing to do with the deep-down joy that kept welling up within my soul during those dark days. Joy has nothing to do with whether or not you are pleased with your particular life situation. Joy is that deep-seated sense of well-being that's in you and that sustains you *no matter what's happening on the outside.* Whatever your set of circumstances, you can sing with all of your heart, "It is well with my soul."

What do you say to someone so deep in sorrow that they can hardly speak? Jesus looked around at His men, eleven guys who had (finally) understood that their Lord was about to be betrayed and killed. And then He said these words:

> "Therefore you now have sorrow; but I will see you again and your heart will rejoice, and your joy no one will take from you." (John 16:22)

Do you have that kind of joy? If you have the Real Thing—I don't mean just a happy arrangement of circumstances, but joy in Jesus—then listen to me: *nobody can take that from you.* Nobody can steal it. It's yours. And no matter what kind of difficulty you're going through, no matter what kind of problems you're facing, if you have Jesus, you have His joy.

You say, "Does that mean I'm walking around laughing and chuckling like a crazy person? Not at all. Joy isn't always laughter. It isn't always noisy. It isn't always hilarity. Sometimes it may be very, very quiet and personal. Sometimes it may be mixed with some tears. But it is real, because it is centered in Jesus.

I penned this next verse in my journal. It's been a great encouragement to me in recent years. Nehemiah 8:10 says this: "The joy of the LORD is your strength." Do you have that strength? It is your birthright as a child of God.

The fruit of the Spirit is peace

Peace completes the first "trilogy," the first cluster of fruit that relates to personal experience. This is Godward fruit. If I am filled with the Spirit of God, I will be described as a loving person, I will have joy and peace in my life.

The word for *peace* in the Greek language is the word *iranai,* and it means "to join together." It is a picture of two opposing forces once separated but now reconciled. Do you know what peace is? Peace is knowing that the God you were once separated from, you are now joined to through Jesus Christ. And that's why Romans 5:1 says, "Therefore, having been justified by faith, we have peace with God through our Lord Jesus Christ." We have been joined together. We will never be separated again, in time or eternity.

This is a peace that has the very same attributes we listed for joy. First of all, it's centered in Jesus Christ, isn't it? He says, "Peace I leave with you, My peace I give to you; not as the world gives do I give to you. Let not your heart be troubled, neither let it be afraid" (John 14:27).

Whose peace is this that we possess? It's Jesus' peace. It's My joy, and it's My peace, said Jesus. And it is complete and absolute peace. Do you know how absolute it really is? Listen to the way David describes it in Psalm 4:8. "I will both lie down in peace, and sleep; for You alone, O LORD, make me dwell in safety."

Can you do that? Do you lie down in peace and sleep? I'm thankful to God that I've never had much trouble sleeping. I'm one of those annoying people you've heard about who hardly ever loses any sleep. It's a wonderful thing to pillow your head at night, have a sense of peace in your heart, and be able to sleep. I can take a nap in the middle of the afternoon for five to ten minutes and be totally refreshed. It drives my wife crazy! I say, "I'm tired. I think I'll take a little nap." And just like that, I'm out. I sleep for five or ten minutes, and I wake up refreshed and ready to go again.

You may not have that gift of instant slumber, but the more important question is, do you have peace in your heart that no matter what's going on, you can still pillow your head and sleep? Are you able to release those anxieties and worries that rob your peace and steal your rest?

Finally, just as we said with joy, this peace is certain in spite of circumstances. Remember what our Lord said? "These things I have spoken to you, that in Me you may have peace. In the world you will have tribulation; but be of good cheer, I have overcome the world" (John 16:33).

Isn't that an encouraging expression? *Be of good cheer!* Take heart! Have courage! Why? Because our Lord is bigger than any circumstance in which we could ever find ourselves. He is the Overcomer, and we are in Him. What a wonderful Savior!

Spirit-filled believers have this peace no matter what may be going on around them. It controls their emotions. It gives them a calmness when their human spirit would rush into panic. As a pastor, I've been called on again and again to walk into a home or a waiting room where people have been shaken by tragedy. Sometimes I am with people who are enduring the most awful moments of their entire lives—something has crashed into their experience that they never dreamed could happen to them. Those are tender, often wrenching moments, and they are never easy. Yet at the same time, I can't even describe how awesome it is to be with believers and to sense that deep-seated peace that moves into a room and just takes over. Yes, there is sorrow. Yes, there is concern and stress. But there is something else there too. Something so real and solid you almost feel as though you could reach out and grab hold of it.

While I was a student at Dallas Seminary years ago, I served as the student chaplain at Baylor Hospital for a few months, during the night shift. One of my tasks was to talk with people in the family room of the hospital whenever a crisis happened. Sometimes if there was an accident, they would call the chaplain's office and say, "Would you go down and talk with these people?" Maybe someone had died in surgery or been seriously injured or killed in an accident.

You never really knew what you were going to encounter when you walked through that door…but I could walk into that room and *immediately* know if I was with believers. I remember going into some rooms after a tragedy and watching someone on the floor, banging his head into the carpet, screaming in despair, because there was no hope. At other times, I'd walk into a room after an accident every bit as terrible and encounter a completely different scene. Yes, there would be some crying and hugging, but as soon as I stepped into the room, I would sense a peace you could not comprehend.

That is the kind of peace you get when the Spirit of God controls your life—Spirit-filled peace. In Philippians 4:7, Paul says it is a peace that "surpasses all understanding." In other words, it doesn't make a bit of earthly sense. It isn't logical. It doesn't add up. It doesn't square with the circumstances.

But friend, it is as real as this morning's sunrise.

Philippians 4:7 goes on to say that this peace will "guard your hearts and minds through Christ Jesus." Praise God for His peace.

You might be asking, "Are those things—that love and joy and peace—ever interrupted?" Of course they are! We are flawed human beings, and sometimes we have to go through spiritual breathing again, don't we? We have to exhale sin and inhale the fullness of the Holy Spirit. But when you're filled with the Spirit, when you're walking the Spirit-filled life, these three things will characterize your personal experience. They'll be there on the branches of your life, just as oranges grow on orange trees. And once you've tasted His love, His joy, and His peace, no imitation, man-made substitute will ever satisfy you.

OUR PERSONAL RELATIONSHIPS WITH OTHERS

The first three fruits—love, joy, and peace—are Godward. The second three are manward. These are three characteristics that will be exhibited in your life with regard to other people.

The fruit of the Spirit is longsuffering

Isn't this a great word? In several of the newer translations it's rendered as *patience*. In the Greek language, it's actually two words blended into one term. *Macrothumia.* The word *macro* in the Greek language means "long," and the *thumia* means "heat" or "temper" or "explosion."

The word *longsuffering,* then, means to have a long temper. What's the opposite of long-tempered? Uh-huh. Short-tempered. Do you know anybody with a short temper? The Bible says that a person who is filled with the Spirit has a l-o-n-g temper. They're not like nitroglycerin that tends to explode if it's jostled. These people have self-control over their emotions.

When I grew up in the Midwest, firecrackers were both legal and plentiful. Did you ever light a firecracker with a short fuse? You touch a match to it and— BLAM!—it goes off in your face or in your hand. Some people have short fuses too. It's not much fun to be around someone like that. You find yourself wincing when something goes wrong. *When will he blow? When will she go ballistic?* The slightest little spark will trigger an explosion...and people get hurt in explosions.

One writer defines longsuffering as self-restraint that doesn't hastily retaliate wrong. Paul prayed for this when he spoke to the Colossians. He wrote: "[I want you to be] strengthened with all might, according to His glorious power, for all patience and longsuffering with joy" (Colossians 1:11).

When you are filled with the Spirit of God, you *relate* to other people. You don't just blow your stack every time something doesn't go your way. Yes, you may have a little trigger that goes off inside of you, but the Spirit of God gets control of it every time before it releases. You start to say something but the words die in your throat. You write that hot letter then throw it in the fireplace and never send it. You plan that sharp-worded speech, and you never deliver it.

The Spirit of God keeps you in control of that situation. There are times when we will find ourselves in very volatile situations, with sparks flying every which way. But the Spirit of God can give us the strength to display this virtue in our lives. And when you are keeping your cool at the very moment when everybody else is losing theirs, believe me, the spiritual fruit of longsuffering will be very, very evident.

The fruit of the Spirit is kindness

The King James Bible lists this quality as *gentleness,* but the Greek word really is closer to the word *kind.* Someone has said that kindness is like the impress in a coin which tells us who the owner is. Kindness is the impress of God upon His creatures. God's person, a man or woman walking in God's Spirit, will be moved by a spirit of kindness toward other people.

Sadly, the virtue of kindness is becoming more and more unusual in our world. What were once "common courtesies" are becoming most uncommon. We live in an angry world. A world with a chip on its shoulder. A world that's in a big hurry.

Incidents of "road rage," those horrible crimes where someone gets angry in traffic and shoots another driver, are increasing all over the country. A recent story from the *Philadelphia Daily News* stated that aggressive driving accounted for half of that city's auto accidents. A survey of accidents during the 1990s showed that four of the top six causes for accidents were not carelessness, but aggression: running stoplights, tailgating, improper turning, and failure to heed a stopped vehicle. Aggressive drivers, the paper concluded, kill two to four times more people than do drunks.[2]

Between January 1, 1990, and September 1, 1996, a total of 12,828 people were injured or killed as the result of aggressive driving, including 94 children under the age of 15.[3]

We're living in an era that is forgetting what it means to be kind, and people get run over by other people in a hurry to meet their own goals. Especially children, who haven't learned to get out of the way. So kindness is rare today...and you know what happens when something becomes increasingly rare, don't you? It also becomes increasingly valued and treasured. A person of Spirit-filled kindness is a great treasure.

I remember a verse on a little placard from some of my earliest years in

Sunday school. It was from Ephesians 4:32, and we only learned that first little phrase: "Be kind to one another."

John Wesley was said to be one of the kindest men who ever lived. He was a strong preacher and a vigorous champion for the faith. And yet, on an individual basis, those who were around him knew they were in the presence of a deeply kind man. Wesley had a little rule of life for himself that he sought to live by in the strength of the Spirit. This was his motto: "Do all the good you can by all the means you can in all the places you can at all the times you can to all the people you can as long as ever you can."

In other words, be kind. Be kind in your home. Be kind in your workplace. And yes, be kind when some arrogant, aggressive driver deliberately cuts you off in traffic and seeks to provoke you! When we're filled with the Spirit of God, our relationships with others are long-tempered, and they are filled with kindness.

The fruit of the Spirit is goodness

When we're filled with the Spirit, our relationship to one another is described as a relationship that is good.

Two women, rivals in their social circle, met at a party. "My dear," said the one, "are those *real* pearls?"

"They are," replied the other.

"Of course," said the first, smiling, "the only way I could really tell would be to bite one of them."

"Yes," agreed the bejeweled woman, "but for that you would need real teeth!"

Seems as if there was a bit of goodness lacking in that relationship. Don't you agree?

The word for *goodness* is found four times in the New Testament. It's a profound word. Have you ever heard somebody say, "He's a *good* man" or "She's a *good* woman"? That's what they should say about us when we're Spirit-controlled. That doesn't mean we're perfect. That doesn't mean we don't make mistakes. But men and women who are filled with the Holy Spirit are simply good people. The fruit of their goodness is obvious wherever they go.

Don't you just like to be around good people? People with long tempers? People who are courteous and considerate? Praise God for people like that. They bring glory to the name of their Master, the One who called Himself the "Good Shepherd."

OUR PERSONAL DEVELOPMENT AS PEOPLE

Now let me add the final part of this trilogy. There are three sets of three. First of all, in our experience with God there should be love, joy, and peace. Secondly, in our relationships with others there should be longsuffering, and kindness, and goodness. And then, third, the fruit of the Spirit in our personal development. This is what we might call selfward fruit. And here, again, we have a branch with three pieces of surpassingly beautiful fruit.

The fruit of the Spirit is faithfulness

When I began to study this characteristic, I expected Paul to be talking about faith—believing great things from God. But no, what he is really talking about is faithfulness.

Faith is a theological term. *Faithfulness* is an ethical term. What Paul is saying is when you are filled with the Spirit of God, you will be growing more and more into the kind of person about whom it is said, "He's a faithful guy. He has integrity." Or "When she says she'll do it, she gets it done." In other words, this is fidelity produced in your life by the Holy Spirit, as you walk with Him and in Him.

Proverbs 20:6 asks a sobering question: "Who can find a faithful man?" Pastors—and leaders of every sort—are always looking for such people. The Bible says when the Spirit of God controls you, one of the developing virtues in your life is the virtue of faithfulness. You become a person who can be counted on, trusted in, relied upon. You become, as Western writer Louis L'Amour might have put it, "A man to ride the river with."

Is that something that's going on in your life? Are you developing the quality of faithfulness as you walk with the Lord controlled by the Spirit?

The fruit of the Spirit is meekness

Whenever you and I hear the word *meek*, our minds tends to think *weak*.

But meek is not weak. Not even close.

Meek is one of the most powerful words in the New Testament. Meek means to have great power always under control. Picture a champion racehorse submitting to the bit. Picture a mighty reservoir leaping through the spillway of a great dam in a measured flow. Picture an Olympic weight lifter brushing a tear out of his little daughter's eye.

Strength under control.

Power under discipline.

Jesus is the prime example of a meek person. Was Jesus weak? Well, go back and watch Him as He cleans out the temple. With a whip made out of cords, He drove everyone out of the temple courtyard in extremely short order. No one struggled with Him. No one challenged Him. I find it hard to believe some wimp could have accomplished this. No one wanted to mess with the Man from Nazareth. He was very strong and had great authority...but He also characterized Himself as a meek person. In Matthew 11:29, Jesus extended His hand and offered this invitation: "Take My yoke upon you and learn from Me, for I am gentle and lowly in heart, and you will find rest for your souls." The prophet Isaiah said of Him: "A bruised reed he will not break, and a smoldering wick he will not snuff out" (Isaiah 42:3, NIV).

Aristotle wrote, "A meek person is neither too hasty tempered, nor too slow tempered. Meekness doesn't get angry with people it ought not to get angry with, nor does it fail to get angry with people it ought to get angry with. The man who is meek is the man who feels anger on the right grounds against the right persons in the right manner at the right moment for the right length of time. At all times, he will err on the side of forgiveness."

Jesus was meek. He had the greatest possible strength under the greatest possible control. While He was on the cross, He could have called ten legions of angels to come to His aid. But He stayed on that cross and held His vast power in check...out of love for you and me.

That's meekness. And that's the quality of the Lord Jesus the Holy Spirit wants to form in you and me.

The fruit of the Spirit is self-control

Self-control is a word in the Greek language that means "to grab hold." That's what the word means. The word self-control, therefore, means to take hold of your life. Have you taken hold of your life by the power of the Holy Spirit? Are you constantly getting chewed up and beat up in the same places because the discipline the Spirit of God wants to develop within you is lacking?

Paul may not have been the first (and he certainly wasn't the last) preacher to make use of sports illustrations in his sermons. Nevertheless, his analogy in 1 Corinthians 9:24 is classic:

Do you not know that in a race all the runners run, but only one gets the prize? Run in such a way as to get the prize. Everyone who competes in the games goes into strict training. They do it to get a crown that will not last; but we do it to get a crown that will last forever. Therefore I do not run like a man running aimlessly; I do not fight like a man beating the air. No, I beat my body and make it my slave so that after I have preached to others, I myself will not be disqualified for the prize. (1 Corinthians 9:24–27, NIV)

Who receives the prize? The person who enters into strict training. The person who is temperate and self-controlled. In athletics you have to discipline yourself for the goal. And Paul says that when you're filled with the Spirit, you take control of your life.

Who is my greatest enemy? It's *me,* isn't it? Who is my greatest challenge in ministry and in life? It's that fella named David Jeremiah. The Spirit of God wants to gain more and more and more control over my life. It's not really "self" control as much as it is *Spirit* control through myself.

Amy Carmichael, who has given us so many wonderful thoughts of our walk with the Lord, wrote this little poem as her prayer.

God, harden me against myself,
The coward with pathetic voice
Who craves for ease and rest and joy.
Myself, arch-traitor to myself,
My hollowest friend, my deadliest foe,
My clog whatever road I go.

When I am self-controlled by the power of the Holy Spirit, I don't allow the things of the world to destroy my walk with God. I spend time with God. I take care of business with regard to my church. I do the things I'm committed to do, because God's Spirit has literally come into my life and is exhibiting a control over me which the Bible calls temperance or self-control.

FRUIT IN SEASON

Paul says that when you walk in the Spirit, constantly depending on Him, you will begin to notice certain things in your life. As a matter of fact, so will others.

It may begin with a little bit more love, a little more joy, and a little more peace. And in your relationships with other people, it may show itself with a longer fuse than you used to have. You're not as touchy as you used to be. There's a spirit of kindness within you that you didn't notice before—and a desire to help others that shows up as true goodness. In your personal walk with the Lord, you discover a greater degree of self-control than you've known before. Where you used to shrug things off, you're becoming more concerned about faithfulness and integrity.

When you live in the Spirit, those are the characteristics of your life.

You say, "David, will I get all the fruits in one big fruit basket with a bow on top? Will God just lay it on my doorstep? Will it happen all at once?"

Probably not. But you will see the evidences. And so will your wife or husband. So will your kids—and maybe even the neighbor's kids. So will your coworkers and the guy at the gas station. The graces will grow in your life for the rest of your life, because it's the Spirit's job to reproduce those things in you.

But you say, "David, this is so hard!" And you are right. These are rare and beautiful fruits in this old world, and they cannot be cultivated in the energy of the flesh—no matter how sincere you are or how hard you try.

St. George by the Vineyard, according to Richard Wentz, is an old church in the foothills of the Allegheny Mountains. It holds the title deed to a vineyard that produces, the natives insist, the most luscious grapes anywhere in the region. And every year, when those grapes ripen, members of St. George's come to pick and eat the delicious clusters or to make a wine that is allegedly the best available anywhere.

People often wondered about that vineyard because, from the outward perspective, nobody in particular ever seemed to care for it. The old vineyard was just left alone to grow. Then came the day when old Jeremy, the sexton, died. His father had been sexton before him, and his father before him, for many generations. No one could remember a time when the sexton of the church had not been a member of that family.

Jeremy, a taciturn recluse, didn't talk much to anybody, but he very lovingly cared for St. George by the Vineyard. After his death, a note was found alongside his bed. It simply said, "The key to everything is under the altar." So the senior warden went to the altar and looked underneath, and there, sure enough, was a key.

But not only a key.

There was a stone slab under the altar—and beneath that slab were stairs leading down into the crypt. The warden and some of the other officials of the church took flashlights and began to investigate that dark cellar. To their surprise, they could hear the gurgling of a spring. When they reached it, they also discovered beside it a chart and a time schedule. Unknown to anybody else, the sexton had been releasing the waters of that spring regularly and faithfully into the ducts that irrigated the vineyard.

Ah, so that was the secret of its rich productivity, a spring that people did not know about, a secret source of renewal and vitality.

How can you know you're going to be fruitful? It's the secret source of power that God has given you. People outside may not see the source of power, but do you know what they *will* see? They'll see the evidence of it in your life. They'll see your love and joy and peace. They will take note of your patience and kindness and goodness. They will become aware of your faithfulness, your meekness, and your amazing self-control. Why? Because that Spirit who lives within you is producing in you those qualities as you submit yourself to His control.

Walk in the Spirit and you *will not* fulfill the lusts of the flesh.

You'll be too busy growing fruit.

THE GIFTS
OF THE SPIRIT

EMPOWERED TO EQUIP
ONE ANOTHER

fter World War II, a group of German students volunteered to rebuild a cathedral that had been severely damaged by German bombs. As work progressed, they became concerned about a large statue of Jesus with outstretched arms beneath which was the inscription: *Come unto Me.* They had particular difficulty trying to restore the hands, which had been completely destroyed.

After much discussion, they decided to let the hands remain missing and change the inscription instead. When they were finished, it read: *Christ has no hands but ours.*

Have you ever thought about how many hands are involved in a living, working, thriving assembly of believers? Have you ever considered how many tasks are required to keep the vital signs of a local church alive and strong?

I'm not talking about a dead church. It doesn't take anyone at all to maintain a corpse. But in front of any church that is alive, whether it has a hundred members, a thousand, or ten thousand, you could put up a sign out front of the meeting place that says, *God's people at work.* It takes many hands, much skill, and a surprising amount of hard work to keep God's work in a community moving forward.

Several years ago, we were doing some homework on where we were as a church—and where we were going. In the process of the evaluation, I asked our staff to do an audit of all the tasks being done at Shadow Mountain. I don't think any of us realized what a challenge that was going to be.

We asked every person in every department in every aspect of the work to write down the particular duties being attended to week by week. When they were done, they had identified 1,800 jobs.

141

That number didn't particularly surprise me. Obviously, it's a big church and there is a great deal to do. But what did surprise me was that those 1,800 tasks were being performed by just 1,200 people. We found one poor lady in our audit who was doing seven jobs. When I asked to speak with her for a moment in my office, I thought she was going to say, "Well, I can spare a minute or two, Pastor, but would you mind stuffing these envelopes while we talk?" This woman really *looked* like she was doing seven jobs.

I am convinced that God backs the concept of full employment in His work here on earth. He wants every one of us to have busy hands in His service. I do not believe that the personnel problem we face in many evangelical churches today is of God's design. As a matter of fact, He has given to us in His Word the formula to make it all work. But too many Christians, both young and old, are content to sit back and watch others carry the load.

I remember reading a bit of doggerel some years ago that went like this:

There's a clever young fellow named Somebody Else.
There's nothing this fellow can't do.
He's busy from morning till way late at night
Just substituting for you.
When asked to do this or asked to do that
So often you are set to reply
"Get Somebody Else, Mr. Chairman,
He'll do it much better than I."
There's so much to do in our parish,
So much, and the workers are few.
Somebody Else gets worried and worn
Just substituting for you.
So next time you're asked to do something worthwhile,
Come up with this honest reply:
"If Somebody Else can give time and support,
It's obviously true, so can I."[1]

It's so easy for us to look around the church, see the gifts of other people and assume, perhaps, that we have nothing to contribute.

But that isn't true. And I want to show you why it *can't* be true.

THE GIFTS AND THE GIVER

When you begin to explore this business of "gifts," you quickly realize that you're on the Holy Spirit's turf. The Spirit of God is all over 1 Corinthians 12.

Verses 4–5 say, "Now there are diversities of gifts, but the same Spirit. There are differences of ministries, but the same Lord." In verse 7, the apostle adds this: "But the manifestation of the Spirit is given to each one for the profit of all."

The truth of God's Word is this: the very moment you and I were born into God's family we were endowed with a spiritual gift from the Holy Spirit. Do you have any New Year's babies in your family? Sometimes, especially in a small town, the first baby born in a new year will get his or her picture in the newspaper and a bundle of gifts and services from local merchants. One of my friends was a New Year's baby and complained that the gifts didn't benefit *him* a bit. His mom and dad appreciated the free week of diaper service, and his older brothers enjoyed drinking up the free case of soda pop. But what did he get out of it?

In the same way, every single believer—at the instant of new birth—is gifted by God to bring a specific blessing and encouragement to the church of Jesus Christ. You get the gift on your spiritual birthday, but the benefit is for others!

Sadly, many believers live out their whole lives and never really discover that uniquely designed gift from God. They flounder around trying this and playing at that and never really stop to ask themselves, *What is it that God has especially equipped me to do?*

THE PERSPECTIVE ON GIFTS

The perspective on spiritual gifts in the church has seen its ups and downs over the years. At times it has enjoyed a strong emphasis, and in other eras it has been neglected. I can only say this: whenever the church of God has had an interest in the laity—the people in the pew—as opposed to just the person behind the pulpit, the ministry and study of the gifts of the Spirit have always gained prominence.

There are three key biblical passages where spiritual gifts are taught. The first one is Romans 12:6–8.

We have different gifts, according to the grace given us. If a man's gift is prophesying, let him use it in proportion to his faith. If it is serving, let him serve; if it is teaching, let him teach; if it is encouraging, let him encourage; if it is contributing to the needs of others, let him give generously; if it is leadership, let him govern diligently; if it is showing mercy, let him do it cheerfully. (NIV)

Then of course we have the passage in 1 Corinthians 12:

For to one is given the word of wisdom through the Spirit, to another the word of knowledge through the same Spirit, to another faith by the same Spirit, to another gifts of healings by the same Spirit, to another the working of miracles, to another prophecy, to another discerning of spirits, to another different kinds of tongues, to another the interpretation of tongues. But one and the same Spirit works all these things, distributing to each one individually as He wills.... And God has appointed these in the church: first apostles, second prophets, third teachers, after that miracles, then gifts of healings, helps, administrations, varieties of tongues. (vv. 8–10, 28)

There is one final listing in Ephesians 4:11–12:

And He Himself gave some to be apostles, some prophets, some evangelists, and some pastors and teachers, for the equipping of the saints for the work of ministry, for the edifying of the body of Christ.

THE PARTICULAR GIFTS

Depending on who does the study, there are somewhere between fifteen and twenty gifts of the Spirit in Scripture. Sometimes they are summarized and lumped together, but I thought it might be helpful to place them into four different categories:

1. Special gifts

These are gifts that were used in the early days of the church, and include apostles, prophets, evangelists, and pastors/teachers. These gifts had a very special part in the founding of the church, and some remain in operation today.

2. Speaking gifts

These are gifts that use the mouth, and include prophecy, teaching, exhortation, the word of wisdom, and the word of knowledge.

3. Serving gifts

This third category is where most of us find our place. I like this list best because this is where most of us find full employment. All of the gifts on this list come from the three passages we just looked at. The list includes serving, helps, leadership, administration, giving, showing mercy, discerning of spirits, faith, and hospitality. You may be busy serving in one or more of those capacities without even realizing you've been gifted! You are involved in serving God, and you didn't even know you are gifted to do it, but you have followed your inclinations to do what God has called you to do.

4. Sign gifts

The final list seems to be where most of the controversy arises. Beneath this heading are tongues, interpretation of tongues, miracles, and healings.

In this chapter, I want to give you a quick aerial survey (we'll circle the airplane and give you a pair of binoculars) so you can begin to grasp where this all fits into the plan of God. Even though we will only take a wide-angle look at a complex subject that could fill many, many volumes, I do believe this chapter has something very specific just for you.

Never doubt it: You have a place in God's great plan for His people.

THE PURPOSE OF THE GIFTS

Each one of these categories—special gifts, speaking gifts, serving gifts, and sign gifts—has a special purpose in the economy of God. One of the reasons there is so much controversy over spiritual gifts in our churches is because we have thrown these gifts together on one big mixing bowl list, without understanding that God has a specific use for each category of gifts.

What is His use for *special gifts?* The special gifts of apostles, pastors/teachers, and evangelists are used to equip God's people. I believe God has given me the gift of pastor/teacher. As such, I seek to equip you to be the people God wants you to be. That is what God has called *me* to be. And I, in turn, am equipped by others who have the gift of pastor/teacher. So the purpose of the special gifts is to equip the people of God.

The purpose of *speaking gifts* is to explain God's truth. It isn't just a gift that you use on yourself to tell everybody how gifted you are! It is given so that you can explain and make clear the truth of God.

The third kind of gift, the *serving gifts,* enable God's work to get accomplished. Look down the list: serving, leading, administrating, giving, showing mercy... If you have a serving gift, the purpose is so that you can make God's work *work,* so that you can enable the work of God through ministry to His people.

The purpose of *sign gifts* was to establish God's authority. One of the reasons why there is so much controversy today over whether or not you should be using these gifts in the church is simply because men and women haven't sat down with their Bibles to determine why the gift was given in the first place. Why was there a sign gift?

When Jesus was preaching, and when the apostles followed Him in the afterglow of His ministry, there was no New Testament as we have it today. How would a person know if the word of this young rabbi from Nazareth was authoritative? The only way they would know that was if His preaching was authenticated in such a way that they could not miss the miraculous nature of His communication. How were the apostles to be identified and authenticated after Christ went back to heaven? It was only because of their use of sign gifts. The sign gift was a visible demonstration that what they spoke was the Word of God. That was its purpose.

Now, one of the reasons those gifts have moved out of center place in the church is because when the Word of God was finished and God put a period at the end of Revelation, He told us that there was no higher authority than His Word. And, my friend, there will *never* be a higher authority than the Word of God.

Not church tradition.

Not contemporary culture.

Not human leadership.

Not denominational conventions or decrees.

Not "we've always done it this way."

Not individual spiritual experiences, no matter how dramatic or deeply felt.

Perhaps someone approaches you and says, "This is what God says." All you have to do is open the Bible and *see* if that is what God said. The authority for life and practice today is the Word of God. So when I preach the Word of God, you don't have to say, "Well, David Jeremiah didn't do any miracles, so I'm not sure if he's speaking the truth." You and I need to be like the people Dr. Luke pointed out in the book of Acts.

> Now the Bereans were of more noble character than the Thessalonians, for they received the message with great eagerness and examined the Scriptures every day to see if what Paul said was true. (Acts 17:11, NIV)

We need to go home and search the Scriptures to see if what a speaker has said stacks up with the Bible. If he speaks the truth according to the Word of God, then we must submit to the authority of that truth.

One of the reasons why we don't exercise the sign gifts at the church where I pastor is because we have elevated God's Word to its rightful place of authority within the church—and there is no higher authority than the Word of God. The Bible says that God has exalted His word higher than His name. God's Word is the highest authority to which anyone can appeal. And if you are appealing to a source in your life or experience that is higher than the Word of God, then you have a serious problem. You will end up with a situation where you are pitting your experience against *his* experience…your experience as compared to *her* experience…your experience versus *their* experience. Where will your authority be? There won't be an authority, because your experiences are subjective.

God's Word is the objective truth.

Whenever you find the Word of God central in an assembly of believers, you will find people coming to Christ, growing, nurtured, and being built up in their faith. Whenever you move it out of the center, you will find confusion, constant controversy, and experience-centered discussions.

WHY DISCUSS THIS AT ALL?

Why were gifts ever given in the first place? What's the purpose of them? Why do I say to you that you have a gift and need to use it? There are several reasons.

Gifts are given to us for the equipping of believers

I am a pastor/teacher who has in turn been equipped by others with the gift of pastor/teacher. I was with our staff this week in my library, and (with a smile) pointed around the room at all the volumes. "You see all these books?" I said. "These are all my friends. I walk in here, pull F. B. Meyer down off the shelf, and he ministers to me. Then I get G. Campbell Morgan, if I don't understand what F. B. Meyer said, and G. Campbell Morgan helps me. Sometimes I call on more recent expositors like W. A. Criswell, and I sit down with them and let them instruct me, correct me, and minister to me."

What are those men doing? They are equipping me. These men have been pastor/teachers who have written down their teachings, and through their teachings, I am being built up and equipped as a person. In turn, I am equipping our congregation through the teaching gift God has given me, so that these men, women, and children can grow in the nurture and admonition of the Lord. Teaching the Word of God is both my highest calling and my greatest privilege.

Gifts are given to us for the edifying of believers

An edifice is a building. So what does it mean to be "edified"? It means you are being built up. The purpose of gifts, then, is to build up the Church. Here's how Paul expressed it in Ephesians 4:

> For the equipping of the saints for the work of service, to the building up of the body of Christ…from whom the whole body, being fitted and held together by that which every joint supplies, according to the proper working of each individual part, causes the growth of the body for the building up of itself in love. (vv. 12, 16, NASB)

The purpose of spiritual gifts is to cause the church to grow and be built up in Christ. Gifted believers enable the church to become what God wants it to become.

Gifts are given to us for the establishment of believers

Are you established? Are you sound in your faith? Are you stable in what you believe? Do you know why so many people are all over the ballpark when they talk about their faith? They don't have any knowledge of the Word of God. Their roots aren't down deep, so they are blown about by every wind of doctrine.

Paul told the Romans, "I long to see you that I may impart to you some spiritual gift so that you might be established." You and I need to be established.

I was at my home recently when one of those El Niño storms that have plagued Southern California for the last few months ripped through. Upstairs, standing by some large windows, I began to feel a little alarmed. The wind and rain became so severe it seemed they would push right through those windows, roar into the house, and just take over. I thought to myself, *Is this house going to wash right down into the valley?*

But then I remembered something. I had been present when the builders put in the house's foundation. With my own eyes, I saw how the foundation was embedded deeply into underlying rock. No, there was no guarantee the windows would survive, but I wasn't worried about the foundation. The foundation was established.

Are you established in your faith? Are you ready to withstand the sometimes violent storms that descend on our lives? How do you get established? When people use their spiritual gifts within the church, they help you and me to be established in what we believe.

Gifts are given to us for the effectiveness of the whole church

Have you ever wondered why some churches seem to just limp along instead of accomplishing everything God has called them to do? One of my coaching friends thinks church ministry looks an awful lot like a football game: you've got twenty-two thousand people in the stands who desperately need exercise and twenty-two people on the field who desperately need rest!

That's the problem with the church. We've got twenty-two exhausted men and women, pushing, pulling, and laboring for all they're worth, and we've got twenty-two thousand spectators in the stands, cheering them on. "Yea!! Go for it! Let's score!"

People come to me and say, "Pastor Jeremiah, you look tired."

Let me clue you, I don't just look tired, I *am* tired. Why? We need more people involved in my church, just as you need more people involved where you fellowship. The plan of God was never for the "clergy" to do the work of ministry while the people in the body cheered them on. God's plan is that everyone should be involved in serving Him.

Scripture tells us that "the manifestation of the Spirit is given to each one *for the profit of all*" (1 Corinthians 12:7). What you do as you minister your gifts profits the whole church. What God has given you to do, He has not given me to do. What He has given me to do, He has not given you to do. But He has given each of us a gift, and I am convinced that within every local assembly are all of the gifts needed for that church to flourish and to grow. That's how it's supposed to work.

Gifts are given to us for the exaltation of Christ

Did you know that Christ is exalted when we use our gifts in the right way? Peter says, "If anyone speaks, he should do it as one speaking the very words of God. If anyone serves, he should do it with the strength God provides, *so that in all things God may be praised through Jesus Christ.* To him be the glory and the power for ever and ever" (1 Peter 4:11, NIV).

What is Scripture saying?

If you have a gift of speaking, speak for the glory of God, and He *will* be glorified.

If you have a gift of serving, serve God with all your heart, and He *will* be glorified.

If you have a gift of teaching, study diligently, teach creatively, do it with all the strength and skill within you, and the God of glory will gain even more glory.

Bringing glory to His name is our chief occupation in this life, and on into eternity. We might as well roll up our sleeves, and in the power of the Spirit, get after it.

PRINCIPLES FOR THE USE OF GIFTS

Let me just give you four simple principles for the use of gifts.

Gifts are distinct from natural abilities

Do you realize that in all of the New Testament listing of gifts, no mention is made of music? In the Old Testament, we read about some people who were gifted musically. Obviously, many people have *natural abilities* in music. And these natural, God-given abilities or bents can be beautifully blended with spiritual gifts. One of the pastors where I serve has an obvious natural ability in music, but he has the *spiritual* gift of administration and leadership. He takes the natural gift of music and with the spiritual gifting of administration, he has built a wonderful choir and orchestra.

On the other hand, I have known many people who have had wonderful natural gifts of music who couldn't put a trio together! To do what he does, you would have to have the natural gift *with* the spiritual gift.

Gifts are different from the fruit of the Spirit

Remember our discussion of that beautiful, ninefold fruit of the Spirit in the last chapter? Love and joy. Peace and patience. Kindness and goodness. But the gifts of the Spirit are not the fruit of the Spirit. The gifts of the Spirit are ways we serve. The fruit of the Spirit is character traits of who we are.

Gifts are determined by the sovereignty of God

You may be sitting back in your chair a bit right now, feeling a little put out because you've just figured out your gift *and you don't like it!* You wanted to be a teacher. God made you a helper. Or maybe you really wanted to be someone who serves and stays in the background, yet God has made it clear that He has gifted you as a teacher.

What right do we have to complain? None of us have gifts because of who we are or what we have done. God *gives* His gifts to us. First Corinthians 12:11 tells us that "one and the same Spirit works all these things, distributing to each one individually *as He wills.*"

When I was a boy, God didn't look down and say, "Look at that Jeremiah kid down there delivering papers. He's going to be a preacher. I see all these wonderful things in him! I'm going to encourage him in that direction." No, God said, "I am going to gift him by My Spirit to be a preacher. Then, as he develops that gift, I will use him."

He gives you the gift. You develop it according to the principle of your giftedness. But it is God who makes the decision. You can't argue with Him.

Years ago, I remember hearing E. V. Hill preach at Moody Church in Chicago. He was speaking on the subject of how God gifts us. Pastor Hill had a pile of books beside him on the platform, and as he was speaking, he began pulling books off the top of the pile and hurling them into the congregation.

"Every once in a while," he explained, "God looks down and says, 'Here, have *this!*'" And with that, he tossed another book into the fifth or sixth row. Somebody caught it. Before the sermon was over, he went through the whole pile. The last thing in the stack was a *Ryrie Study Bible.* That was too much for Moody's president Dr. George Sweeting. He got up and took it himself, so Hill wouldn't toss it like a Frisbee into the pews.

In his own inimitable way, E. V. Hill was illustrating God's sovereign determination in the giving of His gifts. He has His own reasons for what He does—reasons that may make no sense to us. We may not figure out why He has gifted us as He has until we get to heaven. Why do you have the gift you have? Because God determined that was what He *wanted* you to have. And what should you do with it?

Receive it. Embrace it. Thank Him for it. And use it with all of your might for His glory.

Gifts are distributed by the Holy Spirit to every believer

If you are a believer, don't ever come to me and say, "Well, I just wish I had a gift." Don't insult the Giver like that, because you most certainly *do* have one. You may not have figured out what it is, but that doesn't mean you were "behind the door" when the gifts were passed out! Listen to 1 Corinthians 12:7: "But the manifestation of the Spirit is given to *each one*...."

Is there any room for doubt there? Are you in that group? Are you one of the "each ones"? Yes, you are! And you do have a gift from God.

First Peter 4:10 says, "As each one has received a gift, minister it to one another, as good stewards of the manifold grace of God." Listen, friend, whoever you may be, the moment you received Christ as your Savior, God gave you a gift that you can use in serving Him. You need to ask God what that gift is. I would imagine if you stopped for a moment to think about it, you might already know what it is. You just haven't seriously contemplated it.

We have a little joke at our church about music, that if you believe God has gifted you in music, there should be at least one other person who agrees with you. If you are gifted, God will begin to confirm that in your heart.

I remember when I started to preach in a little church in Ohio. My dad had asked me to go there to "fill in" for a few Sundays. At that point in my life, I didn't know that I was going to be a pastor. Truthfully, I was doing my best to run in the opposite direction. But I did what my dad asked me to do, and as I did, a strange thing happened. I couldn't get around the fact that God seemed to be *using* what I taught. People would come up to me after one of my messages and say, "You know, I've heard that before, but today, I *understood* it."

That was a confirmation to me (whether I wanted it or not) that God had given me an ability to explain the truth. I began to realize and to admit to myself that this was indeed the gift God had given me.

When you begin to use your gift, you will find that God confirms that with others. What you need to do is look into your own heart and say, "What has God gifted me to do?" begin to do it, and watch what happens!

We have some people in our church who have the gift of serving in such a way that it is written all over them. They get so much joy out of serving because that is what God has uniquely equipped them to do. Where does the joy come in? The joy bubbles up from the Holy Spirit within you as you begin cooperating with His purposes and touching other lives in the body of Jesus Christ. That's an experience He earnestly desires for you. He knows very well you have a gift, because He gave it to you!

THE PROBLEM WITH THE GIFTS

There are a couple of problems that sometimes surface along with the exercise of the Spirit's gifts.

The "spirituality" problem

Have you ever encountered somebody who believes himself to be "spiritual" because he flaunts a particular spiritual gift?

Here's one that always gets to me: Someone comes up to you, gets in your face, rips you up one side and down the other, and then informs you that he or she has the "gift of exhortation." Exhortation is certainly a legitimate gift, but I doubt very much that is the way God intended it to be used!

Having a spiritual gift doesn't mean you are "spiritual." Far from it. The fact is, most of the truth about spiritual gifts is recorded in Paul's first letter to the Church at Corinth...easily the most carnal church in the whole New Testament! The Bible says of this church that they came short in no gift (1 Corinthians 1:7). The Corinthian church had 'em all! Yet they were tragically, embarrassingly immature and carnal.

The ironic fact is, you can be greatly gifted and still not be walking with the Lord. Once you find your gift, it isn't so you can *brag* about it or draw attention to yourself. It is so you might serve.

The "specialist" problem

Someone will say to me, "Well, Pastor, you've been talking about witnessing to neighbors, but I can't do that. You see, I don't have the gift of evangelism." That may be true, but that doesn't let you—or any of us—off the biblical hook. I recently discovered that almost every one of the specific gifts of the Spirit that is best performed by specifically gifted people also has a general application. We're all supposed to do these things to the best of our ability.

Yes, He has called you to teach. And exhort. And serve. And administer. And speak wisely. And evangelize. And show mercy. *All* of those things are part of your job description as a son or daughter of the living God.

There is a gift of giving. Suppose the only people who gave were those who have that gift! God has commanded *all* of us to give. There is a gift of exhortation. We're *all* commanded in the New Testament to exhort one another. Please don't tell me, "I don't have the gift of evangelism so I don't have to witness." Yes, you do! The Bible says, "Go into all the world, and preach the gospel to every creature." He was talking to everyone. And if you don't heed Him in this, you will be in disobedience.

Certainly, we can all rejoice that God has gifted people like Billy Graham, who knows how to reach people at the level of tens of thousands—and even millions—even while you and I seek to reach people at our own level in the apartment building or cul-de-sac. But don't allow yourself to slip into an unbiblical specialist mind-set.

The self-centered problem

There are other people who fall into a self-centered problem. "My spiritual gifts are for me." That's not true. God didn't give you spiritual gifts for *you*. That's not what God is up to. God gave you gifts to help others. Once again, Scripture says that these gifts are "to profit all."

There is an adage that goes something like this: "If God has given you a gift, use it, don't abuse it, or you will lose it." It's true…you can let a gift atrophy. A gift that isn't used is ultimately lost in terms of its effectiveness for God. Once you figure out what God has gifted you to do, your goal should be to polish that gift, sharpen that tool, and use it all that you can for the glory of God…while there is still time.

Over a hundred years ago, the Holy Spirit sovereignly gifted an Irish farmer named Jeremiah Meneely with the gift of evangelism. The great Northern Ireland awakening began with Jeremiah and three other young men meeting every night in an old schoolhouse to pray for revival. The men prayed for three solid months without any visible results. Then, on New Year's Day, they saw one conversion. After that there were conversions every night. By the end of the year, there were fifty young men taking part in the prayer meetings.

When crowds of unconverted people began to come to those meetings, they decided that Jeremiah Meneely should preach to them. The farmer agreed—only on the condition that the others would pray for him. God brought the whole community under conviction and many people were coming to Christ. Not long after that, Meneely was asked to preach in a town about five miles away.

When he arrived, the building was jammed with people. He made his way to the front and preached. When he told the crowd they were dismissed, no one left. So he preached another sermon and again dismissed the people. They still didn't want to leave. The same thing happened again. After preaching four times, he stepped outside, took off his shirt, and wrung the perspiration out of it. He put his shirt back on, went inside, and preached one more sermon before walking the five miles home.

By then it was after midnight. He had only been home a few minutes when he heard a knock on the door. There stood a man asking how to be saved. Meneely took him to his neighbor's house, shouting, "What, lying in bed and souls seeking Christ!"[2]

There will come a time when the harvest will be over, and the opportunities to reach the lost and strengthen the Lord's people for service will be gone forever. Jesus Christ will return for His own, and the era of grace will end. Now is not the time to leave our tools to gather dust in the barn.

The Holy Spirit has placed a tool in your hand. For the Lord's sake, *use* it.

Chapter Ten

THE BEST
EVIDENCE OF
THE SPIRIT

AN ATTITUDE OF GRATITUDE

It is good to give thanks to the LORD,
and to sing praises to Your name, O Most High;
to declare Your lovingkindness in the morning,
and Your faithfulness every night.

PSALM 92:1–2

Dr. W. A. Criswell pastored his first church in Chickasha, Oklahoma. One day in the course of calling on residents of that town, he went to see a woman who lived by herself in a dilapidated house. He knocked at the door, and as Dr. Criswell described it, "There came to the door a woman who looked more like wretchedness than any countenance or figure I have ever seen."

The young pastor introduced himself and said, "I have come to see you."

"Well," she replied, "what do you want?"

"I am a pastor," he told her, "and I have come to visit with you."

"There's no need for anybody like you around here," she replied.

"But," Dr. Criswell said, "I have come to visit you and I want to come in."

Seeing that he wouldn't be dissuaded, she reluctantly invited him in and he sat down. "Where do you preach?" she asked, and he told her. "You say you believe in God?" she asked gruffly.

"Yes," Dr. Criswell replied, "I believe in the Lord."

"Well, I do not believe in God," she said, and she cursed Him.

As he visited with her, the terrible story of her life came out. Ever since she and her husband had moved to Oklahoma it had been, as Criswell put it, one wretchedness after another. Her husband had died and her children had scattered, leaving her alone. She lived in poverty, and her eyesight was almost gone. She was bitter and angry at everyone.

Then the woman startled the young pastor by suddenly saying, "I write poetry. Would you like to hear some of my poetry?"

Criswell politely replied that he would. The poem she recited made such an impression on him that he went out to the car after the visit and wrote it out so that he wouldn't forget it. This is what the woman had composed:

I hate Oklahoma!
Not the land of my native birth
But a land by all the gods that be
A scourge on the face of the earth.
I hate Oklahoma!

I hate Oklahoma!
Where the centipede crawls in your bed at night,
And the rattlesnake lifts its fangs to bite,
Where the lizard and the scorpion play on the sly,
And the lonesome vultures sail high in the sky.
Where water and food are an eternal lack,
And a man's best friend sticks a dagger in your back.
I hate Oklahoma![1]

Dr. Criswell said that all of her poetry was like that. She was an unthankful, bitter old woman who saw only the difficult things in life and dwelled on them.

Just a few weeks after the pastor's visit, he was called and told that the old woman had died and had requested before her death that he hold the funeral service. Dr. Criswell said it was the only service he could remember where *no one* came. There was just one somebody there besides the pastor, and it was the woman in the plain pine box.

Ingratitude, said Dr. Criswell, has no friends.

Think for a moment of your own friends and circle of acquaintances. What if I were to ask you this question: What is the greatest evidence of someone being filled with the Holy Spirit? How would you recognize a truly Spirit-controlled individual if you ran into him or her this afternoon and had an opportunity to chat for a while?

What would tip you off?

You might say, "Well, I know that man has a powerful witness for Jesus Christ, and that proves that he's Spirit-filled." Or "I've heard that she speaks in tongues frequently, so that must mean she's filled with the Spirit of God."

But what does the Word of God say? How can we really determine if a person has been filled, or is controlled, by the Holy Spirit? You may find what I'm going to say in this chapter rather strange, and yet as I began to chase this concept, it showed up again and again in the principle texts of the New Testament. For me, it was one of those "Aha!" principles of Scripture where you sit back in your chair and say, "Yes, it makes sense—but I'd never considered that before."

I believe the strongest evidence for a Spirit-filled life is *gratitude*.

"THANK GOD!"

I don't know whether it has been a good thing for God's people that we have one day a year when we celebrate "Thanksgiving." Does that mean that we can be as ungrateful as we want to be through the other 364 days? In this chapter you will discover that the attitude of gratitude is the very beating heart of a Spirit-controlled life.

It was December of 1914 when Thomas Edison's great laboratories in West Orange, New Jersey, were almost entirely destroyed by fire. In one night Edison lost 2 million dollars' worth of equipment and the record of much of his life-work. Edison's son Charles ran frantically about trying to find his father and finally came upon him standing near the fire, his face ruddy in the glow, and his white hair blown by the winter winds.

"My heart ached for him," Charles Edison said. "He was no longer young, and everything was being destroyed. Then he spotted me. And he said to me, 'Where is your mother? Find her. Bring her here. She will never see anything like this again as long as she lives!'"

The next morning, walking about the charred embers of so many of his hopes and dreams, the sixty-seven-year-old Edison mused, "There is great value in disaster. All our mistakes are burned up. Thank God! We can start all over again."[2]

What a perspective on life! The Bible speaks very strongly to the Christian about the importance of a grateful spirit. In fact, it very carefully links the spirit of gratitude with victory in the Christian life. I don't know if you have ever connected these two thoughts, but in 2 Corinthians 2:14 we read these words: "Now thanks be to God who always leads us in triumph in Christ."

Did you see it? Gratitude and triumph in the same verse. There is something about the attitude of gratitude that seems at home in the scenario of triumph.

That same concept blazes across the biblical sky again in 1 Corinthians 15:57. "But thanks be to God, who gives us the victory through our Lord Jesus Christ." There it is again! Victory and triumph in the same context with gratitude. You show me somebody who is experiencing spiritual victory, who just exudes a sense of triumph, and I can promise you, as you get to know that individual, you will find a man or woman who is permeated with a spirit of gratitude.

Gratitude, you see, is one of the evidences that God is in us and that He is working in our lives. Why do I say that? Because in the world in which we live today, there are so many reasons to be ungrateful. So many reasons to complain. But if the Spirit of God is in us, He will triumph over that. He will give us victory over those negative, self-pitying thoughts, and genuine, heartfelt gratitude will spill through the cracks of our soul like sunlight through venetian blinds as we explain to people what God is doing in our life.

Unfortunately, the doctrine of gratitude, which is paramount in the New Testament, has been relegated by some to an optional and seasonal spirit. Gratitude, as I have watched it, is sometimes looked upon as that which good Christians sometimes do, instead of that which should mark the life of *every* believer. The spirit of gratitude should be true of all of us if we know Jesus Christ and if God's Holy Spirit is in control of our lives.

Walk with me for a few minutes through some biblical thoughts about gratitude. It may prove as revolutionary to your life as it did to mine.

THE CONTROL OF THE SPIRIT RESULTS IN GRATITUDE

The following passage in Ephesians began this revolution in my thinking. Please take special note of the highlighted words.

Do not be drunk with wine, in which is dissipation; but be filled with the Spirit, **speaking** to one another in psalms and hymns and spiritual songs,

singing and making melody in your heart to the Lord, **giving thanks** always for all things to God the Father in the name of our Lord Jesus Christ, **submitting** to one another in the fear of God. (Ephesians 5:18–21)

The words that end in -ing are called participles. In this passage, these are words that describe what goes on in the life of a man or woman who is being filled with the Holy Spirit. Zero in with me for a closer look.

Speaking and singing

When we're filled or controlled by the Spirit, we will be *speaking* to one another in psalms and hymns and spiritual songs, and we will be *singing* and *making melody* unto the Lord.

That sounds like worship to me!

One of the things that happens when you are a Spirit-filled Christian is that you are filled to overflowing with worship to our Lord. Our churches ought to be singing churches. A Spirit-filled congregation will really *sing* when they sing. It won't be a mechanical mouthing of words while we check out so-and-so in the next row or let our minds drift. We will be entering into those words, climbing into that melody, and the music will be coming up from our toes. It will be immediately evident to the visitors and seekers in our midst. They will think to themselves, *My goodness, these people really BELIEVE what they're singing!*

I have been in some churches where they say "stand up and sing," but all they do is stand up! Have you ever been in a church like that? I feel like looking around and saying, "Hey, doesn't anybody *sing* in this place?"

The experts on preaching will tell you that pastors are supposed to save their voices; they aren't supposed to sing along during worship time. Sorry, I choose not to comply. I choose to *worship,* and then I preach with what's left over. I sing my preaching voice right out of tune. Sometimes I have trouble finishing the message, but I'll tell you what…I get worship done! It isn't an option with me. I can't help myself because I love the Lord, and the Spirit of God is in my heart. I can't sit on the sidelines when God's people are worshiping before God's throne—I want to be right in the middle of it!

Whenever I read Psalm 42, I am reminded how the psalmist was sustained in moments of loneliness and deep discouragement by memories of joyful praise among God's people.

These things I remember as I pour out my soul:
how I used to go with the multitude,
leading the procession to the house of God,
with shouts of joy and thanksgiving
among the festive throng.
(Psalm 42:4, NIV)

How he missed that "festive throng" of worshipers, singing and shouting praise to the Lord! And so would I, if I had to be away from joyous worship with brothers and sisters in Christ. One of the evidences that you are a Spirit-filled Christian is that you will find yourself singing and speaking to one another in psalms and hymns and spiritual songs, making melody in your heart to the Lord. Not just on Sunday, but all week long.

Submitting

Submitting (Ephesians 5:21) is as much an evidence of God's Spirit in a life as singing and rejoicing. A man or woman who is controlled by the Holy Spirit will have a submissive attitude. Do you know why I know that is of the Spirit? *Because I am absolutely certain it isn't of the flesh.* It isn't "normal" to submit to one another, whether in the family or in the church or in the business world. But you show me a person who is filled with the Spirit of God, and I will show you a man or woman who has a submissive spirit.

Giving thanks

One of the evidences of a Spirit-filled Christian is the gratitude in his heart—so very evident to those who are around him—gratitude to God for all that He has done. Literally, the text says, *"Be being filled* with the Spirit, giving thanks always for all things to God the Father in the name of our Lord Jesus Christ." God says that when we are controlled by His Spirit, we will be grateful people, thankful for what we have, anxious to share it with others, always overwhelmed with gratitude for God's goodness to us.

Do you realize what God has done for you? Has it gripped you lately? Has it pushed you to your knees? He gave His Son for you, He put His Spirit in you, and He has given you life everlasting. When you come to grips with those things (who can understand them?), you can't help but be thankful.

William Law, writing centuries ago, made a very good point when he said, "Would you like to know who is the greatest saint in the world? It isn't he who prays most or fasts most. It isn't he who gives most. But it is he who is always thankful to God, who receives everything as an instrument of God's goodness, and has a heart always ready to praise God for it."

The greatest saint is the one who is always thankful.

To be candid with you, I have drifted in and out of this attitude of gratitude in years past. But it's all different now in my life. Every day is a gift. Every moment is a precious treasure. If you haven't been through something like cancer, you can't know what I'm talking about. Sometimes I think God has to beat us up a little bit so we can learn about this grace of gratitude. And then, when He tenderizes us, when He allows circumstances to knock away that ugly cocoon of ingratitude, the Holy Spirit can begin to do His work in us and enable us to take flight in our gratitude and praise.

Somebody said to me recently, "You walk around all the time with a smile on your face."

Amen! I'm grateful to be alive. Grateful to have my family around me. Grateful to have the opportunity to minister to a wonderful church. Grateful for the California sunshine that spills through my bedroom window every morning.

People say, "I'm glad to see you." And I smile and say, "I'm glad to be seen!"

I'm alive! My Lord has saved me, healed me, and filled me with His Holy Spirit. How could I keep from smiling? It is a wonderful thing. I'm even grateful for my gratitude because I know it is a gift of the Holy Spirit and not something that naturally dwells in the heart of David Jeremiah.

Don't you like to be around grateful people? Isn't it wonderful to be around folks who exude this spirit of gratitude? Sometimes you find yourself thinking, *Is he for real? Is she really genuine about this?* And then when you discover that it is real, you find yourself just wanting to hang around that person.

Ephesians 5 says that when you are filled with the Spirit, gratitude is the result. But there is something else I want you to see too.

A COMMITMENT TO GOD'S WORD RESULTS IN GRATITUDE

Colossians 3:16–17 is yet another passage rich in gratitude...but I want you to notice something special about it.

Let the word of Christ dwell in you richly in all wisdom, teaching and admonishing one another in psalms and hymns and spiritual songs, singing with grace in your hearts to the Lord. And whatever you do in word or deed, do all in the name of the Lord Jesus, giving thanks to God the Father through Him.

You say, "That sounds similar to what I just read in Ephesians." It is very similar. And why not? It had the same human author (Paul) and the same divine author (the Holy Spirit). But did you notice the change? In Ephesians it is being filled with the Spirit that creates gratitude in us. In Colossians, it is because we are filled or indwelled with the Word of God.

Did you ever notice that a Spirit-filled Christian is a *Scripture*-filled Christian? If you meet somebody who claims to be filled with the Spirit and yet never has time to read or study or meditate on God's Word, something's out of sync. If a brother or sister in the Lord is full of the *Los Angeles Times* or *Newsweek* or even *Christianity Today*, but never mentions the Word of God, something isn't right. You can't be filled with the Spirit of God without also being filled with the Word of God. The Bible is the Holy Spirit's toolbox! It is the instrument He uses to change us and conform us into the image of our Lord.

Paul is saying that when you spend time as a Spirit-filled Christian reading the Book, you will come out a grateful person. It is the natural result of being filled with the Word of God.

But there is a third evidence you may not have considered.

A PEACEFUL HEART RESULTS IN GRATITUDE

Did you know that? I couldn't believe it when I saw this in Colossians 3:15. Let's go back and read it.

And let the peace of God rule in your hearts, to which also you were called in one body; and be thankful.

A Christian is the only one who has peace with God, because Christ has solved the issue of enmity with God. A believer is the only one who *can* have the peace of God, the peace that passes understanding, according to Philippians. Therefore, when a person is characterized by peace, the result is exactly the same as a person who is controlled by the Spirit and a person who is committed to the Word of God. He will be filled with gratitude.

Do you ever experience gratitude that you are not at war with God anymore? Maybe you were at war with God for a long time but God saved you out of it. I think sometimes people who are saved out of a tough life, saved out of ugly circumstances, and saved when they didn't know anything about God possess a deeper sense of gratitude than others who grew up in the church.

But it takes the same amount of grace to save all of us, doesn't it? No matter what has happened in our lives, when we fully understand what it's like to be at peace with God, our hearts will overflow with a spirit of gratitude.

I have to laugh when I think back to my early years as a pastor and some of my frustration with the apostle Paul. I would be studying my way through one of his epistles, just caught up in what a clear, orderly, logical teacher he is. Then, all of a sudden, he would seem to launch himself into the ionosphere. And I would say to myself, "Paul, I know a rabbit trail when I see one, and that is a rabbit trail! That's not on the subject at all!"

Yes, I know that some preachers are famous for rabbit trails. But *Paul?* The great apostle? In the very text of God's infallible Word? How could it be?

I finally realized something about those "rabbit trails"…and it made me feel a little ashamed.

Whenever Paul did those quick turns in the text and seemed to head down a different track, it was always because he was overcome with a sense of gratitude to God for what He had done for him. He would come to a place in his teaching and his reasoning where the reality of what the Spirit of God was leading him to say would suddenly overwhelm him. He couldn't go on to the next point until he had a little praise party, giving thanks to the Lord for His wisdom and longsuffering and mercy.

Logic, I learned, isn't everything. It has to leave room for praise.

When you are filled and controlled with the Spirit of God, you will be a grateful man. A grateful woman. A grateful boy or girl. The same thing happens when you are controlled with the Word of God. You are grateful. And when you have peace… Remember, now, peace is a fruit of the Spirit—one of the ninefold evidences of being Spirit-filled. And as you enjoy the peace that wells up in your heart and floods the landscape of your life, you will be filled with gratitude…just as I am right now. Praise God for His peace!

A PRAYERFUL LIFE RESULTS IN GRATITUDE

Are you seeing how the wagons are circling here?

That's the very thought I had while I was studying this. It is almost as though God is saying, "I'm not going to let you escape this. Because everywhere you turn in My Word, I'm going to place this concept right in front of you."

You want to talk about being filled with the Spirit? Then you had better be talking about gratitude at the same time. Do you sense a spirit of ingratitude and complaining in your life? Then you had better search your heart and find out if you have been grieving or quenching the Holy Spirit of God.

Where the Spirit is, there is gratitude. Think of it as the cologne of heaven. When a Spirit-filled man or woman walks through a room, you catch a whiff of a heavenly fragrance…the aroma of a thankful heart.

Notice yet another piece of evidence in a very familiar passage.

Be anxious for nothing, but in everything by prayer and supplication, with thanksgiving, let your requests be made known to God. (Philippians 4:6)

Many people read the verse like this: "Be anxious for nothing, but in everything by prayer, and supplication, and thanksgiving…"

But the word before *thanksgiving* isn't *and,* is it?

The word is *with.*

Don't overlook that distinction! It's so important. The *with* in this verse means that whether it is prayer or supplication or any other kind of praying to God, it is always to be mixed with thanksgiving. Thanksgiving belongs to all of the properties of prayer.

When you are asking God for something, it is always with thanksgiving.

When you are praising God for something, it is always with thanksgiving.

When you are interceding for someone, it is always with thanksgiving.

When you are a "watchman on the wall" for your church, or for your family, or for your nation, don't forget that with all those requests, all of them should be mixed and blended generously with thanksgiving to God for all He has done.

In Philippians 4:6, Paul seems to be mentioning several kinds of prayer, but he focuses in on one kind of response. And that is the response of gratitude. It is to be present in all of our prayers, no matter what the content might be.

Have you seen one of those automatic bread makers, that sits on a counter-top in your kitchen and turns out beautiful loaves of freshly baked bread? I've heard it's a fun gadget to have around. It comes with a little recipe book for all different kinds of bread. You can add raisins and cinnamon. You can add garlic and parmesan. You can add sugar and spice and everything nice. But you'd better not forget the flour! Flour is a basic ingredient in any kind of bread you make. In the same way, gratitude is the indispensable ingredient in every prayer we offer before the throne of God.

A CONCERN FOR GOD'S WILL RESULTS IN GRATITUDE

You may find yourself saying, "Jeremiah, I don't know if I'm with you yet on this. I've never heard anything quite like this before. How do I know if this gratitude thing is really God's will for my life, or just one of your personal hobby horses?"

Let me bring you back to another familiar verse, a powerful little prescription for life.

In everything give thanks; for this is the will of God in Christ Jesus for you. (1 Thessalonians 5:18)

How could God make it any plainer? Would it be more obvious if He sent a couple of angels to hold a banner over the side of an overpass for you to see on the way to work? How obvious does He have to be? A Spirit-filled Christian who is concerned about the will of God must be concerned about gratitude! The text says, "THIS IS THE WILL OF GOD." Wouldn't you like a statement as clear as that when you're trying to figure out whether you should move, or take a new job, or marry someone? Can't you just see stumbling across that in Scripture?

This is the will of God...that you move to Cleveland.

This is the will of God...that you marry Bill (or Betty) Jones.

People come to me all the time wishing they could find that kind of specific direction in Scripture. They want God to jot them out a neat little prescription: "Do this on Tuesday morning at the corner of Seventh and Main Streets."

Do you want a prescription? Do you want specific direction? Do you want to know the will of God? Here it is! *Be thankful.* Gratitude is the will of God for your life. If you are not a grateful person (and in your heart right now, you know very well whether you are or you aren't), you are not walking in the Spirit. You are out of the will of God, no matter how many gifts of the Spirit you might be exhibiting in your life. To be ungrateful is to be out of the will of God.

You say, "Well, I don't like that." I don't like it much either, but I didn't say it. God said it. The Bible isn't only a sword, it is a hammer. Have you ever been hammered by the Word of God? Let's say you find yourself grousing some afternoon. You're singing a sad story about how bad things are, how your talents are unappreciated, how your kids aren't measuring up, how your job is going south on you, how rotten the weather is, how the government did you wrong…and you work yourself into a really bleak, foul mood.

Friend, according to 1 Thessalonians 5:18, you are out of the will of God.

Let me show you how powerfully this is taught in God's Word. In Romans chapter 1, Paul begins describing a culture sliding toward disintegration. We hear a great deal about evolution in the media and in our public school classrooms, but this is *devolution,* a culture sliding backward into darkness. We don't hear much about that, do we? Yet here in Scripture, as the apostle sets the scene, he adds these significant words in Romans 1:21–22 (NIV):

> For although they knew God, they neither glorified him as God *nor gave thanks to him,* but their thinking became futile and their foolish hearts were darkened. Although they claimed to be wise, they became fools.

Paul told the Romans, "Let me tell you what happens to a culture that rejects God and rejects His natural revelation. They will head down, down, down. And one of the evidences of their decadence, of their rebellion against God, will be their lack of gratitude."

That's at the beginning of the process. Now let me tell you what it's going to be like at the end. Paul wrote to his young friend in the ministry and said, "Timothy, let me tell you what it's going to be like just before Jesus Christ comes back.

Let me describe to you how decadent the society is going to be in those days just before He returns."

> But mark this: There will be terrible times in the last days. People will be lovers of themselves, lovers of money, boastful, proud, abusive, disobedient to their parents...

What are the next two descriptive words?

> ungrateful, unholy... (2 Timothy 3:1–2, NIV)

Ingratitude travels in some pretty bad company, doesn't it? Ingratitude is comfortable with all the sins listed in these verses. I think sometimes we try to shrug it off as if it were no big deal. "Well, that's just my temperament." If that's the case, I want to tell you something. You need to get your temperament fixed! You need to let the Holy Spirit take control of your temperament. We excuse ourselves so often, don't we? We say, "Well, that's just the way I am." Or "It's my environment." Or "It's what I experienced when I was growing up."

Listen to me: if I understand the Bible, the Holy Spirit cuts through all that stuff. He slices right down to the center of you and begins to create within you a spirit that isn't your own, because it is God's Spirit, God's own characteristics in you. When you are controlled by the Spirit of God, gratitude will start to exude from your life. It may even catch you by surprise. It will certainly catch others by surprise when they notice your change in attitude. And you will know that what is coming forth from your life is not something that is naturally and normally yours. It is the supernatural evidence of the Spirit of God at work in your life.

This might not be the sort of teaching you were looking for when you purchased this book. Maybe you were looking for something spectacular instead of this nitty-gritty, rubber-meets-the-road sort of attitude exam. But if the Bible is anything, it is an extremely practical book. Yes, it deals with cosmic issues. Its story reaches into eternity past and cracks open the door to eternity future. But in between, there is a great wealth of help and correction and encouragement for day-to-day life in the trenches.

You and I have both met people who say they are believers and yet have all the signs of being ugly, bitter, mean-spirited folks. How could that be? If you are filled with the Spirit of God, your life is going to be marked by a spirit of gratitude that runs to the very core of who you are. And if that isn't true, whatever else you've got, you haven't got the Holy Spirit controlling your life.

One more thought on this matter of God's will and gratitude. Not only is the will of God clear, but the will of God concerning gratitude is comprehensive.

In Ephesians 5:20, Paul says that the Spirit-filled believer gives thanks to God for *all things*.

In Colossians 3:17 he expands "all things." He writes: "And whatever you do in word or deed, do all in the name of the Lord Jesus, giving thanks to God the Father through Him."

> Whatever we do
> in word
> or in deed
> do all
> …giving thanks.

In other words, in *everything*. And Paul was the kind of man who practiced what he preached. Some of the "all things" in his life would curl your hair! Yet Paul stayed grateful right up to the end. Do you know where Paul wrote most of his words to the Ephesians, to the Colossians, and to his friend Timothy? He wrote them in prison. He wrote them while in chains.

Now, wait a minute! Gratitude belongs in the palace, not in the prison! You get grateful on a cruise ship, maybe. You feel gratitude when you have a soft bed with clean sheets and three square meals a day. But in a Roman prison? In a cell?

Paul got it done. In whatever you do, in whatever you say, he tells us, be grateful. When I read his letters and think over the events of the man's life, I am overwhelmed. Sometimes people in our fellowship say to me, "I know I ought to be grateful, Pastor, but you don't know what's going on in my life. This has been a killer of a year, and I'm not in a grateful mood."

Yet the plain fact is, the man who wrote these letters so permeated with thanksgiving had a killer of a *life*. Listen to this small recitation he gave to the Corinthians from earlier in his career:

I have worked harder than any of them.

I have served more prison sentences!

I have been beaten times without number.

I have faced death again and again.

I have been beaten the regulation thirty-nine stripes by the Jews five
    times.

I have been beaten with rods three times.

I have been stoned once.

I have been shipwrecked three times.

I have been twenty-four hours in the open sea.

In my travels I have been in constant danger from rivers and floods,
from bandits, from my own countrymen, and from pagans. I have faced
danger in city streets, danger in the desert, danger on the high seas,
danger among false Christians. I have known exhaustion, pain, long
vigils, hunger and thirst, doing without meals, cold and lack of clothing.
(2 Corinthians 11:23–27, Phillips)

To top it all off, he spent his last days in a Roman dungeon and was martyred for his faith. But let me tell you this, Paul was a thankful man. Paul's life
trailed the fragrance of gratitude that we can still smell drifting up from these
pages two thousand years later.

You see, gratitude isn't something that develops within us because of the
good things that happen in our lives. When writing to the Romans, Paul wrote
a similar list of "woes" that can happen to a believer. Have you read those words
in Romans 8? He writes of tribulation, and distress, and persecution, and famine,
and nakedness, and peril, and sword. But then he seems to shout at the end of
that long list, "Yet in all these things we are more than conquerors through Him
who loved us!"

In all of *what* things, Paul? Distress and persecution, famine and nakedness,
sword and peril. He said in all these things we're not just conquerors, we're *more*
than conquerors. How can you have a spirit like that? How do you explain it?

The Holy Spirit.

That's the only explanation I have. The Holy Spirit comes to create within
you that which is unexplainable in any other terms. When you are filled with the
Spirit of God, He gives you a sense of victory and triumph over the issues of life

so that you can live in the prison in the same way that you live in the palace.

That's why Paul was able to say, "I can handle it when I abound and I can handle it when I am abased...I can enjoy the good, sweet times, and I can take the dark, difficult times in stride, because my contentment is in the person of Jesus Christ."

Henry Nouwen once wrote, "Where there is a reason for gratitude, there can always be found a reason for bitterness. It is here that we're faced with the freedom to make a decision. We can decide to be grateful or to be bitter."

When we are filled with the Spirit...

We learn how to count our blessings instead of our crosses.
We learn how to count our gains instead of our losses.
We learn how to count our joys instead of our woes.
We learn how to count our friends instead of our foes.
We learn how to count our smiles instead of our tears.
And our courage instead of our fears.
And our full years instead of our lean ones.
And our kind deeds instead of our mean ones.
And our health instead of our wealth.
We count on God instead of ourself.

It's all a matter of perspective. Helen Keller once made an observation when she was growing up. She said, "I have often thought it would be a blessing if each human being were stricken blind and deaf for a few days sometime in early adult life. Darkness would make them more appreciative of sight and silence would teach them the joys of sound."

God has to beat on us sometimes before we wake up to what we have and how grateful we ought to be.

In Africa, I am told, there is a little berry called the "taste berry." It is called by that name because it changes your taste so that everything you eat tastes sweet and pleasant. Someone has said that gratitude is the Christian's taste berry. If you take the attitude of gratitude and devour it in your being, it turns even the difficult, sour things into the sweet.

When you are filled with the Spirit of God, you will be grateful.

Yes, you may live in a shack on a dead end in Chickasha. But oh, those Oklahoma sunrises! God brings a new one every day and delivers it to your window, free of charge.

Pull back those curtains and take a look. Then give Him thanks.

Chapter Eleven

SPIRIT-CONTROLLED CHURCH MEMBERS

SUBMITTING TO ONE ANOTHER

Be filled with the Spirit...
submitting to one another
in the fear of God.
EPHESIANS 5:18, 21

recently saw an ad for "Classic Faux Jewelry."
The ad featured an elegant-looking lady in a black evening gown wearing the company's products...a faux diamond necklace, a faux bracelet, and matching faux earrings.

Faux, I take it, is a fancy-sounding French word for fake.

The ad promises a collection of "the most stunning and affordable jewelry available...inspired by Cartier, Bulgari, Tiffany, and more." The text goes on to assert that "the look is so real, only your jeweler will know it's *faux*."

You can fake a great many things in life. You can even wear around a *faux* Spirit-filled life, for a while, and fool your friends and family. If you wear it long enough, you might even begin to convince yourself. But there is one quality I can't help believing would be very, very difficult to counterfeit.

And that is the quality of joyful submission.

You can have grudging submission, you can have bitter submission, you can have gloomy, resigned submission, you can have grit-your-teeth, plastic-smile submission. But joyful, willing submission? I don't think so. That is a jewel that only the Master Jeweler can produce in our lives.

In Ephesians 5, the apostle Paul has been telling us that when we're filled with the Spirit of God, certain things will be true of us. We've seen that there will

175

be speaking and singing, worshiping and giving thanks. But Paul doesn't leave this passage until he has listed one more outcome of the Spirit-controlled life.

...submitting to one another in the fear of God. (Ephesians 5:21)

One of the things that will be true of a person who is filled with the Spirit of God is an attitude of submission. Now, I don't have to tell you that we're living in a world where such a spirit isn't a very common thing. You don't see it in the workplace, do you? Just imagine sitting on an airliner and noticing some sharp, buttoned-down business type across the aisle from you reading a book titled *Joyful Submission in the Corporate Arena*. It doesn't work, does it? It's a little difficult to visualize.

You certainly don't see submission in the sports world. We recently learned that an NBA basketball player can actually attack his coach in anger, put his hands around the man's neck and choke him, get kicked out of the league, and then be quickly reinstated by a court of law. Not much submission there, either.

When you think about it, willing submission to authority in any area of the world, in any area of life, is highly unusual. It's rare, like a precious stone. And so here we are as Christians with an open Bible before us, reading that when we're Spirit-filled, we're to have an attitude of willing submission to one another.

We say, "That's not normal." No, it isn't. It is neither normal, natural, nor human. That's because it isn't coming out of the human nature at all. To be filled with the Spirit is to have the Spirit of the Lord Jesus within us, running our lives, instead of our own spirit.

As we wade deeper into this truth, I want you to note that an attitude of willing submission was an unknown truth before Christ began to set His principles in motion. When Jesus explained it to His men, I can almost visualize their mouths dropping open. They'd never heard anything like it...and it wasn't easy to swallow!

"Among the heathen, kings are tyrants and each minor official lords it over those beneath him. But among you it is quite different. Anyone wanting to be a leader among you must be your servant. And if you want to be right at the top, you must serve like a slave. Your attitude must be like my own, for I, the Messiah, did not come to be served, but to serve, and to give my life as a ransom for many." (Matthew 20:25–28, TLB)

In this text Jesus says, "Here's the way it shakes down out in the world. But that's not the way it works when you belong to Me." He called His men—and you and me—to live in a different way, with a different spirit. If you study the Bible carefully, you will discover that this principle cuts straight across the grain of our lives. Our Lord is calling us to walk in His steps through every area of our experience.

BE SUBMISSIVE IN THE MUNICIPALITY

As believers we're to have a submissive spirit within the government restraints under which we live. Romans 13 puts it this way:

> Everyone must submit himself to the governing authorities, for there is no authority except that which God has established. The authorities that exist have been established by God.... Therefore, it is necessary to submit to the authorities, not only because of possible punishment but also because of conscience.... Give everyone what you owe him: If you owe taxes, pay taxes; if revenue, then revenue; if respect, then respect; if honor, then honor. (Romans 13:1, 5, 7, NIV)

The Bible calls upon believers to offer willing submission to the authority God has placed over us. Perhaps you find yourself saying, "Well, I don't happen to like or respect that authority. I happen to believe that some of those people in authority right now are ungodly."

Let me remind you of something that may help you put this matter in perspective. When Paul wrote these words to the Romans, Nero sat in the emperor's chair. He wasn't exactly the epitome of a godly ruler. You wouldn't want to put his mug on Mount Rushmore between Jefferson and Lincoln. He was a wicked, cruel tyrant who murdered his own mother after she had helped him come to power. Yes, things have deteriorated pretty badly in Washington, D.C., but at least we haven't come to the place where they're dipping Christians in pitch and using them as human torches at garden parties, as Nero did.

Even so, Paul still instructed Roman believers to keep a submissive attitude toward their government. It amazes me, and it may amaze you. But that's what the Bible says.

Peter weighs in on the subject too. He wrote:

> Therefore submit yourselves to every ordinance of man for the Lord's sake, whether to the king as supreme, or to governors, as to those who are sent by him for the punishment of evildoers and for the praise of those who do good. For this is the will of God. (1 Peter 2:13–15)

The supernatural attitude of submission to government raises some serious questions for some of us with regard to the whole concept of civil disobedience. We need to walk very carefully when we move into that realm, because the Lord God says to us that if we're controlled by the Spirit of God, we will have an attitude of submission to the authorities who are over us in the municipality.

Even when we don't like those authorities.

Even when those authorities are ungodly.

Even when we don't feel like it.

BE SUBMISSIVE IN THE MARKETPLACE

You may feel like debating me on this one too. You may be saying, "You don't know my boss, Jeremiah. He's unreasonable. He's a tyrant. He's got a foul mouth." Or "She's so petty. She's into control games. I don't like being submissive to my boss. You need to cut me a little slack on this one."

Yet on this very issue, where we would *love* to have a little slack, the Word of God gives us none at all. In the days when the New Testament was being written, the rule of the day was master-slave relationships. In Ephesians, Paul writes:

> Slaves, obey your earthly masters with respect and fear, and with sincerity of heart, just as you would obey Christ. Obey them not only to win their favor when their eye is on you, but like slaves of Christ, doing the will of God from your heart. Serve wholeheartedly, as if you were serving the Lord, not men, because you know that the Lord will reward everyone for whatever good he does, whether he is slave or free. (Ephesians 6:5–8, NIV)

The Bible says that when we're in a relationship with someone in authority over us, we're to have a submissive attitude toward that man or woman, just as the slaves had to their masters in New Testament days.

Paul drives the point home even further in the book of Colossians. (This passage is so rich with practical counsel that we could camp here for weeks.)

> Slaves, obey your earthly masters in everything; and do it, not only when their eye is on you and to win their favor, but with sincerity of heart and reverence for the Lord. Whatever you do, work at it with all your heart, as working for the Lord, not for men, since you know that you will receive an inheritance from the Lord as a reward. It is the Lord Christ you are serving. (Colossians 3:22–24, NIV)

Peter speaks up on that point too: "Servants, be submissive to your masters with all respect, not only to those who are good and gentle, but also to those who are unreasonable" (1 Peter 2:18, NASB).

Do you see what I mean? Scripture doesn't give us any wobble room. We're to be submissive even when the individual in authority over us is *unreasonable*. No matter whom we find in authority over us, we are to do our work with all our strength, with all our heart, as unto Jesus Christ.

The fact is, everyone is submissive to someone.

If Scripture has a word for the employee break room, it also has a word for the executive suite. In Ephesians 6:9 (NIV), we read, "And masters, treat your slaves in the same way. Do not threaten them, since you know that he who is both their Master and yours is in heaven, and there is no favoritism with him."

Every person is under authority to someone. Paul underlines this idea yet again in Colossians 4:1: "Masters, give your servants what is just and fair, knowing that you also have a Master in heaven."

The thread that holds all these biblical directives together is the attitude of heart, isn't it? It isn't, "Well, I'm not going to let *him* rule over me...I'm not going to let *her* tell me what to do." The fact is, if God says I am to have a spirit of willing, joyful submission to the authorities in my life, then by the Holy Spirit's power, I *can* live in that way. No, He isn't saying we should be Milquetoasts and doormats, and let people disrespect us and mistreat us. But He is saying in the very warp and woof of life, the thing that ought to be true of us as believers is that God has put within us the inward power to have a submissive spirit.

That submissive spirit comes to bear within the municipality and within the marketplace. It is also within marriage, which we will deal with extensively in the next chapter. Within the church, Scripture teaches us to...

BE SUBMISSIVE WITHIN THE MEMBERSHIP

When Paul says to submit to one another in the fear of God, he's talking to the whole church...and to all who would read his epistle down through the years. Whether we're man or woman, boy or girl, child or parent, folks ought to see within us a gentle, submissive spirit, one toward another.

Here is how this truth works its way through a body of believers.

We're to have a spirit of submission as leaders to our followers

That's a good thing for me to know as a pastor—and for all pastors to know. In 1 Peter 5:2–3, Peter writes, "Shepherd the flock of God which is among you, serving as overseers, not by constraint but willingly, not for dishonest gain but eagerly; nor as being lords over those entrusted to you, but being examples to the flock."

The spirit of a pastor, the spirit of the undershepherd within the church, is to be one of submission, submitting to the needs of the people, to the demands of the task, to the call of God upon his life. That is my challenge as a pastor, to fulfill my tasks as a servant-leader, depending on the power of the Holy Spirit.

The mighty Son of God, who could command legions of angels greater than the combined armies of every world power since the beginning of time, said, "I am among you as the One who serves" (Luke 22:27). He is my example.

We're to have a spirit of submission as followers to our leaders

But if it is true for the leader to the follower, it is also true for the follower to the leader. The writer to the Hebrews offers the following words of tough love: "Obey your leaders, and submit to them; for they keep watch over your souls, as those who will give an account. Let them do this with joy and not with grief, for this would be unprofitable for you" (Hebrews 13:17, NASB).

What is the writer saying? Have a submissive attitude toward those in the church who have been put in a place of leadership. Why? Because they've got a big job to do. They're going to have to stand before the Lord of the universe and give an account of how they watched over your soul. Besides that, they care about you. (Why else would they be in ministry?) Don't make their job hard by being rebellious. But make their job easy, knowing that their heart for you is that you will be what God wants you to be.

Peter offers this word of insight to some of the younger men within a flock: "Young men, in the same way be submissive to those who are older. All of you, clothe yourselves with humility toward one another, because, 'God opposes the proud but gives grace to the humble.' Humble yourselves, therefore, under God's mighty hand, that he may lift you up in due time" (1 Peter 5:5–6, NIV).

And what if that kind of submission causes stress in a young man's heart? Peter has the answer for that in the next verse. "Cast all your anxiety on him because he cares for you "(1 Peter 5:7, NIV).

We're to have a spirit of submission to one another

You say, "How can this work? How can everybody submit to everybody else? Wouldn't that just be chaos?" Have you ever been around two very submissive, nonassertive people who are trying to decide where to go to lunch?

"Wherever you want to go is fine."

"No, I'll be happy with whatever you choose."

"Oh no, you choose. I insist."

"No, no. I don't care. Goodness, I just want to do what you want to do."

Some of us more take-charge types feel like interrupting the conversation and saying, "Hey, *I* will choose! Just get on with it, will you?"

I'm not talking about being indecisive or directionless. But I am talking about an attitude of the heart that has a direct effect on our actions. Here's what I mean. Sometimes we go into a meeting and we have our own agenda—the points we want to drive home, the words we want to say, and the impression we want to leave.

Fine. But...do we care as much about the opinion of the other person as we care about our own? Are we seeking to understand his heart? That's the whole issue: having a heart of submission born out of the supernatural power of the peace of God which is in us by the indwelling Holy Spirit.

You say, "Boy, that's hard for me!"

It's hard for all of us. And I will tell you very candidly, without the Spirit of God, it is *impossible* for all of us. All of this sweet submission talk is just so much pie-in-the-sky-by-and-by unless and until He moves in our lives and makes it reality. But when He does...when God's Holy Spirit controls us, oh, what a wonderful impact it has on our attitude about life. Things that used to irritate us and upset us and cause us inner strife no longer have that effect. We begin to enjoy the peace of God.

PETER'S PRINCIPLES

I want to show you how the apostle Peter takes this concept and delineates it for us so that we can see how it works.

Notice 1 Peter 3:8: "Finally, all of you be of one mind, having compassion for one another; love as brothers, be tenderhearted, be courteous." That little verse is a whole sermon in itself. It contains some very key terms that tell us how to live in a submissive way. These are the nuts and bolts that make this thing work. First of all...

Submission demands a commitment to one another

This is a disposition to "mind the same things." That's what it says. "Finally, all of you be of one mind." Romans 8:5 says, "For those who live according to the flesh set their minds on the things of the flesh, but those who live according to the Spirit, the things of the Spirit."

What does that mean? If we are in the body of Christ and submitting to one another, it begins with spiritual oneness, having the same focus in our lives. We're to attend to the interests of Christ and His kingdom. Our Lord wants us to tap into a common longing, a common eagerness, and common concerns.

No, this doesn't mean we'll all have the same opinion on every subject. That would be b-o-r-i-n-g. Who would want to be in a community where everybody agreed about everything? What a bland, vanilla life that would be. But what happens so often to us in the church is that we get our opinions ahead of God's Word and ahead of God's principles. We take the things that are not absolute and elevate them to the status of absolutes, sometimes forgetting the *real* absolutes in the process.

I have bumped around the evangelical church almost all of my life, and I am ready to go on record with this observation: Most of the difficulties we have in church, if you do a postmortem on them, arise from the fact that people have not developed a real commitment to one another. Our commitment to each other is so shallow! We are much more committed to our own interests. As a result, we're ready to go to war over the most trivial things. We're ready to *die* for green carpet or padded pews or the type of music that gets played during communion.

Yes, you and I may disagree about certain things. But don't we love the same Lord? Aren't we both committed to the power of the Spirit in our lives? Don't we have the same goal to reach the world for Christ? We can disagree about some of the peripheral things, but we had better stay focused on the things that bind us together. We can't have a submissive attitude if we don't do that.

I had an interesting conversation with one of the older members of our church some months ago, in which he honestly confessed that he "wasn't too sure" about some of the new worship music. But just that quickly the clouds lifted from his brow and he smiled at me.

"But do you know what, Pastor Jeremiah? When I look around the congregation, I see that it's really ministering to a lot of the younger families in our church—and a lot of the young people too. It's kinda funny. The more I try to get into their hearts, the better I like that music."

A conversation like that can make a pastor's week—or maybe his whole year. I saw the fingerprints of the Holy Spirit all over that exchange.

What had this dear man just done? He had taken his own opinions, his own preferences, his own prejudices, and deliberately placed them on a lower shelf, while he took the needs of others and put them on the top shelf. And he did it with a wink and a smile.

That's not natural. That's not expected. That's not the way it usually works in this old world. No, it is *supernatural.* And God gains the glory!

Submission demands a concern for one another

Continuing on in 1 Peter 3:8, notice how he builds on this principle: "Finally, all of you be of one mind, having compassion for one another." *Compassion* is a poignant word in the language of the New Testament. It means to suffer together with other people.

Romans 12:15 says we're to rejoice with those who rejoice and mourn or weep with those who weep. Most people find it is easier to rejoice with those who weep and to weep with those who rejoice. Isn't that a strange thing? It gets inverted somehow. The Bible says when we have concern for one another, if someone is hurting, we hurt too. Listen to me, we actually *feel* it. We are moved by it.

First Corinthians 12:26 says, "If one member suffers, all the members suffer with it; or if one member is honored, all the members rejoice with it." That's how we enter into this submissive attitude within the church. We have compassion one for the other, sharing the joys and sorrows of our lives.

A little girl came home from visiting a neighbor whose young daughter had died just a few weeks before. When she got home her father said, "Why did you go over there?"

"Well," the little girl said, "I went over to comfort the mother."

"Well, honey, what in the world could you do to comfort the mother?"

She said, "I climbed up in her lap and I cried with her."

That's what you do when you have compassion for one another.

Grace Noll Crowell expresses what we're talking about here in a little bit of verse:

Let me come in where you are weeping, friend, and let me take your
    hand.
I, who have known a sorrow such as yours, can understand.
Let me come in. I would be very still beside you in your grief.
I would not bid you cease your weeping, friend. Tears bring relief.
Let me come in. I would only breathe a prayer and hold your hand,
For I have known a sorrow such as yours, and I understand.[1]

That's what it means to have compassion.

Submission demands charity one to another

Again, it says in 1 Peter 3:8, "Finally, all of you be of one mind, having compassion for one another; love as brothers."

Isn't that a great thought? The New Testament uses the word brethren over two hundred times to describe who we are in the body of Christ. Did you know we're brothers and sisters in the family?

You say, "Well, then, why do we have so many disagreements?"

Because we're brothers and sisters in the family, that's why!

But oh, what a wonderful thing to be in the family together. Brotherly love is the badge of Christian fellowship, and because God our Father has first loved us, we love Him and then we love one another. We're in the family together.

Blood is thick, isn't it? I would do anything for my family. Not just the family that lives in my house, but my extended family. Family is special. Part of being in the family is to love one another, and when you love one another you submit to one another.

Without submission in the family, all would be chaos. If you grew up as a boy in a family with two girls, as I did, you learned that you could only get into the bathroom on certain rare occasions. We had a small house with one bathroom, and the operating principle was this: you waited. You submitted. You didn't always like it, but you submitted. Then, when you finally got smart, you learned that you could get up a little earlier and get into the bathroom before sleepyhead girls got out of bed! It's all a part of learning how to live together, isn't it? Submitting, growing, and learning within the family.

Submission demands compassion for one another

Peter says to "be tenderhearted" toward one another. The Greek word translated *tenderhearted* in verse 8 is very graphic. It's something visceral. It says, *feel it in your gut*. It's something deep down, below the surface.

In Romans 12:9 (Phillips), Paul says, "Let us have no imitation Christian love." No *faux* love to go with your *faux* jewelry. No shallow, phony stuff. Our compassion must be the genuine article.

Ephesians 4:30 says, "Do not grieve the Holy Spirit of God, by whom you were sealed for the day of redemption." Then it goes on to say we're to be kind to one another. It grieves the Holy Spirit when we are unkind to one another. It grieves Him when we are so wrapped up in our own goals, our own plans, and our own worries in our own little world that we do not feel for one another and offer those priceless little acts of kindness.

Are you too busy to write a note to that brokenhearted dad whose son is in trouble with the law? Then you're too busy.

Are you too swamped to send a bouquet or a card to the family that has suffered a miscarriage? Then you'd better get out of that swamp. What are you doing there, anyway?

Are you too much in a hurry to stop on the sidewalk or in the hallway to encourage a friend who is "under the pile" and heavy of heart? Then friend, you're in too big a hurry.

Submission demands humility toward one another

Peter writes, "Be submissive to one another, and be clothed with humility" (1 Peter 5:5). The Phillips translation give this verse an extra twist:

> All of you should defer to one another and wear the "overall" of humility in serving one another.

I like that. No matter what you wear at home, wear to school, or wear to the office, put on those overalls of humility last. Zip yourself into 'em. Wear 'em on top of everything else. Then, when the opportunity to serve someone comes along, you won't worry about getting dirty or rumpled. You'll already have your overalls on! You can plunge right in, for Jesus' sake.

Peter (who learned some hard lessons before he came to this attitude) says we're to have a spirit of willingness to *bend* to one another. That's what it means to be submissive. It isn't a limp acceptance of whatever comes along, it is a willingness to flex for the sake of another. Does that describe you? Are you bendable? Flexible? Willing to lower-shelf your plans to place someone's need on a higher shelf?

Humility is a trait in our lives that is so rare and precious that when you finally realize you have it, you have already lost it! That's the truth! And yet it is the very quality the Holy Spirit desires to develop as He works within us. It is a jewel beyond price that catches the reflected glory of Jesus Christ.

Submission requires taming the tongue

Sometimes when people discuss a transaction of some sort, they will speak of "deal makers" and "deal breakers." In 1 Peter 3:10, Peter brings up a deal breaker when it comes to this matter of submission to one another. This is something that can destroy submission in any context.

In verse 10, quoting from the Old Testament, he writes: "He who would love life and see good days, let him refrain his tongue from evil, and his lips from speaking deceit." When we're in a submissive environment, the thing that will blow it away more than anything else is what we do with our tongue. When we start talking the way we shouldn't, when we start putting on airs and posturing in front of everyone, we are trying to make people think we're something we're not.

And that's a lie. That's a tongue that is full of deceit. It may certainly be the standard operating procedure of people in the world, but Peter warns us not to live in such a way.

When the Spirit of God comes to live within us, old things pass away, all things become new. And while we may not feel like we have "arrived," the minute Jesus Christ comes to live within our heart and the Holy Spirit comes to indwell us, we start down the road to become what He wants us to be instead of what we have always been. And along the way, as we yield to the Holy Spirit in more and more areas of our life, that is what it means to be filled. We say to the Holy Spirit every day, "Oh, Spirit of God, fill my life, and control me, and make me to be the person that Jesus wants me to be."

And little by little, He does just that. Our attitudes begin to change.

I have watched that process in many lives over the years. One of the great joys of being a long-term pastor is to see what God does in people's lives as He grows them up in the Spirit of God.

THE BENEFITS OF A SUBMISSIVE LIFE

Perhaps you're saying to yourself, "Why should I bother with this? Why should I let the Spirit of God work me over in this area of submission? It's so hard for me. It really goes against the grain. Why should I seek to change?"

I'll tell you why. Because the joy and blessing it will bring into your life is incomparable. Remember the old TV game show *Let's Make a Deal?* Contestants would win prizes then had to choose whether to keep what they had or swap it for something behind Door Number One, Door Number Two, or Door Number Three. And they knew that behind *one* of those doors was a prize much, much greater and more wonderful than the one they held in their hands.

God doesn't do that to us. He tells us straight out what will happen to us if we hold on to our old flesh life, and what will happen if we exchange it for the Spirit-filled life and Spirit-filled submission one to another.

For instance…there is a door marked "Psalm 34," with wonderful benefits for those who give themselves to God. What do we receive when we choose Door 34?

We receive God's angelic safety system

This poor man cried out, and the LORD heard him,
and saved him out of all his troubles.
The angel of the LORD encamps all around those who fear Him.
(vv. 6–7)

Donna and I flew home together recently from the East Coast, and somewhere midway across the continent we met up with our old California friend El Niño. This climatic condition is no longer just a West Coast phenomenon; it has disturbed the air waves all over the world. Almost anywhere you fly, you're in for a bumpy ride.

Maybe you don't think of such things, but it became so turbulent on that flight I couldn't help wondering if the wings were going to come right off that 737. What do you do with that fear? You just give yourself to the Lord. You remember that the mighty angel of the Lord is encamped all around you. You couldn't be in better hands.

But you don't only receive God's angelic safety system. Look what else is behind Door 34. I love this one!

We receive God's ample supply system

Oh, fear the LORD, you His saints!
There is no want to those who fear Him.
The young lions lack and suffer hunger;
but those who seek the LORD shall not lack any good thing.
(vv. 9–10)

You say, "If I live in the will of God and adopt this principle of being a submissive, Spirit-filled Christian, what am I going to get out if it?" You are going to get the sense of God's involvement in your life. There are many who receive God's salvation, but all they really care about is avoiding hell and making sure they go to heaven. They trust the Lord Jesus Christ, and then they go AWOL for the rest of their lives. Just think what they are missing! They miss the deep artesian well of joy that God wants to put into our hearts. He came that we might have life and have it more *abundantly*.

We receive God's amazing support system

He gets involved with us.

> I sought the LORD, and He heard me,
> and delivered me from all my fears. (v. 4)

> The righteous cry out, and the LORD hears,
> and delivers them out of all their troubles.
> The LORD is near to those who have a broken heart,
> and saves such as have a contrite spirit. (vv. 17–18)

Isn't that a wonderful truth? You may feel uncomfortable and your flesh may rebel about yielding to God's Spirit, but if you do, you're going to love the benefits! The benefits of living God's way far outweigh any efforts or sacrifices we make along the way.

We receive God's absolute security system

> The LORD redeems the soul of His servants,
> and none of those who trust in Him shall be condemned.
> (v. 22)

When you walk with the Lord in the light of His will and you let the Spirit of God control your life, God takes His big arms and wraps them around you. He says, "You are My child. You are in My family, and I'm going to watch out for you. I'm going to take care of you."

Reuben Welch was for many years associated with Point Loma College in San Diego. He has written some wonderful things about the way the church functions. Some years ago, he wrote these free verse lines about submitting to one another in Jesus Christ.

> You know something? We're all just people who need each other. We're
> all learning and we've got a long journey ahead of us. We've got to go
> together, and if it takes us until Jesus comes, we better stay together. We
> better help each other. And I daresay that by the time we get there, all
> the sandwiches will be gone, all the chocolate will be gone, and all the

water will be gone, and all the backpacks will be empty, but no matter how long it takes us, we've got to go together because that's how it is in the body of Christ. It's all of us in love, in care, in support, in mutuality and submission. We really do need each other.[2]

That's how we are to function within the body.

When I was growing up, my grandfather and grandmother taught me to play dominoes. In this high-tech world of computer and video games, you don't see dominoes being played much anymore. Once in a while when we go to see my wife's mother in the care center, we'll see some older people sitting around playing dominoes.

Dominoes is a game unlike almost any other game you will ever play, because the only way you can ever win is to spend everything you have. The person who wins isn't the person who has the most dominoes left, but the person who gets rid of all of his first.

It seems to me that living the Christian life is something like playing dominoes. Your friend plays a two, and you need to play a two to identify with him. She plays a six, and you have to play a six to identify with her. And the more you identify with what's played, the faster you get rid of your dominoes. Then, when you've given yourself away and you've submitted to everything and all your dominoes are gone...you're the winner!

When we give ourselves to God and let His Spirit fill us and control us, we will give ourselves to others, rather than protecting ourselves and holding on to what we have. And then, when we've given it all away, we win.

When we are in eternity together, what we have won will be so much greater and more radiant than what we gave away that our small sacrifices will hardly be worth remembering.

Except to the One who never forgets.

Chapter Twelve

SPIRIT-CONTROLLED MARRIAGES

THE FOUNDATION FOR LIFELONG JOY

part from the indwelling Spirit of God, marriage can be tough sledding.

My buddies and I used to do some sledding during those long Ohio winters. We had some easy runs (good for a few laughs and a mild thrill), and we had some pretty scary runs (the kind you would have never done except on a dare). My definition of tough sledding would be a hill where two kids get on the sled at the top of the hill, and only the sled makes it to the bottom. When that happens on over half the trips down a particular hill, that's tough sledding.

Similarly, when over half the marriages in our country today end in divorce, that's a pretty hazardous ride. That's a challenging sled run. Without the Spirit of God in a marriage, it's going to be tough to maintain any peace and joy and beauty and happiness. It's going to be a challenge just hanging on to the relationship.

One of the reasons for these tensions is that God has created man and woman in such uniquely different ways. If the Spirit of God doesn't provide the glue for intimacy within the home, those differences will create hurt and misunderstanding, pulling the man and woman apart from one another.

One of my friends snagged this anonymous broadside from the Internet. Exaggerated perhaps, and certainly politically incorrect...but do you discern a grain or two of truth between the lines?

And now, for the question of the day: "Is your computer male or female?" You decide!

As you are aware, ships have long been characterized as being female (e.g., "Steady as she goes" or "She's listing to starboard, Captain!").

Recently, a group of computer scientists (all male) announced that computers should also be referred to as female. Their reasons for drawing this conclusion are as follows:

No one but the creator understands their internal logic.

The native language they use to communicate with other computers is incomprehensible to everyone else.

The message "Bad command or file name" is about as informative as "If you don't know why I'm mad at you, then I'm certainly not going to tell you."

Even your smallest mistakes are stored in long-term memory for later retrieval.

As soon as you make a commitment to one, you find yourself spending half your paycheck on accessories for it.

However, another group of computer scientists (all female) thinks that computers should be referred to as if they were male. Their reasons are as follows:

They have a lot of data but are still clueless.

They are supposed to help you solve problems, but half the time they *are* the problem.

As soon as you commit to one, you realize that if you'd waited a little longer, you could have obtained a better model.

In order to get their attention, you have to turn them on.

The truth is, if God didn't give us some help in all of this male-female relationship business, we'd be in a lot of trouble, wouldn't we? It's like having an Apple computer and an IBM in the same house—and trying to get them to communicate with each other. Sometimes it seems like men and women are from different solar systems!

Isn't it great that God has a word for us to help us? We often hear about what it means to be filled with the Spirit in theological terms, and yet when you read the Bible carefully, you will discover that God has also put it in very *practical* terms. This is the stuff of everyday living.

It rings true to life. And it works.

Look with me again at how Paul lays the foundation for all of our relationships in the book of Ephesians:

> Be filled with the Spirit, speaking to one another in psalms and hymns and spiritual songs, singing and making melody in your heart to the Lord, giving thanks always for all things to God the Father in the name of our Lord Jesus Christ, submitting to one another in the fear of God. Wives, submit to your own husbands, as to the Lord. (Ephesians 5:18–22)

What does a Spirit-filled person look like? Will we know that person because of all the miraculous signs and works of wonder that follow his life? Yes, that might be an indicator…but that's not the way most people will respond to the work of the Spirit. Paul tells us that when someone is controlled by the Holy Spirit, he will first of all be committed to worship. He will find himself speaking about God, singing to God, and making melody in his heart to the Lord. Further, his life will be dominated by an attitude of gratitude, giving thanks to his Lord in everything and through everything.

In the last chapter we talked about the word *submitting,* in verse 21. Submitting to one another is that spirit of sweet reasonableness that God gives to us within the body of Christ. Instead of constantly seeking to promote our own interests and our agenda, we defer to the needs of others.

The Bible takes this to the next logical step. When we're filled with the Spirit, Scripture says, we will have mutual submission *within the home.*

This is the subject that always tends to put people on the defensive. When these truths are misunderstood or misapplied, the damage to relationships can be devastating.

I heard a story recently about a married couple who attended a marriage seminar. The speaker was teaching on the ramifications of submission in the home, but he was one of these demagogues who had it all wrong. (Whatever you might think about submission, the Bible says we are first of all to submit *one to another.*)

When the couple left the meeting that night, the husband could tell his wife was really upset. She had not appreciated the message at all, and after sitting through nearly two hours of it, she was fuming.

The husband, however, felt drunk with fresh power as he climbed into the car. Driving home, he said rather pompously, "Well, what do you think about *that?*" His wife didn't say a word. When they arrived home, she got out and followed him silently into the house. Once inside, he slammed the door and said, "Wait right there. Just stand right there."

She stood tight-lipped and stared at him. "I've been thinking about what that fellow said tonight," he began, "and I want you to know that from now on, that's just the way it's going to be around here. You got it? That's the way things are going to be run in this house."

Having said that, he didn't see his wife again for two weeks. After two weeks he could just start to see a little bit out of one of his eyes.

Misapplied Scripture can be dangerous…in more ways than one!

If you look closely at verse 21, it says *Submitting,* and what is the rest of it? *"To one another in the fear of God."* Then in the next paragraph, it shows us how that "one another" submission works in the family. And while it is true that a husband, as head of the home, must resolve an impasse in those times when a decision has to be made, in practice those standoff situations are very rare.

I've talked to literally hundreds of people who have lived in Christian marriage, and most of them can't even remember coming to such an impasse. Neither can Donna or I. Instead, there has been a gradual growing together in the Lord, resulting in a mutual sense of submitting to one another.

This whole concept of the wife's submission to her husband—and the reciprocal responsibility of husband to wife—are not isolated here in Ephesians. Paul wrote something similar in Colossians 3:18–19: "Wives, submit to your own husbands, as is fitting in the Lord. Husbands, love your wives and do not be bitter toward them."

In Titus 2:3–5, Paul was giving some instructions to an associate in the ministry, telling the younger man how the church was supposed to function. He wrote:

"Likewise, teach the older women to be reverent in the way they live, not to be slanderers or addicted to much wine, but to teach what is good. Then they can train the younger women to love their husbands and children, to be self-controlled and pure, to be busy at home, to be kind, and to be subject to their husbands, so that no one will malign the word of God" (NIV).

But the best commentary on mutual submission appears in Peter's first letter. Here the text calls for a spirit of sweet reasonableness within the heart of the wife *and* the heart of the husband. Wherever this doctrine gets derailed, wherever you see some guy beating his chest and taking a chauvinist position about the family because he's a Christian, you can be sure he doesn't understand the biblical text (and probably doesn't want to).

The Bible leaves no room for the abuse of authority. Remember what Jesus said?

"You know that the rulers of the Gentiles lord it over them, and their high officials exercise authority over them. Not so with you. Instead, whoever wants to become great among you must be your servant, and whoever wants to be first must be your slave." (Matthew 20:25–27, NIV)

Those who attempt to use Scripture as a club to "lord it over" another do violence to the teaching and ministry of the Lord Jesus.

Peter, however, begins his instruction on mutual submission by turning first to wives.

THE SUBMISSION OF A CHRISTIAN WIFE

Wives, be submissive to your own husbands, that even if some do not obey the word, they, without a word, may be won by the conduct of their wives. (1 Peter 3:1)

A Christian wife submits to her husband willingly

The *New English Bible* says it like this: "You women must accept the authority of your husbands so that if there are any of them that disbelieve the gospel, they may be won over without a word being said."

Do you know what will make the biggest difference in the heart and attitude of an unbelieving husband? It is how his Christian wife responds to him—her love for him, her attitude toward him. The wife's attitude toward her husband has a far stronger impact than her words.

Someone might ask, "But how can I show that kind of attitude and response to him when he doesn't even know the Lord?"

You can do it because God tells you to do it, and the Spirit of God will enable you to do it. When I speak about the willingness of a wife to submit to her husband, I would quickly add that this is not to be in any way harmful to her, or in any way that violates the Word of God. But truthfully, most issues in day-to-day life don't lie in those questionable areas, do they? And so God says to the woman who is married to an unbeliever, if you want to win him, the way you do it is with your willing spirit of submission.

Saint Augustine said of his mother, Monica, "When she came to marriageable age, she was bestowed upon a husband and served him as her lord, and she did all she could to win him to Christ. Speaking to him by her deportment, whereby thou madest her beautiful and reverently loveable, and admirable to her husband. Finally, when her husband was now at the very end of her earthly life, she won him to thee, because of the way she had lived before him all of her life."

The great Dr. Harry Ironside, one of my favorite Bible commentators, had a woman approach him during a series of evangelistic meetings at Moody Church in Chicago. "Dr. Ironside," she said, "I have talked until I am blue in the face trying to get my husband to come to these meetings."

In reply, the great expositor gently pointed the lady to these verses in 1 Peter 3 and suggested she put this advice into action.

The next morning when her husband got up, he smelled bacon and eggs. That could only mean his wife had struggled out of bed early in the morning to fix him a lip-smacking breakfast. In the afternoon when he came home, she had prepared a fish dinner. He enjoyed fish, but since she didn't like it, she hardly ever cooked it. But on this day, she cooked it with style. Then in the evening she said, "Honey, they're having some special services at the church, and I wondered if you would mind if I went."

Well, that was something new. In years past—and even in the month just past—she just told him she was going and left. This time she asked. This whole pattern continued for a number of days. During the second week of the crusade, the wife went into her bedroom after supper to discover her husband getting dressed to go out.

SPIRIT-CONTROLLED MARRIAGES   197

"I'm going over to the church with you tonight," he told her. "I have never seen such a change in my life as what's happened to you, and any man who can do *that* is worth listening to."

Of course, it wasn't the preacher at all. It was the Holy Spirit who had made a difference in this woman's life. But that unbelieving husband went to the meeting because of the attitude he saw in his wife, a willing spirit of submission.

A Christian wife submits to her husband reverently

Notice what it says in verse 2. "...When they observe your chaste conduct accompanied by fear." Some of the translations have rendered the Greek phrase "in fear" as "reverence" or "respectful behavior." The bottom line, I believe, is that there should never be any occasion within your marriage where your husband has any reason to suspect your fidelity to him. And he should be able to see that your incentive for giving him this loyalty is that you hold God in such high esteem.

The wife submits to her husband reverently. In Ephesians 5:23, Paul explains, "For the husband is head of the wife, as also Christ is head of the church; and He is the Savior of the body."

A Christian wife submits to her husband spiritually

> Do not let your beauty be that outward adorning of arranging the hair, of wearing gold, or of putting on fine apparel; but let it be the hidden person of the heart, with the incorruptible ornament of a gentle and quiet spirit. (1 Peter 3:3–4)

You have to understand what was going on in the society where Peter was teaching. Some in that day were given over to incredible outward extravagance in their dress and appearance. One of the Roman satirists mocked the practice of the women of his day. He said: "They build up their hair tier upon tier until they are as tall as the mythological wife of a Trojan hero."

Clement of Alexandria said that "sleep comes to such women with terror lest they should accidentally spoil their hair."

Seneca tells of women who carried several fortunes attached to their ears.

Paulina, the wife of Caligula, the Roman emperor, wore a dress covered with pearls and emeralds that cost over a million dollars.

Peter wasn't saying it is wrong to look good or to dress attractively. Referring to this verse, Dr. Tim LaHaye used to say, "If the barn needs painting, *paint* it!" But he always added, "Don't let that be the source of your beauty."

Peter's prescription was simply this: Don't let outward appearance be the focus of your attention. I have heard preachers use this passage to preach against wearing jewelry or doing anything ornate with the hair. But I can tell you right now, they're on very shaky ground. Why do I say that? Because in the same place where it mentions wearing jewelry, it also mentions the wearing of clothes!

Peter isn't saying you aren't supposed to wear clothes. He's just saying let the beauty shine from *within*. The outward stuff is going to fade over a period of time. It is the inward beauty that will endure. I can close my eyes right now and visualize certain elderly women through the years of my life. Some of these wonderful ladies had stooped bodies and wrinkled skin…but they also had a beauty that just seemed to radiate right out of their person.

One of the nationally advertised facial creams for women purports to be based on "ancient beauty secrets." How ancient? Back as far, perhaps, as 1972? Here in Scripture is a beauty secret at least two thousand years old—and dating back thousands of years before that to Sarah, wife of Abraham, known for beguiling beauty into her nineties! Once again, Peter speaks of

> …the unfading loveliness of a calm and gentle spirit, a thing very precious in the eyes of God. This was the secret of the beauty of holy women of ancient times who trusted in God and were submissive to their husbands. (1 Peter 3:3–5, Phillips)

Do you know how that inward beauty develops? All through your life you concentrate on caring for the inside, just as you care for the outside. You look intently into the mirror of Scripture, just as you look intently into the mirror in your bedroom. And you do it every day, letting what God is doing in your heart become dominant in your spirit. *That* sort of beauty, my friend, never fades. Age has no impact upon it. The passing years take no toll. On the contrary, that beauty gets lovelier and lovelier the longer you walk with the Lord and absorb the fragrance and radiance of His presence.

So here is Peter's counsel to believing wives: submit to your husband willingly, submit to him reverently, submit to him spiritually, and constantly build the spiritual part of your life. When you do those things, you will be doing your part to bring beauty and blessing to your marriage.

But Peter is by no means finished with the subject of submission. Having addressed the Christian wife, he now sits down at the kitchen table and points the man of the house to a chair. Eyeball to eyeball he speaks candidly to that man about…

THE SUBMISSION OF A CHRISTIAN HUSBAND

> Likewise you husbands, dwell with them with understanding, giving honor to the wife, as to the weaker vessel, and as being heirs together of the grace of life, that your prayers may not be hindered. (1 Peter 3:7)

I'd like you to note three truths in this passage directed at believing husbands.

A Christian husband submits to his wife's physical needs

The American Standard Version of the Bible instructs a husband to dwell with his wife "according to knowledge." You are to meet your wife's needs with an understanding of the mutual interests that are involved. Usually this pertains to the physical aspects of the marriage relationship.

You have to understand again, what Peter was saying ran completely counter to the culture of his day. In Peter's day a wife was regarded as a thing, not a person; as property to be owned, not a partner to be loved. Yet Peter states that when Christ comes to live within your heart, and the Holy Spirit takes up residency within you and you allow Him to control your life, your wife becomes a partner in the grace of God. She isn't a female slave, she is a coheir of Jesus Christ.

A wife is God's precious gift to a Christian man. She is to be treasured, loved, and honored, and her husband is to dwell with her according to knowledge. In other words, we men are to treat our wives with respect and thoughtfulness. We need to ask God to help us understand them…even though we will spend the rest of our lives doing that. Just when you think you've got it all figured out, some little nuance comes out of left field that you never saw before, never thought of before, and you think to yourself, *Where did that come from?*

So you go through all your notes again, and you start over on a fresh page. That's a process that will never stop…and that's okay. We must make it our covenant and our lifelong commitment to study this woman God has placed at our side.

Bill Hybels, who pastors a huge church in the Chicago area, is a very vulnerable teacher. I love to listen to him preach because he doesn't care about protecting his own ego. He tells about himself (and tells on himself). In one of his recent books, he penned this story:

Romance was never my strong suit. I proposed to Lynne in her parents' garage; I took my Harley-Davidson on our honeymoon; I thought our best anniversary was the one we spent watching a video of *Rocky III*. I had to grow in the gentle art of romance.

So, for starters, I figured that meant flowers. Beyond that, I didn't have a clue, but I knew I could get the flower job done. As confirmation from God that I was moving in the right direction, who do you think set up shop right out of the trunk of his '58 DeSoto at the corner opposite our church? The flower man!

So, quite regularly, on my way home from work or from meetings, I would pull over to the side of the road, buy a bundle of roses or carnations from the flower man, and take them home to Lynne. What a husband! I thought as I handed over my three bucks.

Yet when I proudly presented these flowers to Lynne, fully expecting her to hire the Marine Corps Band to play "Hail to the Chief," her response was rather lukewarm.

"Gee, thanks," she said. "Where'd you get these?"

"Where else? My buddy, the flower man—you know, the guy with the '58 DeSoto at Barrington and Algonquin. I'm a volume buyer now. Because I stop there so often he gives me a buck off, and if they're a little wilted, he gives me two bucks off. I figure they'll perk up when you put them in water."

"Of course," she said.

I did that regularly for quite some time—until Lynne's lack of enthusiasm for the gift drained my enthusiasm for the practice.

Some time later, at our regularly scheduled date night, Lynne and I decided to clear the air on anything that might be bothering either of us. We do that now and then. We sit down in a cheap restaurant (not only am I unromantic, I'm also Dutch) and say, "What's going on? Is there anything we need to talk about? Is there anything amiss in our relationship?" On that particular night, Lynne took out her list and started checking off the items, and I said, "Ooooh, you're right on that one. Sorry. Eeeh, that one too. Yep. Guilty as charged. Guilty. Guilty. You're right again." She ended her list, and I was in a pile. I said, "I really am sorry, but trust me. I'm going to do better."

She said, "Now, what about you?" I really didn't have any complaints, but after hearing her grocery list, I thought I should say *something*. I scrambled. "Well, I do have one little problem. Have you noticed the absence of the flowers lately?"

"No," she said. "I haven't really paid attention." *How could she say that?*

"We have a problem. I can't figure it out. Hundreds of thousands of husbands pass by that corner. Do *they* stop for flowers? No. Do I stop? Yes! …What gives? What is your problem?"

Her answer made my head spin. She looked me straight in the eyes and quietly said, "The truth is, Bill, I'm not impressed when you give me half-dead flowers that come out of the trunk of a '58 DeSoto that you were lucky enough to run into on your way home from work. The flowers are cheap and the effort is minimal. The way I see it, you're not investing enough time or energy to warrant a wholehearted response from me. You're not thinking about what would make me happy; you're just doing what's convenient for you."

I said, "Okay, let's get this straight. You would be happier if I got up from my desk in the middle of my busy day, threw my study schedule to the wind, walked all the way across the parking lot, got in my car, made a special trip to Barrington where I'd have to pay quadruple the price just because it said Barrington on the bag? And you wouldn't mind if the extra time that took would crimp my work schedule at the Y…. And you wouldn't mind if I came home late because of *all* the extra running around I would have to do to get you *expensive* flowers? Is *that* what you're telling me? *That* would make you happy?"

…Without batting an eyelash, Lynne said, "Yes, that would make me happy."

I couldn't believe it! "What're you talking about? What you're asking for is neither practical, economical, nor an efficient use of time."

"That's a great definition of romance, Bill. You're learning!"[1]

I think that's what it means to submit to your wife in the physical sense. We need to take time to discover ways we can minister to her. God and Donna know I could do better in that department.

Maybe, just maybe, this shoe fits on your foot, too.

A Christian husband submits to his wife's emotional needs

The text says, in effect, that he will be sensitive to his wife's frailty. Now, that isn't to be construed as a slam against women at all. It has nothing to do with questions of superiority/inferiority. The differences between men and women are always to be viewed in terms of *function,* not in value or status. Peter is simply saying that the disparity of physical strength between husband and wife calls for a gentle and courteous attitude on the husband's part. It forever rules out anything that is even a distant cousin to abuse. Nothing resembling a bullying, strong-arm tactic has any place whatsoever in your home or my home. A husband should never, ever lay his hand upon his wife in any physical way to hurt or harm her. We are to dwell with our wives according to the grace of Christ, and when the Spirit of God fills our hearts, we will treat them with gentleness.

A Christian husband submits to his wife's spiritual needs

Even though husbands have been given a place of authority in the home, the Bible says that we are "heirs together of the grace of life." What does that mean? That means we have *identical* standing before the Lord. Yes, there may be those rare occasions when the head of the home has to have the "last word" on a given decision, to resolve a deadlock. But what of that? That has nothing to do with our standing before God. Each of us stands before the Lord as an individual.

Galatians 3:28 reminds us that "there is neither Jew nor Greek, there is neither slave nor free, there is neither male nor female; for you are all one in Christ Jesus." It is so important for Christian men to grasp this truth. Scripture says further that if we *don't* grasp it, our prayer life will suffer damage.

I sometimes tell people that one of the occupational hazards of being a pastor is that you don't have the luxury of staying angry at your wife. Some men can go off to work in a huff and nurse their wounded pride along all day. I can't do that.

Why? Because it's a pastor's job to walk into *his* office in the morning and to read the Bible and pray. You try to do that when something isn't right at home! You can't do it. At least, not with a genuine heart. When things are wrong at home, the Bible says your prayers will just bounce off the ceiling until that relationship is set right again.

Before Peter ever spoke to that subject, the psalmist had the same idea. He wrote: "If I regard iniquity in my heart, the Lord will not hear" (Psalm 66:18).

The principle is this: when the Holy Spirit of God fills and controls our lives, one of the evidences of that will be a submissive spirit of sweet reasonableness with one another as we walk together through this life. It will be evident on the job. It will be evident in our church fellowship. It will be evident in our attitude toward government. And it will be evident within our home and in our marriage.

You might find yourself saying, "That's all well and good. But what if I do my part and my husband doesn't want to do his part?" Or "What if I'm doing my best to follow the biblical model but my wife isn't interested?"

What you and I have to determine in our hearts is this: "I will do my part, and I will let God deal with the other part of this relationship."

When each person in the relationship submits, the result is truly beautiful. As I have read and studied the Bible over the years, I have learned that many of the truths of God's Word are held in dynamic tension. By that I mean whenever you have a truth that could be carried to an extreme, if you just keep reading, you will find another truth that holds that first truth in balance—usually in the same context. So you never can get out of balance if you are a faithful student of the Word of God. If you keep studying the Book, God's truth will keep you from tilting into an unbiblical extremism.

Biblical balance is the best kind of "tension" to have in our homes. And it is God in you, the Helper and Counselor who is the third member of the Trinity, who will keep you in balance as you depend daily upon Him. Before we leave this subject, let me wrap up with just a few more principles.

When a wife commits to authority and a husband understands equality, there is beauty.

Some lady might say to me, "Well, if I submit to my husband, what will keep him from going off the deep end and setting himself up as dictator in our family?" I can only answer this: if you understand biblical authority and he understands biblical equality before God, that simply won't happen. When you do your part and he does his part, there is beauty in your family and in God's family. When you think about it, we're talking about more than a husband-wife relationship here. Your husband is your brother in Christ; your wife is your precious sister in the Lord. We are brothers and sisters in the forever family of God. The husband-wife relationship lasts until "death us do part." But the brother-sister relationship is for eternity.

When a wife is concerned for her purity and her husband understands her personality, there is beauty.

The text says here that a woman is to live in such a way that her husband never has any reason to doubt her fidelity. And then Scripture urges a man to understand his wife, or to live with her in an understanding way. Men are to make a lifelong study of their brides. When those two truths come together and each of us do our part, the result is beauty.

When the wife's concept of spirituality is matched by her husband's knowledge of her frailty, there is beauty.

Every one of these truths that play off against each other in 1 Peter 3 guarantees us that if we do what God has called us to do—if first of all we submit to the authority of the Word of God and to the power of the Holy Spirit in our life—God can do marvelous things to bring marriages back together and to keep them strong through all of the challenges and pressures of these days.

Without the Spirit of God working underneath, over top, and through a marriage, it won't just be tough sledding, it will be a long slide into a dark crevasse.

No, you can't answer for your spouse's lack of responsiveness to the Word of God and the Spirit of God. But don't give up hope! If the Holy Spirit truly has 100 percent of *you*, almost anything can happen!

A prayer such as the one that follows is a good way for *all* of us to begin each day.

O God, here I am in Your presence this new day. I thank You that I am Your child, that You have made me part of Your family. I know through Your Word that Your Holy Spirit lives right inside me. So Lord God, as I begin this day with You, I want You to know that it's not enough for me for the Holy Spirit just to be resident in my heart...I want Him to be the president of my heart. So Lord, I give You permission to control my life. Holy Spirit, I give You permission to control my emotions, to control everything there is about me. I totally yield myself to You, Lord. My life, my health, my finances, my marriage, my family, and the hours and minutes of this new day before me. Lord God, control my life, for Jesus' sake and in His name. Amen.

When we do that, when we yield to the Spirit of God and walk in faithfulness to the Word of God, He causes us to live in a way we could not normally, naturally live. He gives us the supernatural qualities that make a marriage a thing of beauty.

Chapter Thirteen

SPIRIT-CONTROLLED FAMILIES

STRONG HELP FOR PARENTS AND CHILDREN

I remember a time in our family when we had a teenager eat dinner with us two or three times a week. He'd just show up before dinner, and we'd put an extra plate on the table.

He was lonely. Between work and other commitments, his mom and dad were hardly ever home. So, since nothing was happening at his place, he showed up at the Jeremiahs' place, where something usually *was* happening. He was always welcome, of course, but the situation grieved me. Where were his parents? I knew in my heart that this was not what God intended for our homes and families.

Busy parents. Two-income homes. Lonely kids left to shift for themselves. These things are not uncommon within the Christian community...and it stirs my heart.

Listen, if we're a people who are filled with the Spirit, it's going to make a difference where it really counts, not just sitting in some church pew, not just on parade in front of our Christian brothers and sisters.

The real test is what happens to us when we're inside those four walls of home. That's where we find out the *reality* of the Christian life. If it isn't real for you at home, friend, then you'd better begin to wonder if it's real for you at all.

I'm sure you've heard Mark Twain's succinct advice about rearing children. "When they're one year old," he opined, "you put them in a barrel, put the lid on the barrel, and drill a hole in the barrel so you can feed them. Then, when they turn sixteen, you plug up the hole."

I for one don't subscribe to Twain's cynical counsel.

It reminds me of a story I heard about a preacher, a priest, and a rabbi who were having their usual morning cup of coffee at a local coffee shop. On this particular morning they were discussing the point at which life begins.

The priest slapped the tabletop. "Life," he asserted, "begins at conception."

"No, no!" said the rabbi, waving his hand. "I believe life begins at birth."

The preacher sipped his coffee as he pondered the question. Finally he said, "You're both wrong. Life begins when the last child has left home and the dog dies."

I don't agree with those sentiments, either! Our life has been filled through the years with the joy of children. We are now starting on the second generation of that whole process, and it gets better and better all the time.

Praise God, He did not entrust us with families and then just leave us to our own devices. He has given us a very adequate instruction book to help us know what to do and how to do it. Yet in spite of the biblical riches on this subject, we hear very little teaching on the family these days in the pulpits of our land. Is it any wonder that so many of our Christian families are falling apart at the same rate as families outside of the church? I believe with all of my heart that I could give a series on the family every single year in our church, and it would be profitable, and probably preventive, in many cases, of family breakdown.

In Ephesians 6:1–4 we have clear instructions both to children and their parents.

> Children, obey your parents in the Lord, for this is right. "Honor your father and mother," which is the first commandment with promise: "that it may be well with you and you may live long on the earth." And you, fathers, do not provoke your children to wrath, but bring them up in the training and admonition of the Lord.

In these verses, Paul continues to show us the practical implications of the commmand in Ephesians 5:18: *"Be filled with the Spirit."* What a rich portion of Scripture this is!

Back in the gold rush days of California, an old sourdough digging into a hillside on his claim might tap into something every miner dreamed about but only one in a million experienced—a vein of pure gold. Digging into that vein, he would have no idea how far into the hill it reached or where its end might lie. He would know in an instant he was a wealthy man. But only time and days of profitable labor could tell just *how* wealthy.

That's how I feel about a passage like Ephesians 5:18–6:9. You dig and dig and dig, piling up the practical applications to life, and you think to yourself, *How much gold can be in one place?* I don't think anyone will ever find the end of it. Throughout this whole context we find the wonderful theme of submission to God, to His Word, and to His principles for living. Submitting to Him, then, we learn how to submit to one another in the fear of the Lord.

There is a beautiful, creative balance in all the Word of God, and this text is a prime example of it. Children, be sure to obey your parents in the Lord, *but...*you fathers, don't provoke your children. In other words, children are certainly to be submissive to their parents. But listen, you dads, you need to be submissive to the emotional and spiritual needs of your sons and daughters.

Do you see the balance? Do you see the Holy Spirit's safeguards in this instruction? Children who obey a tyrant father are often abused and misused. But when a father loves his children and seeks to lead them in the way of God according to the principles of this Book, he will not have angry, disobedient children. At least, not over the long haul.

Paul's emphasis on mutual submission is like a lovely, joyous refrain, repeating in each of our relationships. *Submit to the Word of God...submit to the Spirit of God...submit to one another in the fear of God.* It is a melody that will bring peace to our homes, happiness to our marriages, and great power and joy to our individual lives.

In Ephesians 6:1–4, we have two truths to explore: the children's compliance, and then (here's that balance again) the parents' conduct.

THE CHILDREN'S COMPLIANCE

It is the fundamental duty of children to obey their parents. Period.

Some might ask, "Whether those parents are Christians or not?" Yes, whether they are Christians or not. For obedience to parents is a fundamental, universal law. It is an integral part of a home. It is like electricity in the wires and water in the pipes—and even more so. A family could get along without electricity and indoor plumbing, but it cannot get along without obedience. Obedience and mutual submission are those elements that make the family work. Without them, you have chaos.

How important is this principle of obedience? The Bible makes it clear that this is not only critical to our families, but to the very fabric of our culture. Two passages in the Word of God remind us that this is one of the foundational building blocks of society. In Romans 1, where the apostle Paul is describing the iniquities that prevail in the heathen world, you will find disobedience linked with the vilest kinds of sin. Read these words:

> Being filled with all unrighteousness, sexual immorality, wickedness, covetousness, maliciousness; full of envy, murder, strife, deceit, evil-mindedness; they are whisperers, backbiters, haters of God, violent, proud, boasters, inventors of evil things, **disobedient to parents,** undiscerning, untrustworthy, unloving, unforgiving, unmerciful…. (Romans 1:29–31)

Whatever you may think about obedience or disobedience to parents, please note it isn't in very good company on this list. I wouldn't want my name included on that list. Disobedience to parents falls into a category of very, very bad things.

The same unsavory associations are revealed over in 2 Timothy 3, where we're told what our world will be like in the last days before the Lord comes back.

> But know this, that in the last days perilous times will come: For men will be lovers of themselves, lovers of money, boasters, proud, blasphemers, **disobedient to parents,** unthankful, unholy, unloving, unforgiving, slanderers, without self-control, brutal, despisers of good, traitors, headstrong, haughty, lovers of pleasure rather than lovers of God…from such people turn away! (2 Timothy 3:1–5)

Isn't that interesting? When the wheels begin to fall off a culture, according to 2 Timothy 3, one of the inevitable outcomes is that there is no glue in the family; you have disobedient children. And in those terrible days just before the Lord's return (are we there right now?), one of the evidences of the breakdown of the culture will be children who refuse to honor or obey their parents.

Where do you think we are on that continuum right now? Have you been to the grocery store lately? Taken any cross-country flights lately? Have you watched the current philosophy of "family" being played out in our world today? Parents have either neglected discipline out of carelessness and laziness, or we have made them fearful to lift a finger, lest they be written up for child abuse. The inevitable result is a shameful chaos.

I was in Wal-Mart recently in the proximity of a little girl who didn't get something she wanted from her mother. And she went *crazy*. (I don't know how else to say it.) Believe me, she had the attention of that whole section of the store. Unfortunately, I ended up checking out right behind her and her family. And while this little one screamed and raged and clawed, her mother acted like nothing was going on at all. (I had all kinds of temptations going through *me*, let me tell you.) And finally she dragged the writhing, screaming little child out of the store to the car.

When I got to the counter, the checkout clerk rolled her eyes. She said to me, "If that had been me when I was growing up, I would not be alive today." I can identify with that. Can you? The tantrum might have lasted a minute or so, but not much longer than that! The consequences of my actions would have quickly closed in over me. From earliest memory, I knew that if I did something I wasn't supposed to do, I would pay the price. And it was a price I wouldn't want to pay more than once.

Sometimes it amazes me to remember that our Lord Jesus Christ was also a child once who had to submit to the authority of earthly parents. Did you ever stop to think that the God-man was once the God-teenager? Do you ever think about the fact that He grew up in a normal home and went through the stages of adolescence? Yet in Luke 2:51 we read these amazing words:

> And He went down with them, and came to Nazareth; and He continued in subjection to them; and His mother treasured all these things in her heart. (NASB)

Can you comprehend the Lord of glory, coming to this earth, being born as a human being, and growing up in a neighborhood with brothers and sisters and neighbor kids? Here is the Ruler of the universe, the One who hung the stars in place, but so committed to the Word of God that He put Himself in submission to his mother Mary and to his foster father Joseph.

He lived in submission to His parents. We've taken this for granted for so long that it no longer awes and amazes us. But it should! The very God of creation willingly obeyed two of His own creatures, a human mom and dad. And if

I want to be like Christ, if I want to grow up to be a Christlike young person, I will follow His example. I will understand the importance of obeying my parents.

I can hear some kids say, "Well, my mom and dad aren't exactly Mary and Joseph. What if my parents aren't always right?" It's true; neither your parents nor any set of parents will always be right. They'll mess up sometimes. They'll make the wrong calls. They'll say the wrong things. They'll push the wrong buttons. But the dominant principle of the Word of God is still submission to our parents by the power of the Holy Spirit.

Right here in this text we're given four good reasons for doing that.

Because it is right

Notice what it says: "Children, obey your parents in the Lord, for this is right."

It's just *right!* I'm not sure our nation knows what that means anymore. In this culture and in this country, nobody seems to care what is "right." If polls are to be believed, morality doesn't seem very important to the general population. I hear this over and over again when we talk about the sleaze and immorality in the lives of high government officials. The dominant reaction of American culture is a big yawn. As long as employment is high, the stock market keeps climbing, and inflation stays in check, *who cares* what our leaders do in their private lives? They can do whatever they want to do and live however they want to live, just so long as it doesn't affect *me*.

"Leave the man alone and let him do his job!" We hear people say that over and over again. Well, I'm okay with that leader doing his job, but I'm not okay with the attitude that morality really doesn't matter. Let me try to say this as plainly as I can. Some things are right and some things are wrong. And if you are wrong there is still hope. You can step up to the line and say, "I was wrong, and I want to do better. Now let's move on from here." But you can't just say right and wrong don't matter. Here in this text it says, "Children, obey your parents in the Lord." Why? Because it does matter. And because it is *right*.

There is an order in nature, ordained of God, and it argues for the rightness of certain actions. Since parents bring children into the world, and since they have more knowledge and wisdom than the child, it is right that the child should obey his parents. Even young animals are taught to obey their parents.

Why are children to obey their parents? Let's just say it again, and not be ashamed, intimidated, or back down a single inch. *Because it is the right thing to do.*

Maybe as a young person you're at a point in life where you say, "Well, I'm not going to obey." Okay. So you choose to do the wrong thing. You've made a conscious, willful choice to rebel against God's standards, just as many, many others have chosen since the beginning of time. And since the beginning of time, there have been consequences for those wrong actions.

Kids are always telling me, "Well, I'm going to get my kicks." And I always like to tell them, "You can choose your kicks, but you don't get to choose the kickbacks." Right? The kickbacks come of their own volition. You can choose your actions, but you cannot choose the consequences.

Colossians 3:20 adds an important little phrase. It isn't only right, but notice:

Children, obey your parents in all things, for this is well pleasing to the Lord.

Do you want to make the Lord happy? Then do what is right. Isn't that a true principle in all of life? If you want to please the God who formed you and gave you life, then why don't you just do what's right? "Children, obey your parents in the Lord, for *this* is right." It's a moral principle.

Because it is a precept of Scripture

Ephesians 6 goes on to say, "Honor your father and mother, which is the first commandment with promise." That's a very interesting text; refers back to Exodus 20:12, where we have this commandment given to children as part of the Ten Commandments. I know that we don't know very much about those anymore. We treat them more like the "Ten Suggestions." Nevertheless, here is what the Lord said:

Honor your father and your mother, that your days may be long upon the land which the LORD your God is giving you.

God had given Moses four commandments up to this point, and there was no promise attached to any of them. But when you get to this fifth commandment something changes.

Why the promise? If for no other reason, I believe it is evidence that God has placed great priority upon this command. It shows the importance He attaches to our obedience to our parents. We're to do this with the realization that this is God's design, and somewhere down the road, we will look back and be glad we did, even though we may chafe under it right now. That chafing under obedience to parents is part of the unhooking process that we go through as we get older and ultimately learn to make our own decisions. But if we try to push that process ahead of schedule, we will cause great harm to ourselves and to our families.

Because it is a protection for the child

Ephesians 6:3 says, "That it may be well with you."

Do you want it to be well with you? Do you want to have a good life? I'm sure there are rebels out there somewhere who have grown up disobeying their parents from the time they were little, never changed their attitude about anything, and somehow made it through life unscathed. They may be out there...but truthfully, I've never met one.

The simple fact is, everybody has to report to somebody. And it doesn't stop when you get to be twenty, does it? *Everybody* has to learn the principle of submission to authority. And if we don't learn that all-important concept at home, if we don't let God help us get a grip on it in that sheltered environment, then we will struggle with it throughout our entire lives.

We'll struggle with it at school. We'll struggle with it on the job. We'll struggle with it in the armed forces. We'll struggle with it in obeying the laws of the land and respecting the police. We'll struggle with it in our own marriage and family. And someday, there will be a notation in a file with your name on it that says: "Struggles with authority," or "Has a problem with authority."

Sometimes young people will say to me, "But Pastor Jeremiah, it's so *hard* to live by mom and dad's rules at home." And they imagine if they could just get out from under their parents' authority, life would somehow get easier. Yet the truth is, it gets harder. You have to deal with that tough-as-nails gym teacher. You have to submit to that foreman who's always on your back. You have to salute and say "Yes sir" to that army drill instructor screaming in your face. You have to pull off to the side of the road when those blue lights begin flashing behind you. You have to shell out taxes on your hard-earned income.

Where do you learn to deal with authority? You learn at home when you are growing up. And when you learn to deal with authority at home, then you can learn to deal with it in the other venues of life. And you can learn how to live in the fabric of society that God has created. If a child gets no instruction, he is going to be perfectly miserable and socially intolerable. And we see it all the time, don't we?

Sometimes after an incident like the one I witnessed at Wal-Mart, I find myself thinking, "My word! What will that kid be like when she's seventeen? I don't think I want to be anywhere near her." Does that mean every child who totally rebels in his or her teens comes from a family where there was no discipline? No. But generally speaking, what we learn in the earlier years of our life will be reflected in our attitudes through the rest of our years.

I can assure you that I never, ever thought of smart-mouthing my dad. Never even considered it! Intuitively, I knew what would happen to me if I ever did, and it just wasn't worth it. And do you know something? It was a *good* thing for me to grow up with that knowledge. It has helped me all the way through life.

Because it is a promoter of long life

Again quoting from Exodus, the text says, "That it may be well with you and you may live long on the earth." Obedient children in the Old Testament did live longer. And discipline in a child's life is usually conducive to good health. Does that mean that a person who is disobedient always dies young and a person who is obedient always lives into his nineties? No. This is not an ironclad promise of Scripture, it is a proverb. And proverbs tell us what life will be like under normal conditions. For instance…

In the month of April in Portland, Oregon, you would do well to carry an umbrella.
When you see a sleeping pit bull, you would do well not to yank on his ear.

Will it always rain in Portland on an April day? Will the pit bull always bite your arm off if you pull his ear? No, perhaps not. But these are truths of life you can generally count on!

And let's face it. A person who grows up rebellious against every fabric of control has put himself on a path that leads to discouragement and destruction, not a good life. Those rebellious ways usually have a way of taking a toll on the years you spend on the earth. People who grow up within the fabric of God's system have a much better chance of living a reasonably good life for a reasonably long period of time.

Now, having spoken to the children, Paul addresses his attention to the fathers in the fourth verse.

THE PARENTS' CONDUCT

And you, fathers, do not provoke your children to wrath, but bring them up in the training and admonition of the Lord.

Home can't be run by loving words alone. There have to be law and discipline, too. The nature of children demands discipline.

Years ago, the Duke of Windsor said, "Everything in the American home is controlled by switches except the children," and he was right about that! The late Dr. Benjamin Spock may have been a worthy man in many respects, but his "no spanking" counsel confused and confounded generations of parents and kids. It wasn't until the early 1970s, when Dr. James Dobson came out with his landmark book *Dare to Discipline,* that the murky skies over American homes saw a little daylight.

The Bible offers many true, unvarnished stories of families who got discipline right…and those who got it terribly wrong. I remember a study I did years ago on the theology of the family in the Bible. I started in the book of Genesis, and wherever I saw families in the text, I noted their relationships and recorded them in my journal. Do you know what I concluded? There are more examples of bad families in the Old Testament than there are of good ones. And the breakdowns in those families were always associated with parents who violated clearly understood principles of parenting.

David the king pampered Absalom and refused to discipline him or intervene in the prince's life. And that young man's ultimate rebellion and death not only turned the kingdom upside down, it sent his father to the grave as a broken man.

Every Father's Day, pastors across the country preach sermons on Eli, a leader and priest who failed to discipline his sons and reaped a harvest of both personal and national shame because of it.

Isaac pampered Esau, and it tore his home in two.

Jacob allowed favoritism and jealousy in his home to set his sons against one another.

Through page after page of Scripture, you see many illustrations of families where the father neither took control of the family nor provided the necessary discipline. But I also noticed something else when I was studying this text. The word *fathers* here in Ephesians 6 is the exact same Greek word that is translated *parents* in Hebrews 11:23. The Scripture there says, "By faith Moses, when he was born, was hidden three months by his *parents*."

In one place the word is translated "fathers," and in another place it is translated "parents." That leads me to believe that this "training and admonition" business isn't *just* the father's responsibility. Single mothers, for instance, bear the heavy responsibility of being both father and mother to their children. But those who lay the weight of these responsibilities at the feet of the Lord will find both hope and strong help as they trust in Him.

One negative prohibition

Paul begins by telling us what *not* to do. He says, "Do not provoke your children to wrath." Don't irritate them. Don't exasperate them. Don't discourage them by unreasonable demands. There are some fathers who are always on their kids' backs. No matter what their son or daughter does, it's wrong. Constant fault-finding, criticism, sarcasm, unceasing don'ts, and unreasonable commands will not generate respect in a child's heart. Within that exercise of parental authority, there is a crucial need for understanding and love, justice and self-control.

Sometimes a kid steps out of line, but the parent steps even *further* out of line by overreacting. Yes, the child needs some correction, but sometimes our response is like trying to shoot an ant with a bazooka. I'm talking about major explosions touched off by relatively small provocations. The penalty is way out of perspective to what actually happened in the family.

The Bible says that fathers are to administrate their homes in love. They are not to push their children away, but they are to do a sensitive job of bringing the children up in the nurture and admonition of the Lord. When Paul was writing in Colossians he used the same little instruction, but with this poignant added insight: "Fathers, do not provoke your children, *lest they become discouraged*" (Colossians 3:21).

Sometimes kids come to see me and say, "Pastor, the only time I ever hear from my dad is when I've done something wrong. He never has anything to say to me unless I'm doing something he doesn't want me to do. And boy, *then* I hear from him!"

That's discouraging. That's disheartening. That could cause any of us to want to throw in the towel. And it moves me to see how the Holy Spirit included that little phrase, "Lest they become discouraged." God cares about discouraged kids. Did you know that? His heart goes out to them. And He knows that kids don't have to be disheartened, if they have parents who really take time to communicate in a loving and sensitive way.

Let me tell you something else I've learned. For every time you have to say no, if you've worked hard to say yes eight or ten times before that, the *no* will have much greater power. I've tried to teach people, not just in the family, but in administration, too, that even though we all have to say no at times, we ought to create the atmosphere where it's obvious we *wish* we could say yes. It isn't no because we delight in saying no.

You exasperate your children when you are always on their case. You know what I mean. Let's face it, we've all had days like that: days when we're feeling irritable and we're just not pleasant to be around. It happens to most of us, when we neglect to walk in the Spirit. But God forbid that we should ever have a lifestyle like that, because that will discourage a kid quicker than anything I know.

So Paul says to parents, don't discourage your kids. Don't exasperate them. Don't provoke them to anger. But then he gives us three principles that are positive.

The principle of diligence

He says, "Bring them up."

To bring up children is a scriptural phrase that implies a serious responsibility for their spiritual, moral, mental, and physical well-being. This is a very encompassing term. In fact, in Ephesians 5:29, when Paul was speaking to the same group of people, he said: "For no one ever hated his own flesh, but nourishes and cherishes it." The word *nourish* there is the same word for "to bring up."

The Bible says that parents are to nourish their children. It's a big job! It's a mountain-sized task to stay tuned in and show care about everything that's going on in their lives. I'm not talking about controlling every little nuance, but simply caring about it. To care, for instance, about their social life and who their friends are. *Who are you hanging out with, son? Who are your friends at school? Who do you like to be with at youth group?*

Sometimes I see parents who just let their kids go wherever they want to go. When our kids were growing up, if they wanted to stay all night at somebody else's house, they knew there was first going to be a phone call between this house and that house. It's not that we didn't trust our kids, but we just wanted to know what they would be facing at that friend's house. If that family was asking to borrow our child for a night, we wanted to know what kind of environment he or she would be stepping into.

Parent, God has put you in charge! If you have ever doubted it or wavered in this knowledge, let me help you out here: I do hereby, on the authority of the Word of God, empower you to be in charge of your family. Be in charge in a righteous, godly way. Take authority where God has given you authority, and bring them up and nurture them.

The principle of discipline

Paul says, "Honor your father and your mother that it may be well with you. You, fathers, do not provoke your children to wrath, but bring them up...." That's diligence. In other words, the text is saying *take control*. Watch what's going on. Be vigilant. But while you're at it, bring them up in the training, the nurture, of the Lord.

Nurture means correction. It is the same word used in Hebrews 12:6, where the writer says, "For whom the LORD loves He chastens." *Nurture* and *chasten* are the same word. So the Bible says there are times when we need to discipline our children. We need to chasten them.

That's become a controversial subject, hasn't it? Here are what I believe to be the two most important things to remember about disciplining your children.

First of all, *discipline has to be for disobedience, not for mistakes*. It's sad to see kids being punished for some normal, natural thing that happens to all children. I remember hearing about a man eating in a restaurant, sitting across an aisle from a little boy and his parents. And during the course of the meal, that little guy did what so many little boys do at a certain age in their development. He went to reach for something and knocked over his glass of milk. Immediately, those parents began to tear into that boy. They told him how stupid he was, how clumsy he was, and on and on.

Finally, the man across the aisle couldn't take any more. He deliberately took his hand and whacked over his water glass—hard—sending water everywhere.

"Oops," he said, smiling at the family across the aisle. "Well...I guess accidents happen, *don't they?*"

He wanted them to see that even a forty-eight-year-old man can dump his beverage from time to time. He wanted them to be embarrassed for the way they were treating their little boy.

I like the story I heard about a mother whose little boy had tried to take a carton of milk and put it in the refrigerator. It was a noble effort, but he wasn't quite big enough or strong enough to pull it off. He got almost to the refrigerator, dropped the carton, and the milk went all over the kitchen floor in a huge puddle. At that moment, the mom came into the room and said, "What happened?"

The little boy puckered up, and he said, "Mommy...I spilled the milk."

"Well," she said, "in a few minutes, we're going to have to clean it up, aren't we? But would you like to play in it first?"

So this little kid got to splash around in that puddle of milk, having all the fun he could out of his mistake. Then she cleaned it up, cleaned him up, and took him out in the backyard. With the same carton, filled with water, she showed him how to carry it so that wouldn't happen again. When that little guy did it right, she heaped praise on him. Isn't that the way it's supposed to be?

Some of the craziest things that have happened in our family occurred when our kids entered the automobile stage of life—a scary passage, I must admit. One day when Jennifer was first getting started, she backed her Mustang out of the driveway...and straight into my van. Two thousand bucks on each car just like that.

Now, should I get mad over that? Hey, it was a mistake. She just forgot to look. I remember saying, "Oh, my word. Honey, it's all right. Are you okay? Everything's fine."

Another time, my son Daniel left his car out of gear, and it rolled down a bank and right through a chain-link fence here at the church. I drove up to the church, and there was his truck, protruding through the fence. (There was another twenty-five hundred bucks, for truck and fence.) But do you know what my first thought was? *Is he in that truck? Is he all right?* When I found out that the accident happened in his absence, it was okay. No, I wasn't happy about it, but it was okay. Anyone can forget to put on a parking brake—I don't care who you are.

Later, Daniel told me his friends had all gathered around him that day, wanting to know if his dad was furious and how much trouble he was in. And he got to tell them that his dad knew it was just a mistake and that everything was okay at home.

Now, if he'd been messing around, driving through the parking lot at fifty miles an hour, it would have been a different matter. There would have been some consequences—and Daniel would have *expected* such consequences. But that's different. Mistakes are not a matter for discipline—as if any of us could live a mistake-free life.

You make mistakes, I make mistakes, and all of our adult friends make mistakes. So why shouldn't we let our kids be human, too? It is disobedience and rebellion that we need to deal with. Those are the cases in which we must come to grips with appropriate discipline.

There's a second observation I would like to make on this subject. *Discipline should be for individual acts, and not an attack on a child's character.* Here's what I mean: If a child tells a lie, that doesn't necessarily make him a liar. When a kid impulsively swipes a piece of candy from the candy store, that doesn't mean he's a thief, a robber, and a terrible person. No, he did an act that was wrong. Deal with the act, but don't create a character out of an act.

As a man, I am more than the sum of my individual failures. I haven't always acted in character in my life; sometimes, to my shame, I have acted out of character. All of us have failed in some areas. We've done things that we're embarrassed about as we look back on them. But those individual actions didn't create a person out of us in the character of the act.

So when you discipline your children, don't get caught up in creating an exaggerated image of their life. If you keep doing that, they will eventually live up to it! Your prophecy will be self-fulfilling.

The principle of direction

Paul said, "Fathers, do not provoke your children to wrath, but bring them up in the training and admonition of the Lord." The training or nurturing is correction. The admonition is the *instruction*.

We need to teach our kids. A parent needs to instruct and train his child. We all feel inadequate to do that, but we have to do it. God places that responsibility upon us in the areas of character, to teach them right from wrong, and the importance of life's true priorities.

I love the story of the high school senior who went to his father in January, the year he was to graduate. "Dad," he said, "I think I deserve a new car."

His father thought a minute and replied, "Son, I'll get you that new car, but you've got to do three things first: bring your grades up, read your Bible more, and get a haircut."

Just before graduation, the son went to his father and said, "How am I doing? Am I going to get a new car for graduation?"

"Son, you brought your grade average up from a C to an A. That's good. I've also noticed you've been studying the Scriptures every morning before school. That's wonderful. But you still haven't gotten a haircut."

"Dad," the young man replied, "I was studying the Bible, and I noticed that Moses is always depicted in the illustrations as having long hair. And even Jesus had long hair."

And the father said, "Son, you must remember that Moses and Jesus walked everywhere they went…and so will you if you don't get a haircut!"

We dads and moms must never lose the joy of being parents and the sense of humor that comes from interacting with our children. We need to be able to laugh and say, "No, not this time. Not now. No, you won't do that. I love you too much to let that happen." You'll never really know how good your discipline is until it is challenged. If that fence is still standing and the relationship is still intact after a major challenge, you've been doing your job. You can go forward from there.

Paul wrote a bit of exhortation to Timothy that has always been an encouragement to me. He said:

> But as for you, continue in the things which you have learned and been assured of, knowing from whom you have learned them, and that from childhood you have known the Holy Scriptures. (2 Timothy 3:14–15)

I'll tell you something. When you are committed to giving your child the Word of God from childhood—from nursery school—you have given that child a massive head start in life. Yes, see that they're in a good Sunday school, but more important than that, live those truths at home. Talk about them. Illustrate them from daily happenings. Make them the subject of a thousand conversations. And if you do, by the grace of God and the power of the Holy Spirit, God is going to do a work in your family.

In the previous chapter we talked about husbands loving their wives and wives being submissive to their husbands, submitting to the needs of one another. When kids grow up and actually see that going on between mom and dad, it is a wonderful environment for them to learn the principles of obedience and mutual submission. When they see that happening between the two most important people in their lives, they will have a much easier time falling into their place in a Christian family.

That's what God wants for us. That's His plan for every family in the body of Christ: that we live according to the principles of the Word of God. He has given us the truth we need, and He has empowered us by His Holy Spirit to put that truth to work.

What does that look like in our lives? For kids, it looks like this:

Even when I don't feel like it, I'm going to honor my mother and my father and be obedient to them. I'm going to live as Christ lived when He was a boy, submitting to the authority of His parents.

And what does it look like for parents?

Let's hold the line where we need to, but do so without exasperating or discouraging our kids with unneeded rules and regulations. Let's love them so much in the process that the things we ask them not to do will seem as nothing because of the love they feel from us and the nurturing we give them in their lives.

If by the grace of God we do those things, we will really *live* those days while our children are with us…and not wish time away until they are gone.

Chapter Fourteen

SPIRIT-CONTROLLED WORKPLACES

HONORING CHRIST FROM NINE TO FIVE

*I*f the Spirit-filled life works at all, it should work *at work*.

If Christianity doesn't work in the stress and strain, the grit and grind of the marketplace, then where is its practical value?

But it does work. *He* works. The indwelling Spirit of the living God will go with you. He'll sit with you all day long in front of that terminal at your desk. He'll stand with you by the cash register, interacting with the customers. He'll walk with you on the roof of that apartment building under construction. He'll crawl with you under that old house to repair the plumbing. He'll rock the baby with you at three A.M. He'll cruise the city all night with you in a squad car.

He will make a difference in your everyday experience…if you have truly given Him control of this area of your life as well.

Have you ever heard anybody say, "Well, I don't mix my religion and my profession"? I don't like to be around people like that. They may be as "religious" as can be on Sunday, but when they go to work on Monday, you wouldn't have a clue they'd ever been inside a church in their life. They revert to the way the world functions.

The whole scene in the workplace these days is a little scary, both from the standpoint of the employer and the employee. I think you can tell how serious it is as you look at the cards, bumper stickers, and slogans that keep cropping up around the office and job site.

On one bulletin board, someone tacked up a sign that read: "In case of fire, flee the building with the same reckless abandon that occurs each day at quitting time."

Or maybe you've seen this one: "If you don't believe in the resurrection from the dead, you oughtta be here five minutes before quitting time."

And then there is this rather lengthy company directive, uttered with tongue firmly in cheek: "It has come to the attention of management that workers dying on the job are failing to fall down. This practice must stop, as it becomes impossible to distinguish between death and the natural movement of the staff. Any employee found dead in an upright position will be dropped from the payroll."

No, all is not easy in today's marketplace. I heard about a management consultant who gave the following instructions to a group of employees: "Be first in the office every morning, be the last to leave every night, never take a day off, slave through the lunch hour, and the inevitable day will come when the boss will summon you to his office and say, 'I've been watching your work very carefully, Jackson. Now just what in the world are you up to?'"

Yes, there's a problem in the heart of many employers. There's some unfairness and abuse out there. Why else did labor unions arise in our country years ago? But there is also a problem in the hearts of many employees. They don't give their best. They gripe and complain and tear down the boss behind his or her back.

Strange that it should be such a two-sided problem, because that's exactly how God chose to deal with the issue when Paul wrote these verses in Ephesians 6:5–9. Notice what it says:

> Servants, be obedient to those who are your masters according to the flesh, with fear and trembling, in sincerity of heart, as to Christ; not with eyeservice, as men-pleasers, but as servants of Christ, doing the will of God from the heart, with good will doing service, as to the Lord, and not to men, knowing that whatever good anyone does, he will receive the same from the Lord, whether he is a slave or free. And you, masters, do the same things to them, giving up threatening, knowing that your own Master also is in heaven, and there is no partiality with Him.

In the space of just a few verses, the apostle has a quiet, heart-to-heart talk with both labor and management. In verses 5–8, he begins with the employees.

THE HOLY SPIRIT'S EMPLOYEE MANUAL

The word used here for *servants* is a word which means "slaves." This instruction in Ephesians was given in the days when Rome ruled most of the world. And in that day, we are told, there may have been as many as six million slaves across the Empire.

Paul knew that many of the *doulos*, these servants, were coming to faith in Jesus Christ. And all across the Empire, those Christian slaves would be experiencing every manner of treatment at the hands of every sort of master. Some of their masters would be cruel and heartless; others would be kind, treating them like family. Some of their masters would be brother Christians, others pagans or those actually hostile to the faith. Paul's words here embrace all of those situations…and yours and mine as well.

Now, in case you think this is outmoded advice for a different era and a different cultural situation, and that it isn't for employers and employees, please notice how Paul qualifies his comments in verse 8: "Knowing that whatever good anyone does, he will receive the same from the Lord, *whether he is a slave or free.*"

So Paul weighs in here with instruction for anyone who is under authority to another in the marketplace. How should he function? How should he live? How should he work? The apostle sets out to answer those questions. Let's take the time to examine his words a little more closely.

The required action

Servants, be obedient to those who are your masters… (Ephesians 6:5)

In Colossians 3:22, Paul repeats the command, but with this added emphasis: "Servants, obey in all things your masters according to the flesh, not with eye-service, as men-pleasers, but in sincerity of heart, fearing God."

It's interesting to note that the Bible clearly tells us that *how* we work—our attitude—is a testimony to those who watch us. The way we go about our assigned tasks can either prompt admiration in those who watch…or it can be a stumbling block to them. For instance, Paul writes to Timothy that if we don't obey those who are over us, we can do great damage to the cause of Christ.

All who are under the yoke of slavery should consider their masters worthy of full respect, so that God's name and our teaching may not be slandered. (1 Timothy 6:1, NIV)

In other words, guard your attitude so that people won't say bad things about your Lord!

Have you ever heard someone say something like this? "I'll tell you one thing. I'd rather do business with anyone than with one of those Christians!" I hear that sometimes, and it makes me sad. How could it be? It ought not be! Those observing us should see clearly that our ethics are higher, our standards are better, our commitment is stronger, our vision is greater, and our compassion runs deeper. We should *lead* in those categories. And when we don't, we can cause the good name of our God to be sneered at and slandered.

"You say you belong to Christ and THAT'S the way you act? Then faith in Christ must not be worth much!"

But the same New Testament that tells us we can dishonor our Savior's name by the way we work also says we can *declare* Him by the way we work. Notice what Paul writes to Titus: "Teach slaves [employees in our culture] to be subject to their masters in everything, to try to please them, not to talk back to them, and not to steal from them, but to show that they can be fully trusted, so that in every way they will make the teaching about God our Savior attractive" (Titus 2:9–10, NIV).

The way you work for your employer, the attitude you show in your workplace—wherever that might be—can actually make the gospel of Jesus Christ attractive to people. Have you ever thought about that? Are there people at your workplace or school who don't think Chrisitanity is very desirable? The Bible says we can change that opinion by the way we perform our day-to-day work. We literally show forth the dignity of Christ in the marketplace.

You say, "Well, people at work will just think I'm trying to get on the boss's good side." Yes, they might…at first. But as you pursue your work with a submissive, willing spirit, day in and day out—whether the boss is watching or not—they will realize it has to be something more than that. They will begin to understand that something else is driving you, and they will be curious about what that something is.

I've been in vocational ministry as the pastor of a church for over thirty years now, but in my other life, before the pastorate, I worked in the marketplace. When I was a seminary student in Dallas, Texas, I drove a truck to pay my tuition and keep food on the table. When I wasn't driving, I spent most of my time on a dock, loading semi trucks.

Since I was the new man on the list and didn't have any seniority, I got thrown down to the end of the dock where you had to lace truck tires in a truck.

If you ever want to put in a hard day's work, that's a good way to do it. I knew nothing of unions at that time; I'd never met a union steward in my life. Didn't even know there was such a person. I was just a "starving student" trying to make money for school. So I reported to the dock with a mind to work.

The foreman told me, "Go fill that truck up with tires," and he showed me how to lace them, one on top of the other, to load the maximum number in a trailer. I didn't do it very well, at first, but I worked hard at it. I had on a pair of Levi's and an old T-shirt, and after about half an hour of work in that Dallas heat and humidity, I was soaked with sweat and black from the dust off those tires. I was a mess!

It wasn't long before a man walked down to my end of the dock and called me out of the back of that truck. "Come here, son," he said, "I need to talk with you."

"Who are you?" I asked him.

"I'm the steward on this dock," he replied, "and look—you can't be doing this."

"Doing what? What do you mean?"

"You can't get dirty like that."

"What do you mean I can't get dirty?"

"You walk around here on this dock and you see if there's anybody else on this dock that's got a shirt dirty like yours. Our goal is to walk out of here after a shift with a clean shirt. And the way you're workin', you're making us look bad, and I don't want any more of it. You've got to slow down. You've got to cool your heels. You've got to stop doing what you're doing if you want to get along with us."

Whoa! I'd never heard anything like that in my life. I thought a fella was supposed to work hard for his paycheck. Now what was I going to do? Please my employer, or please the union guys? I didn't know a job could be that complicated. (Although I'm sure most union stewards aren't like that.)

Do you know how long a day can be when you're not working hard? I wasn't thinking about a career as a dockhand; I just wanted to earn enough money to get through seminary so I could teach the Word of God. And when I worked at that job as hard as I could, the hours flew by. I went home physically exhausted but mentally ready to hit the books. But some of the old-timers there didn't appreciate this kid in his twenties putting out the work and showing them up.

The men in the trucks and on the dock knew there was something different about me. When they found out I was in seminary, they started calling me

"Preacher Joe." It's kind of funny how that worked. When they were together in a group, they liked to ridicule me or give me a hard time. But when I got alone with one of those guys, it was a different story. Maybe one of them would see me in the lunchroom when nobody was around, and he'd pick up his lunch pail and come over to sit across from me. He'd be having some trouble at home, with his marriage or one of his kids, and he'd look at me kind of sheepishly and say, "Got a minute?"

Or maybe one of them would see me reading my New Testament, and—after looking around to make sure no one was in earshot—would start asking me about some of the problems in his life.

Now, why did those men single me out? How did they know I was "different"? I didn't talk much about the Lord during work hours; there was too much to be done. I didn't make a big deal about being in seminary or studying for the ministry. But somehow they sensed something about me—something that drew their notice.

I think it boiled down to the way I worked.

I showed up on time. I worked hard. I did my best. I kept a decent attitude. I didn't let the world (or the shop steward) squeeze me into its own mold. That's what this passage is all about. It is talking about going to work with a heart that is going to make a difference.

The assignment reviewed

Servants, be obedient to those who are your masters according to the flesh....

The required action is obedience. The assignment is to work for men or women that God has placed in authority over you. And this obedience isn't to be diminished because you and your employer both happen to be Christians.

Sometimes Christian employees think that because their employer is a believer, they can be cavalier in their attitude toward work because they know the boss won't get in their face. Listen to what the Word of God has to say about that.

> Those who have believing masters are not to show less respect for them because they are brothers. Instead, they are to serve them even better, because those who benefit from their service are believers, and dear to them. (1 Timothy 6:2, NIV)

What a happy thing it is when a believing employer and a believing employee know their roles and work hard to accomplish the goals of the company or the community where they happen to be. The Bible says that our workplace can be like that every day as employees and employers alike submit to the Word of God and the Holy Spirit.

A recommended attitude

Servants, be obedient to those who are your masters according to the flesh, with fear and trembling....

"Now, wait a minute," I hear you object. "I'm supposed to go to work every day scared to death of my boss?"

No, this wonderful phrase in the New Testament doesn't speak of fright as much as it speaks of a holy concern. We are to be deeply concerned that if we don't respond and act the way God directs us to respond and act, we will grieve the Holy Spirit. In other words, we should take these things very seriously. Our attitude should be, "There is more at stake here than eight hours of work. There are eternal issues wrapped up in my attitudes and actions in this place."

That's not what you'd call the average nine-to-five attitude, is it? Men and women drag themselves out of bed, go to work, do as little as they can get away with, try to hang in there until five, and then drag themselves home so they can ready themselves to do it all over again the next morning.

What a drag! How monotonous. That's not living, that's just putting in time. You say, "Well, that's all there is. You work, you go home, you go back to work, and eventually you retire and then you die."

No! There is more. No matter where you work, no matter what you do—even if you are a *slave*—there is more. There is another dimension to our work and another dimension to our lives here on earth.

A rewarded ambition

Servants, be obedient to those who are your masters according to the flesh, with fear and trembling, in sincerity of heart, as to Christ.

There it is. That's the secret. The ambition that God rewards isn't that we just show up and punch the time clock, but that we work at our jobs with all of our hearts.

I found my life verse when I was a college student. I was playing basketball in those days and doing some of the other things that I love to do, and I came across a verse in Colossians 3 that motivated my heart and marked my life. It still does.

Whatever you do, work at it with all your heart, as working for the Lord, not for men. (Colossians 3:23, NIV)

Whatever we do, whatever we put our hand to, God wants us to do it with everything we've got. Martyred missionary Jim Elliot once made this statement: "Wherever you are, be *all* there. Live to the hilt every situation you believe to be the will of God."

Are you all there when you are at work? In a sense, to be "halfhearted" is really only to be half alive. (How would you like to get a halfhearted greeting from a close friend or a halfhearted kiss from your wife or husband?) Do you have kids who make their beds halfheartedly? Did you ever see a halfheartedly made bed? The pillow is cocked at an angle. The bedspread is all the way down to the floor on one side, exposing the mattress on the other. And the blankets underneath are so rumpled up it looks like a topographical map of the Rockies. If you didn't know better, you might think someone was still in that bed.

What did the kid do? Well, he knows he's supposed to make his bed before he goes to school, so he gives it a lick and a promise and walks out of the room. And you call out the door, "Did you get that bed made?"

"Oh, yeah, Mom. Made the bed. See ya."

He made it all right—halfheartedly. Did you ever meet anyone who lived his life the way a teenager makes his bed? That kind of person is just going through the motions, isn't he? He isn't putting his heart into it. I know there have been times in my life, too, when I've failed to live by this verse, and those were not happy times in my life. The way my schedule looks these days, I have to ask myself, "If you can't put your whole heart into it, David, why are you even doing it?"

Every coach's dream is that his players would play up to their potential. What a way to live! Leave it all on the floor. Don't walk away from a game when it's all over and say, "My heart wasn't in it. I really could have done more!" That's an awful feeling. And in the same way, don't leave your workplace at the end of the day and say, "I really should have followed through. I really should have been more attentive." Do everything you can with all of your heart. The stakes are higher than you imagine!

The biblical phrase rendered here "in sincerity of heart" is really better translated "in singleness of heart." The Christian employee is to devote full attention to his or her job. Singleness of heart indicates you have a purpose. It is the determination to carry through with orders in spite of the temptation to be led astray by conflicting desires.

Perhaps one application we should make of this principle is that Christians should never use witnessing to their unsaved workmates as an excuse to give less than a full day's work for a full day's wage. Have you ever seen that happen? Some guy wanders away from his workstation, and he's over across the building talking to someone about the Lord.

If I were the employer, I'd feel like saying, "Get over there and get back to work!" That believer isn't being paid to evangelize his coworkers or discuss the fine points of theology. He's drawing a salary to do a particular task. Talking about your faith is something you do on your lunch hour or after work, when you invite someone over to your house. But don't ask your employer to pay you to witness to the people who work alongside you. That's not godly! You'll make a much greater impact by working hard and faithfully than you ever will by stealing time from your company and using it for your own purposes.

I feel very strongly about these things. Do you know why? Because as a pastor, I hear complaints all the time from employers—Christian and non-Christian—who hire believers. "Yeah, he comes to work for me. But all he does is sit around and read his Bible and pass out tracts. He doesn't do much work."

My friend, if you are a believer, you ought to be the hardest worker in your shop. And by your hard work, you will attract people to you who want to know what makes you tick. *Then* take them home and tell them about Jesus.

Nehemiah, one of the great leaders of the Old Testament, accomplished one of the most magnificent feats you will ever read about anywhere. He rebuilt the wall around Jerusalem. Remember how he obtained a leave of absence from the king of Media-Persia and came back to the ruins of his people's inheritance? Observers and enemies all around them said it couldn't be done. They mocked and ridiculed the workers. But Nehemiah and the others just rolled up their sleeves and made it happen. And they did it in just fifty-two days, with swords in one hand and trowels in the other.

What a motivator this man must have been! But when the great task was almost done, this courageous leader penned these words in his journal: "So we built the wall, and the entire wall was joined together up to half its height, for the people had a mind to work" (Nehemiah 4:6).

Don't you like to work alongside hardworking people? I'm not talking about grim, stressed-out types who never know how to smile or have fun. I mean people who work at their jobs with a full heart and a willing spirit. I like having people around me who work so diligently and so faithfully that I am motivated to take it up a notch in my own life and do better work…as unto the Lord.

Solomon had an interesting angle on the subject in the book of Ecclesiastes. He wrote: "Whatever your hand finds to do, do it with all your might, for in the grave, where you are going, there is neither working nor planning nor knowledge nor wisdom" (Ecclesiastes 9:10, NIV).

Isn't that an interesting thought? If you're going to work hard, you'd better do it now because you won't be able to do it later. Do it now.

As Christians, we should know nothing of the dichotomy between the "sacred" and the "secular." I really don't know where that sort of thinking came from. As a child of the living God, I am no more holy when I stand in the pulpit preaching the Word of God than I am when I'm raking the leaves in my yard, cleaning out the garage, or doing whatever chores might be mine. Why? Because I'm God's person. I'm God's person when I preach, and I'm God's person when I take out the garbage. I'm God's person as pastor of a church, and I would be God's person if I retired from the pastorate and started ringing up groceries at the corner market.

Sometimes you hear people say (in a stained-glass tone of voice), "Well, he has gone into the ministry." My friend, if you are a Christian, you are *already* in the ministry. You're either going to be an effective minister or a poor one, depending on how you allow the Holy Spirit to fill you and use you.

I happen to minister in a church in San Diego, California. God has called me to teach His people. That's what I do, and He has given me a passion for that task. God has likely called you to do something else somewhere else. And He has called you to be an ambassador in your workplace, whether that workplace is at home caring for the kids or in an office suite on top of a skyscraper.

Monday is as holy a day for you as Sunday. When you step into the place of His appointment—whether it's flipping hamburgers or delivering the State of the Union Address on national TV—you are to be God's person operating in His strength. We are to do the will of God from the heart.

"Well, Jeremiah," you might say to me, "that's all well and good. But you don't know that foreman of mine," or "you don't know that department manager." I hear people say that sort of thing all the time. "This stuff works every-where except where *I* work."

I remember working in a hardware store when I was in high school. It wasn't much fun. The manager of the place loved to give me all the meanest, most dif-ficult jobs he could come up with. I was always the guy who did the stuff no one else wanted to do. What's more, the man seemed to derive real joy out of seeing me flounder around in those hard jobs.

What does the Bible say about working for a tough boss like that? Let's quickly review a passage we looked at a little earlier in this book. Listen again to Peter's counsel about working for an unreasonable employer.

> Servants, be submissive to your masters with all fear, not only to the good and gentle, but also to the harsh. For this is commendable, if because of conscience toward God one endures grief, suffering wrong-fully. For what credit is it if, when you are beaten for your faults, you take it patiently? But when you do good and suffer for it, if you take it patiently, this is commendable before God. (1 Peter 2:18–20)

If you do something at work that really deserves some disciplinary action...well, you've got it coming, don't you? You did it. Harsh treatment is simply what you deserve.

But Peter says this: Even if you don't do anything wrong—if you're doing the best you can and giving an honest day's work—and he *still* treats you badly, then understand that the way you respond to such treatment is going to set you apart as someone who has a different internal guidance system.

Remember what we said about willing submission in an earlier chapter? It isn't natural, it's supernatural. And it can't help but make an impression.

The Word of God continually amazes me. It's one thing for the Word to shine its bright searchlight on my actions at work—what I do and how I do it. But it doesn't stop there. It also shines that light on the attitude of my heart—*why* I do what I do.

Paul tells us, don't be giving your employer just "eye service," to please him when he happens to be walking by and his eye is on you. In other words, don't be the kind of worker who suddenly becomes diligent and attentive when the boss shows up—only to slack off again when he walks away. The Bible says no

Christian should ever be like that. Why? Because the aim of a Christian employee isn't to please the boss. It is to please God, the One who never leaves the room, the One who never stops watching.

A received appreciation

Knowing that whatever good anyone does, he will receive the same from the Lord (*Ephesians 6:8*).

Somebody says, "Well, I work so hard all the time, and that man never even notices one thing I do. Man, I do the hardest work and put in more time than anybody else around this place. He never says a word to me. He never says he appreciates me, he never says 'good job.'"

Yes, that could be very disappointing. But the Bible reminds us of something that ought to be on our minds all day long: You're not working for *that* boss. You are working for the Lord God Almighty, and He is the One who will reward your service. And nothing ever escapes His notice.

You say you can't get excited about working where you're working and who you're working for? Well…could you get excited about working for the Lord Jesus Christ? Could you get excited about working alongside Him, being in His presence as you perform your tasks all day long? That, says Paul, is where you need to keep your focus each day.

That's quite a bit for the Christian employee to think about. But how does Scripture do with putting the shoe on the other foot? What does the Bible have to say to those who are employers?

THE MARKS OF A CHRISTIAN EMPLOYER

And you, masters, do the same things to them, giving up threatening, knowing that your own Master also is in heaven, and there is no par-tiality with Him. (Ephesians 6:9)

Respect your employees

"And you, masters, do the same things to them." In other words, this is a recip-rocal arrangement. You have men and women working under your authority. You want them to work hard, you want them to respect you, and you want them to give an honest day's work.

Fair enough. But the Bible adds this: If you want respect, then offer your

SPIRIT-CONTROLLED WORKPLACES   237

employees the same kind of respect with which you want to be treated. That's what verse 9 is saying. Do the same things to them. Simply give them what is due.

Colossians 4:1 says, "Masters, give your servants what is just and fair." In other words, don't underpay them. Don't cheat them out of that which is theirs. Don't do to them as employees what you gripe about their doing to you as an employer.

Realize that you, too, are under authority

You may be the boss, but you aren't *really* the boss. What does it say here? "Because you also have a Master who is in heaven." And someday you are going to give an account to Him. In fact, *He is holding you accountable right now.* If you are mistreating those who are under you, and you are a Christian, your Boss isn't happy with you. And remember, in the Lord's eyes, the attitudes of your heart toward your employees are as relevant as your actions toward them.

Refrain from abusive treatment

Notice what it says here: "Give up threatening." The law of the Old Testament sets forth clear guidelines for those who are over slaves. Listen to this illustration from Leviticus: "You shall not rule over them with rigor, but you shall fear your God."

Have you ever known a believer who seems to be a different man or woman in the workplace when the pressure's on? Something happens. Something snaps. She's sarcastic and cutting. He uses vile language and goes ballistic if somebody crosses him.

I've had coaches over the years who would jump down your throat for the slightest mistake, who *never* had a positive word to say about any effort, any sacrifice. Christian, where do you get that stuff? The Bible says you are to be gentle and kind. Yes, you can still be firm when you need to be firm, but you can do that in a godly way. The Bible says we're to *lead* people, not bully or threaten them, the way the world does. The world, of course, has its own methods for squeezing work out of people. But our Lord very clearly tells us, "It shall not be so among you" (Matthew 20:26). We're supposed to be different.

Does that mean you'll always agree with others in the workplace? That you'll always see eye to eye with your boss, or that you'll agree with the employees' suggestions and complaints? Not at all. But we will learn how to disagree agree-ably, and we will work out our differences, and we will move forward. People who have mutual respect and work hard at honoring one another can work together.

You say, "Well, Jeremiah, I think you're a dreamer. That's not the workaday world I know, that's utopia. That isn't ever going to happen." No, it may not happen down here on this earth as part of our culture, but wherever God's people are, it should be happening. It should be happening in our hearts, because if you are filled with the Spirit of God, He will empower you to be different and to make a difference.

When *God* is in you, you can't be the same. "Business as usual" simply doesn't apply to a Spirit-filled follower of Jesus Christ.

One of these days, not so very long from right now, you and I are going to stand before our ultimate Employer. The One who made us for Himself. The One who bought us out of the slave market of sin with His own blood. The One who sent His Holy Spirit to be our Companion and Guide and Helper through all the days of our lives. And every workday of our lives will be spread out before His eyes. He will see every injustice, every slight, every unfairness. He will see those days when we were careless and halfhearted in our work, and He will see those days when we poured ourselves into the task, as unto Him, in our love for Him.

In that moment, "Well done" from His lips will mean more than anything any employer has ever offered in the history of the world.

In the meantime, let's be His people. Let's let the Spirit of God fill us and control us and empower us. And let's go out and make a difference.

Whatever we do, let's do it with a full heart...as unto Him.

Chapter Fifteen

WHEN THE
HOLY SPIRIT
CONTROLS YOUR LIFE

WALKING INTO YOUR FUTURE
WITH CONFIDENCE

*A*t the time of this writing, angels are big business in America. Books about angels have ascended both the Christian and secular best-seller lists. Many Christians have been surprised by the success of a network TV show, *Touched by an Angel*—an intrusion of something almost wholesome into the prime-time wasteland.

Americans are okay with angels. According to a recent national survey, three-fourths of us believe that angels exist. Network executives, however, would do well to avoid casting any shows about two other spiritual entities, Satan and the Holy Spirit. According to the same survey, a large majority of adults do not believe either in the devil or the third member of the Trinity. Nearly two out of three adults, 62 percent, agree that Satan is "not a living being, but a symbol of evil."

Perhaps the most stunning result of this survey is this nation's conclusion that there is no such thing as the Holy Spirit. Six out of ten Americans agreed that the Holy Spirit is a "symbol of God's presence and power, but not a living entity." Even among self-proclaimed believers, the belief in the Holy Spirit as a real being with personality and power is diminished far beneath anything you would ever imagine.[1]

In the pages of this book, we've been considering what it means to be controlled by the Spirit of God. If the Holy Spirit is just a symbol of the presence of God, then obviously He would have no power whatsoever to affect us or to make us over into the kind of people God wants us to be.

In the opening chapters, however, we discovered that the Holy Spirit is indeed a person, not just some vague "presence." He is a part of the Trinity, a person who has the desire and the power to make a difference in the lives of those who yield to His control. We have walked along the avenues of Ephesians and Colossians where we have learned how the Holy Spirit wants to touch us, change us, and make us into the men and women God wants us to be.

He is the Holy Spirit of God who can transform us and make us new. Do you truly believe that?

I remember reading about a man named Charlie Steinmetz, a dwarf, who had a deformed body but one of the greatest minds in the field of electricity the world has ever known. Steinmetz built the generators for Henry Ford's first auto plant. One day those generators broke down and production froze to an immediate halt. A small army of mechanics and technicians pored over the machinery, but couldn't get the generators running again. Every hour of inactivity meant a great deal of lost money.

Finally, Henry Ford called Steinmetz back to the plant. The genius came in, seemed to just tinker around for a few hours, and then threw the switch and put the Ford plant back into operation.

A few days later, Henry Ford received a bill from Steinmetz for ten thousand dollars—a considerable sum of money in those days. Although a wealthy and generous man in his own right, Ford returned the bill with a note. The note said, "Charlie, isn't this bill just a little high for a few hours of tinkering around with those motors?"

Steinmetz returned the bill to Ford. This time it read, "For tinkering around on the motors: $10; for knowing where to tinker, $9,990. Total bill: $10,000."

Henry Ford paid the bill.

The Holy Spirit knows where to tinker, and you need to allow Him to restart the generator in your life. If you have gotten off the path, if you are a Christian and your life has lost its zest for God, the only way to get on track is to seek the One who knows more about you than you do and put Him back in control of your life.

In his letter to the church at Colosse, Paul wrote what I believe to be a powerful summary statement about what happens to us when the Holy Spirit takes control of our life.

Continue earnestly in prayer, being vigilant in it with thanksgiving; meanwhile praying also for us, that God would open to us a door for the word, to speak the mystery of Christ, for which I am also in chains, that I may make it manifest, as I ought to speak. Walk in wisdom toward those who are outside, redeeming the time. Let your speech always be with grace, seasoned with salt, that you may know how you ought to answer each one. (Colossians 4:2–6)

In these few verses, it is as if Paul has taken all that we have learned and wrapped it up in the three areas of our life where we have the most difficult time living consistently for God. He talks to us about how we are to worship, our prayer life, and the nature of our walk in the world—how we live our testimony.

HOLY SPIRIT HELP IN OUR PRAYERS

He begins in the second verse by saying, "Continue earnestly in prayer, being vigilant in it with thanksgiving."

All of us who have struggled at any time with our prayer life have come to understand that prayer is the very breath of spirituality. Its absence is an indication of coldness and deadness in our life. An orchestra tunes its instruments before a concert. A carpenter sharpens his tools before he begins construction. An artist mixes his colors before he paints. And prayer is like the tuning of an instrument and the sharpening of a tool. When we begin the day in prayer, we have tuned our lives in the power of the Holy Spirit to face *whatever* comes our way.

If we put prayer at the beginning of the day, it sets the tone for the day. You may not consider yourself a "morning person." But then again, you *are* a person, and you do have to get up in the morning. And if you begin your day by communing with your God, it will change the nature and character of your waking hours.

Perhaps you've seen this bit of verse on a plaque in someone's home:

I met God in the morning, when the day was at its best,
and His presence came like sunshine, like a glory in my breast.
All day long, this presence lingered, all day long He stayed with me,
and we sailed in perfect calmness o'er a very troubled sea.
So I think I know the secret, learned from many a troubled way:
You must seek Him in the morning if you want Him through the day.[2]

And many of us have discovered that when we launch our day with prayer, it makes all the difference. I've been learning how to begin my workday by praying over my appointments, praying over the tasks that await me, and just asking God to breathe into every situation in a way that will make me a distinct influence for Him in the world in which I live. Let's begin where Paul began with the whole area of our prayer life.

Pray diligently

Paul says, "Continue in prayer." This is an imperative. A command. It means to devote your time, attention, and strength to this task. You are to do it with steadfast continuance. Don't let it be an afterthought, and don't let it be a ho-hum kind of thing you could take or leave. When we learn how to make this the focus of our discipline, then prayer begins to come alive. You don't just say, "A prayer a day keeps the devil away," mumble a few things under your breath, and go on your way. You pray with distinction and determination.

I've learned something interesting about *anticipating* my morning prayer time.

Before I fall asleep, I remind myself, "David, the first thing in the morning you're going to spend time with the Lord. You're going to pour out your heart to Him, and He's going to meet you in a wonderful way." Somehow, when that's the last thought of the day, it becomes the first thought of the morning. Almost as soon as I've opened my eyes I'm thinking, "I have an appointment with God. He's waiting for me."

When I'm on the way to the office where I have my time with the Lord, I try to keep myself in a prayerful frame of mind so that when I walk through the door, meeting with my Lord will be the first order of business. I've learned that I have to do this *diligently;* if I don't I lose that edge in my life and begin to slip back into old patterns of worry, self-doubt, and prayerlessness.

Pray diligently. Keep after it. Persevere. *Fight* for that time with God. As Jesus taught His disciples, pray always and don't give up (Luke 18:1). It's not just a religious interlude. It's not some spiritual luxury. It's not just a 911 number you dial in a personal emergency. It is something that you *continue* in. And if you read the New Testament carefully, you will see that this was the testimony of the men and women who walked with God in the early church.

We read of the apostles in Acts 1:14, "These all *continued* with one accord in prayer and supplication, with the women and Mary the mother of Jesus, and with His brothers."

In Acts 6:4, the apostles insisted, "But we will give ourselves *continually* to prayer and to the ministry of the word."

In Acts 2:42, we're told, "And they *continued steadfastly* in the apostles' doctrine and fellowship, in the breaking of bread, and in prayers."

In Romans 12:12, Paul speaks of the believer as "rejoicing in hope, patient in tribulation, *continuing steadfastly* in prayer."

We are instructed in Ephesians 6:18 to *"pray always* with all prayer and supplication in the Spirit, being watchful to this end *with all perseverance* and supplication for all the saints."

And 1 Thessalonians 5:17 adds that we are to "pray *without ceasing."*

I could give you many more verses, because I have cataloged them all. There is a great deal more about prayer in the Bible than most Christians ever get hold of. But we ought not to look at it as some grim duty we have to experience. Prayer is a great adventure! Walking with God daily, diligently, is a path with more mysteries, vistas, and glories than in any national park in the world.

A friend of mine told me about taking a hike with his family in the mountains of Central Oregon. He hadn't been very excited about the path his wife had chosen from a guidebook and wasn't anticipating much more than a long walk through ponderosa pines with perhaps an occasional glimpse at some distant peaks on the horizon.

Suddenly they came around a bend in the trail and found themselves at a wide-open vista point. Right in front of them, filling the whole horizon, was a craggy, snowcapped mountain soaring into the heavens. It seemed close enough to reach out and touch. My friend said he felt like falling on his knees in awe. It was one of the most spectacular, breathtaking sights he had ever seen. He hadn't been expecting it. He'd had his mind on the long trail and finding some big flat rock where they could rest and eat some lunch. And then the trail suddenly led into a moment of beauty and majesty and awe that will be burned into his memory for the rest of his life.

Prayer is like that, as you persevere in it. It is an adventure of sudden, unexpected vistas, amazing landscapes, and answers beyond your expectations and dreams.

Pray watchfully

Picture a lone army sentry, pacing the perimeters of camp in the night, alert to every sound, every movement. Watchfulness involves mental alertness and spiritual vigilance. It is to be sensitive and aware when you are in danger.

Peter, who criticized our Lord for taking the path of the cross and later failed Him at the most strategic moment, later on had learned his lesson. He knew Satan had gotten control of him on that occasion, so when he wrote his first letter to the church, he penned these terse words: "Be self-controlled and alert. Your enemy the devil prowls around like a roaring lion looking for someone to devour" (1 Peter 5:8, NIV).

Peter, who had not been alert, who had not been watchful and vigilant and prayerful, now offers this hard-won counsel. You'd better keep your eyes open and you'd better keep on your toes. The stakes are too high for you to doze off.

What does it mean to be watchful in prayer? First of all, it means to stay awake! But it's really much more than that. To be awake is to be vigilant. Alert. Observant. Careful. Attentive.

One of the things I've learned, not only in my own life, but in talking with others about praying, is that the discipline of prayer can easily slip away from you if you're not attentive to it. One day without prayer (which can happen to anyone) becomes two days. Two days become three. Three days become a week. And then you wake up and realize with a start that a month has gone by and you've hardly prayed at all. Paul warns us, "Watch over your prayer life."

Do you know what has helped me with my prayer life more than anything I've done in years? It's keeping a journal, so that I can remember what I've prayed, when I prayed it, and how God has answered. This has become very precious to me in my life, particularly in those weeks and months when I was battling with cancer.

Watch God's answers to your prayers. Watch God work in your life. Write it down and remember to remember that He will never fail you.

Pray thankfully

We devoted a whole chapter to "the attitude of gratitude," and here is the same emphasis again in Colossians. Once again, we find that prayer is directly linked with a spirit of gratefulness. Philippians 4:6 tells us that we are to "be anxious for nothing, but in everything by prayer and supplication, *with thanksgiving,* let your requests be made known to God."

When we are Spirit-filled people, we are grateful people, and we pray thankfully. Thanksgiving acknowledges submission to the will of God. First Thessalonians 5:18 tells us, "In everything give thanks; for this is the will of God in Christ Jesus for you."

Did you ever find yourself rushing into your prayer, getting halfway through it and realizing you haven't breathed a single word of thanks to the Lord? We've all got our "gimme lists," don't we? Mine starts accumulating throughout the day, stored in some file in the back of my mind. I want this, I need that, I've got to have such and such. And sometimes, if I'm not careful, I will turn on my spiritual computer and rush my gimme list to the screen without taking time to thank the Lord.

Did you ever wonder about those days in the Garden of Eden, before sin entered the picture to shatter the relationship between God and His two happy tenants? The Bible says God would come to walk with Adam and Eve in the garden, at the cool of the day. Did you ever wonder about those conversations? Do you suppose Adam rushed up to God with a clipboard and pencil in hand?

"Ah yes, there were just a few things I wanted to review with You, God. That new pomegranate orchard by the river, for one thing. Do you think we should hedge it with rhododendrons? Oh, and we've really had our hands full with those crazy gorillas in Sector Two...."

Don't you imagine the first couple would have simply cherished being in God's presence? Don't you imagine them expressing their wonder and gratitude for the beauty He had created...for the cooling wind...for the crimson sunset...for the joys of companionship between husband and wife...for the privilege of walking and talking with the Creator of all?

Oh, what a wonderful thing happens when we stop to reflect upon what God has already done, and ask Him to accept our gratitude as we offer Him our praise and our worship.

Pray specifically

Paul tells the Colossians, "I want you to pray not only for yourselves, but I want you to pray for me, too." And as I read through his letters, I am taken by the *detail* in which Paul asks others to pray. Sometimes we'll agree to pray for someone, but I wonder if we shouldn't be more diligent to ask, "*How* would you like me to pray?"

As I write these words, a certain couple comes to my mind. From the time I first became pastor of the church where I currently serve, they have asked me how they can pray for me. Whenever I see them on the campus, it's almost like a broken record. They will come up to me, put a hand on my arm, and say, "Pastor, how can we pray for you this week?"

Sometimes I don't know exactly what to say when they ask me that, but I'm so glad they keep asking! Because there have been times when I've had some very heavy, important matters I've wanted to put onto their list. I love to bump into these people—I'd go out of my way to do it! They have carried the burden of this responsibility with me from the very beginning.

Do you want to encourage your pastor? Cards and notes and little remembrances are nice, and I'm sure they'll always be appreciated. But the sure knowledge that he can count on your daily prayers—for him and with him—is something that's just beyond price.

Pray for opportunity

Notice what Paul says: "Pray also for us that God would open to us a door for the word, to speak the mystery of Christ, for which I am also in chains, that I may make it manifest, as I ought to speak." Remember, now, Paul is writing this from prison. And he's not asking for an "open door" so that he can walk out of jail. (That would be my prayer!) No, that's not the principal thing on the apostle's heart. In reality, he's asking for several things.

That "open door" phrase appears in Scripture several times. Please note that Paul is not saying prayer opens the door, He is affirming that *God* is the One who opens doors.

He shuts a few, too.

I was reminded of the passage in Revelation 3:7–8 where Jesus is speaking to the seven churches and says, "These things says He who is holy, He who is true, 'He who has the key of David, He who opens and no one shuts, and shuts and no one opens'; I know your works. See, I have set before you an open door, and no one can shut it."

Let me tell you something. When God opens a door, no one shuts it. When we pray for open doors, we ought to pray that God would give us opportunities.

And when God gives you an opportunity, it's big enough to drive a Mack truck through. You don't have to *squeeze* yourself through God's opportunities. You can walk through four abreast!

You and I get ourselves in trouble sometimes because we try to make our own opportunities. I would rather have an opportunity God made than those I try to create. And I'm the sort of person who will try to make my own opportunities, if I'm not careful. I'll run around rattling this door and that door to see if it will open. Paul says, "Pray for an opportunity to minister."

You might say, "I wish I could witness, but I don't know how to do it." Let me give you a little key that someone gave me some years ago. Don't worry so much about the fact that you *ought* to witness and go around trying to create your own opportunities. Some of those forced encounters can be really awkward. Maybe you've been on the other end of one of those awkward moments and know how uncomfortable it can be.

But I dare you to make this thought part of your prayer life every morning as you are on your knees before the Lord: "Lord, make me sensitive to the opportunities that You bring my way, so that I will know that it is *Your* open door."

Have you ever prayed that prayer in your heart as you've boarded an airplane? Maybe you have your whole agenda planned for the trip across the country. Your notebook is out. Your pencil is out. Maybe even your computer is out. And the seat next to you is empty, which is unusual with the way they jam people into airliners these days. But just as the attendant is about to close the door, someone hurries down the aisle and takes (of course) the seat right next to you.

The first thing he or she says to you is, "I'm so-and-so. What's your name?" When that happens to me, I know what the next question will be. *And what do you do?* At that point, I close my book, close my notebook, and close my Bible. Because I know that as soon as I tell that person I'm a pastor, I'm going to be in conversation most of the way across the country.

And that's all right. After all, if I'm going to begin my day by praying, "Lord, open the door of opportunity for me," and He *does* it, I'd better be alert enough to walk on through.

Pray for clarity

Paul went on to ask for prayer that he might "speak the mystery of Christ, for which I am also in chains." Paul's purpose was to have open doors so that he could teach the grace of God. He wanted the ability to explain what to that point in time had been a mystery, hidden in the counsels of God. He wanted to be able to declare how Jew and Gentile had been brought together into one church, one body, one kingdom—and he wanted to make it understandable. He says, "I want to be clear in my teaching. Pray that I'll see the opportunities. Pray that I will have clarity in my presentation."

If you've ever done any teaching, you understand very well what Paul was praying for. Sometimes something seems so clear in your studies, so clear in your notes, and makes perfect sense to you. But then you present it to a group of people and you watch a glaze form over their eyes. With a sinking feeling, you realize that they don't have a clue what you're talking about. Paul was saying, "This is too important to muddle or obscure. Pray that I'll be able to lay it out in a way that people can readily pick it up."

Pray for sensitivity

Pray, Paul went on, "that I may make it manifest, as I ought to speak." Paul knew that the manner in which he presented his message was just as important as the message itself. And so he said, "When you pray for me, pray that God will open opportunities for me to minister, pray that I'll be clear in what I say, but pray also that I'll have a sensitive heart—so that I will minister in the power of the Holy Spirit."

HOLY SPIRIT HELP FOR OUR WALK

Notice Colossians 4:5: "Walk in wisdom toward those who are outside, redeeming the time." Walking is Paul's favorite metaphor of the Christian life. The Christian life *is* a walk, one step at a time.

We've been watching our little grandson in the early stages of locomotion. He isn't crawling yet, and he certainly isn't walking. He's *scooting*. When you put something attractive in front of him, he can get to it—but it's a major effort (and great fun to watch!). Walking is just taking one little step at a time.

And walking is dependent, isn't it? You have to trust when you walk. In Colossians 1:10, Paul says, "Walk worthy of the Lord, fully pleasing Him." He mentions it again in chapter 2 verse 6. He says, "As you have therefore received Christ Jesus the Lord, so walk in Him." This is such a key concept, Paul takes time to explain *how* we ought to walk.

Walk consistently

The Word of God places great emphasis on consistency. The Christian life isn't a hundred-yard dash followed by a long nap. It is a consistent walk. It moves forward at a measured pace. It progresses. It's heading toward a goal. While people around you are drifting or going around in circles, you are *going somewhere* as you walk in the Spirit. Where you are this year is not where you were last year. Where you are today, Lord willing, is not where you will be tomorrow.

Walk carefully

Do you realize how important this is? Even the good things in your life can be ill spoken of if you don't walk carefully. We live in a broken world, and sometimes it's as though broken shards of glass cover the trail before us. We have to pick our way through. We can't shuffle along with our eyes closed, humming a hymn.

David knew this very well when he prayed: "Keep me, O LORD, from the hands of the wicked; protect me from men of violence who plan to trip my feet. Proud men have hidden a snare for me; they have spread out the cords of their net and have set traps for me along my path" (Psalm 140:4–5, NIV).

It's a dangerous world out there. There are traps. There are snares. There are land mines that can blow our lives into a thousand pieces. We need to watch where we're placing our feet.

Walk openly

Paul says, "Walk in wisdom toward those who are outside." What a wonderful picture that is. There are many Christians who think that once you become a Christian, you cut off all your relationships with the people in the world and stay within a little "holy huddle" for the rest of your days.

I don't see one shred of evidence for that thinking in the New Testament. The Lord Jesus Himself associated with sinners, prostitutes, and societal rejects. How are we supposed to win a world we don't even know? How are we going to touch people who don't know Christ if we are never *with* them? As Dr. Joe Aldrich always says, "There is no impact without contact."

Paul says in this passage that when you walk with wisdom, do it openly toward those who are outside of the faith. You may work in a company where, to your knowledge, you're the only believer in the whole place. If I were in your shoes, I'd be on my knees every day praying the same thing Paul prayed. "Lord, help me! Help me today to walk consistently and carefully toward those who are without."

I can promise you this: They will watch your every move! Once it becomes apparent you are a Christian, you'll be on display, an object of curiosity, and they will monitor everything you say and everything you do.

You say, "That sounds like living in a fishbowl. I don't think I like that!" That's tough! That's the way it is. And if you try to live consistently in your own strength, you will fall flat on your face. But the Holy Spirit will empower you to live in such a way in that environment so that when people see you, they will see your good works and will glorify your Father who is in heaven.

Walk urgently

Paul says, "Walk in wisdom toward those who are outside, *redeeming the time.*" Do it urgently! Make the best possible use of your time. It strikes me sometimes that we need a lot more urgency in our lives about spiritual things. We've become comfortable with all that God has given to us...and maybe a little sleepy. That sense of urgency we ought to have toward reaching our friends and our loved ones for Christ needs to be fired up again.

Paul says, redeem your time. Seize every opportunity, like merchants who are buying up a scarce commodity in the market.

Ours must be an alert and industrious discipleship. It is understanding that if God has opened the door for an opportunity, you are going to grasp that opportunity and not let it go. A friend of mine told me that recently he happened to be standing in his driveway looking at the stars on a brilliantly clear night. His neighbor, a somewhat crusty old gentleman, was standing in his driveway too. He walked over to the elderly man and they talked some, touching on subjects of life and death. My friend sensed that inner urgency to open his mouth and speak of faith in Christ. But in his reluctance, he let the moment slip by. And there has not been another such moment.

Don't walk away from those opportunities. Don't let them slip through your fingers. Take a risk. Step out. Break through your fear and reluctance, trusting the Holy Spirit to give you the words. If you're thought of as a fanatic or a fool, so be it. People have been called worse. We must buy up those opportunities, knowing they may never come again.

Sometimes God puts opportunities in your path to minister in the church, to have an impact on others for Christ. Step through those open doors! Don't let those opportunities be lost out of fear, hesitancy to "get involved," or doubt in your own abilities. Don't put yourself in a position of looking back years later, saying, "I wish I had done that."

Paul says we are to walk in this world with a steady consistency, with careful steps, with openness to all who are watching, and with that sense of urgency, so that when the door opens, you are ready to step through.

This whole business of our walk before the world is so critical. Do you realize that many people judge Jesus Christ by what they see in Christians? You say, "But that isn't fair. That isn't an accurate picture of Him at all." Nevertheless, it is true. Our responsibility is great.

I remember reading a story about the Russian writer Maksim Gorky. Gorky was a child when his father died, and he and his mother went to live with his grandparents. His grandfather, Gorky recalled, was a religious man, but stern, irritable, and sometimes cruel. His mother was also religious, but kind, gentle, and understanding. Gorky wrote that when he saw his mother and his grandfather kneeling side by side in church, he could not believe that they were praying to the same God. He felt there had to be two gods, one cruel and vindictive, and the other loving and forgiving.

I think sometimes when people see us, they must wonder about our God. Because, you see, the way we interact with those who are outside the faith paints a picture of the God we worship. The Christ they see in you and me is the Christ they evaluate.

Robert Ingersoll, the famous infidel, had a godly aunt to whom he sent a copy of one of his books attacking the Bible. And on the flyleaf of this book, he wrote these words over his signature: "If all Christians lived like Aunt Sarah, this book would never have been written."

HOLY SPIRIT HELP FOR OUR WITNESS

Paul wrote in Colossians 4:6, "Let your speech always be with grace, seasoned with salt, that you may know how you ought to answer each one."

The Bible states that one of the hardest things you and I will ever have to deal with is the control of our own tongue. The book of James tells us that it's more difficult to bridle the tongue than it is a wild horse. How true that is. You can get those words out, but you can't stuff them back in! You can send them forth, but you can't call them back. You can say something, but you can't unsay it.

The tongue gets many people in trouble. What we say. How we say it. When we say it. So it's not surprising to me that Paul would, in the final verse of this paragraph about living in the power of the Holy Spirit, talk about our Christian witness.

Our witness must be consistent

Paul uses the word *always*. "Let your speech *always* be with grace." Be consistent in how you speak. With the Spirit's enabling, make gracious speech a habit of life.

Our witness must be courteous

Many Christians turn people away from Christ by the very way they present the truth of the gospel. You don't usually persuade people to know and love the Lord when you begin the conversation by telling them they're going to hell. That usually doesn't win you an open door.

We read of our Lord Jesus that He was "full of grace and truth." Truth packaged in grace. That's the way Christ related to men and women in His earthly walk...and so should we.

Our witness should be compelling

Notice he says, "Let it be with grace, *seasoned with salt*." What does that mean? Don't let your words become flat and tasteless. Salt had two particularly important purposes in New Testament times. It was a preservative, to keep things from spoiling. And it was also used to create thirst in animals. At my uncle's farm we used to put salt licks out in the field so the animals would lick the salt and then consume the proper amount of water.

Salt has the ability to create thirst. You eat a bag of potato chips at a ball game, and then you want to go get a soft drink—the biggest one they sell. That's why they sell so many salted peanuts, chips, pretzels, and popcorn at ball games. They want to sell drinks, too!

Paul is saying, "Let there be something in what you say that compels people to know the God you know." Get creative in how you communicate Christ. Talk in such a way that when people are around you, they sense this is not something you've "put on." It is something in you that comes out effervescently, the overflowing life and power of the Holy Spirit.

Yes, let your speech always be gracious, but don't let it be flattened out, pious and syrupy. Don't load it up with canned phrases and Christian clichés. Let your conversation be filled with the wonderful truth of who Christ is and the greatness of the Christian life.

Our witness should be compassionate

He ends this portion of Scripture by saying, "Know how you ought to answer each one." You talk to people differently, not because your message is different, but because *people* are different. You suit your witness to the one with whom you are speaking.

I think one of the most difficult things as a Christian is to witness to people who are in your own family. Someone once told me something like this: When a wife talks to her husband about the Lord, she might be conveying to him—subtly or perhaps not so subtly—that he hasn't been as good a husband as he should have been or could have been. So this "spiritual thing" is a way of saying he's not measuring up.

What a difference when a woman comes to her husband and says, "Honey, you've been everything I could ever have asked for in a husband. You are a great provider, you love me, and I know that. I just wish there was one thing we could share together that is so very meaningful to me."

What a difference a new approach can make!

The same thing may be true with our parents. If you go back and try to witness to your father who is not a Christian, do you know what you might convey to him, if you're not careful? You might convey that you think he was a bad father. After all, what kind of father would let his kids grow up without any religion? So you need to *season* your witness and say to him, "You've been a great dad. I couldn't have asked for better. But you know what? God has given me something that is so special to me, and I love you so much, I can't help but share with you what He's done for me. I wish you knew the God I know."

When you affirm a person's worth without blasting him or her with the gospel right up front, you win an opportunity. The Holy Spirit gives us the wisdom and grace to do that. He empowers you and me to look at every situation and to discern how God wants us to tailor-make our witness to each individual.

When Jesus met the woman at the well in the hot noonday sun, He didn't say, "You must be born again," as He had said to Nicodemus. He spoke to her about thirst—and the deeper thirst for God that we all feel deep within us. He spoke about water—and the water of life that can become an unfailing source of refreshment through the years of our lives.

When Philip encountered the Ethiopian eunuch in his chariot on the desert road, he didn't immediately begin preaching about Jesus. He said, "What are you reading? Does it make sense to you?" And that African official invited him to step up into the chariot and say more.

When the Holy Spirit controls you, He empowers your prayer life, your walk, and your witness.

STANDING FAST IN HIM

At the close of World War II, a series of memorable color photographs appeared in one of the nation's magazines, showing a large tank bearing down on a lone American soldier.

The first picture was terrifying. The camera angle showed that huge, fearsome war machine towering over the soldier, who seemed so small and frail by comparison.

Just as the tank was about to overwhelm him, the picture in the next frame showed the soldier deploying a bazooka rocket launcher in his hands. And then the third picture showed the soldier like some towering giant as the tank melted down to a crumpled pile of metal.

The striking photographs portrayed the power of this new instrument of warfare created for the military, the tank-destroying bazooka. But it is also a great illustration of what we've been talking about in the pages of this book.

Without the power of God released in and through our lives, we are like an infantryman in the presence of a tank. We have no power. The odds are completely against us. We feel the tank bearing down on us, about to crush us. And we can't do a thing! It's too big. It's too overpowering. It's too much for us.

But when we put our trust in the power of the Holy Spirit, and when we ask Him to fill us and take full control of our lives, He then begins to help us pray, help us walk in our world with wisdom, and help us witness. He gives us what we don't have in and of ourselves.

As a result, we live for God in the power for which we were designed.

I want to ask you a question as we reach the last few pages of this book. Is this just so much theoretical information for you? Facts on a page? Another book to slip on your shelf and collect dust?

Friend, it can all be *real* for you. Today. Right now. This is no self-help book where you make resolutions, enter into a new program, or try to pull yourself up by your bootstraps. This is a book about the greatest Power in the universe, who loves you and wants to empower you in the service of Jesus Christ.

Will it be theory for you as you set this book aside, or will it be a life change beyond what you've ever experienced before? It's really up to you.

If you're ready for a new life adventure, pray with me now.

Holy Spirit of God, take control of my life. Sit in the place of power. Pull the switches. Do Your work. Lord, I just want to be available. Holy Spirit, I will be Your suit of clothes. Walk around in my body. Speak through my lips. Empower me to be what I cannot be in myself. I ask You to cleanse me from my sin, O God, and fill me now to overflowing. And I ask it in the name of Jesus.

When the Holy Spirit begins to tinker with your life, you'll see the power come on. And don't worry about the bill.

Jesus paid it all.

CONCLUSION

*D*r. Raymond Edman, former president of Wheaton College, was a very
devout man.

In 1967 he was preaching in the college chapel on the subject of worship. He told his students that several years earlier he'd had the opportunity to
meet the king of Ethiopia. In order to meet the king, he had to observe a very
strict protocol. There were a number of items that had to be done in order that
he might present himself properly to that earthly king.

Dr. Edman used that illustration to remind the students that when they came
to chapel each day, they were coming into the presence of the King of kings. He
urged them to understand what it meant to worship the Lord, and to cultivate
an eternal perspective that would sustain them through the pressures and anxieties of college life. In the midst of offering several suggestions to that end, Dr.
Edman suddenly collapsed to the floor and entered the very presence of the
King.

Some of those who knew the man commented that Dr. Edman probably
experienced one of the easiest transitions into the presence of God of anyone
they'd ever known. He so loved and worshiped God during his lifetime, and so
cultivated an eternal perspective through the years, that stepping into eternity
wouldn't have been much of a shock to his system. He would just flow right into
the worship before God's throne, because he'd spent so much of his life doing
that very thing.

I'm sure Dr. Edman was a very busy man with a great many duties, yet he
lived life with eternity in view.

That's what the Holy Spirit does for us. He is that still, small voice within us,
reminding us that *this life is not all there is*. What we see with our eyes and hear
with our ears, what we touch and taste and smell is not the sum of reality. For
the believer, life is so very much more than our present circumstances.

As Paul reminded the Corinthians, "Eye has not seen, nor ear heard, nor

258 GOD IN YOU

have entered into the heart of man the things which God has prepared for those who love Him. *But God has revealed them to us through His Spirit"* (1 Corinthians 2:9–10).

The Holy Spirit wants to reveal those things to you, too. Are you listening? Scripture tells us, "For you did not receive the spirit of bondage again to fear, but you received the Spirit of adoption by whom we cry out, 'Abba, Father.' The Spirit Himself bears witness with our spirit that we are children of God" (Romans 8:15–16).

He wants to remind you—today, right now—that you are the adopted child of the King of kings. He wants to remind you that you are a former slave, redeemed at great price from the auction block and brought into the eternal family of God. He wants to remind you that you have an eternal destiny that stretches through the years and beyond all years, out to the horizon and beyond the horizon.

How can we not praise and worship such a God, who has given us so much?

As you turn the final pages of this book, you may find yourself in very difficult circumstances. You may be out of work...struggling with serious health concerns...experiencing the disintegration of your marriage, the rebellion of a child, or some other deep emotional pain. In your heart you say, "I don't feel much like worshiping the Lord sometimes."

Yet the Holy Spirit is still within you, gently, quietly urging you to lift your gaze from the present circumstances and hurts and pressures into the face of One who loves you, cares deeply about you, and will one day (not so very long from now) welcome you into His presence.

In Psalm 46:10, the Lord says to us, "Be still, and know that I am God; I will be exalted among the nations, I will be exalted in the earth!"

Be still! Cease striving. Quit trying to put all the pieces together. Quit trying to figure it all out in your own wisdom. Quit trying to carry everything on your own back. Remember that He is God, and that you belong to Him. Bring Him your worship and praise, and remember that He has promised to meet all your needs.

After all we have read in the previous pages about the ministry of the Holy Spirit, I believe that worship is the bottom line. It may be in a Sunday morning worship service, where the Spirit urges you to be a participant, not just a passive observer. For that matter, it may be on a Monday afternoon, when you look up from your pile of work and worries and remember that there is a great and majestic God who loves you and has bought you for Himself.

The Holy Spirit has sometimes been called "the forgotten God," because so few know or understand His ministry. But whether the world acknowledges Him or believes in Him or not doesn't really change a thing. He is *God in you.*

Walk through the days of your life in Him, and you will experience the very fragrance of heaven. And when it comes time to step into God's presence at the end of life, it won't be such a big step at all.

You will have been there all along.

CHAPTER ONE
THE PROMISE OF THE SPIRIT

1. Some of this material has been adapted from *The Biblical Basis for Modern Science,* Henry M. Morris (Grand Rapids, Mich.: Baker Book House, 1984), 82–85.

2. Ibid.

CHAPTER SEVEN
WALKING IN THE SPIRIT

1. A. W. Tozer, *That Incredible Christian* (Harrisburg, Penn.: Christian Publications, Inc., 1964), paraphrased from introduction, 11–13.

CHAPTER EIGHT
THE FRUIT OF THE SPIRIT

1. Sherwood Wirt, *The Book of Joy: A Treasury of Delights in God* (New York: McCracken Press, 1994), 8–9.

2 . Don Russell, "Road Rage: Driving Ourselves into Early Graves," *Philadelphia Daily News,* July 1997. Local Section, 4.

3. Information courtesy of AAA Foundation for Traffic Safety Web site, http://www.aaafts.org..

CHAPTER NINE
THE GIFTS OF THE SPIRIT

1. "Somebody Else" from *Illustrations for Biblical Preaching,* Michael P. Green, ed. (Grand Rapids, Mich.: Baker Book House, 1991), 331.

2. John Bjorlie, "Jeremiah Meneely," *Uplook* 63:3, June 1996, 22.

CHAPTER TEN
THE BEST EVIDENCE OF THE SPIRIT

1.   W. A. Criswell, *Ephesians: An Exposition* (Grand Rapids, Mich.: Zondervan Publishing House, 1974), 165.
2.   Alan L. McGinnis, *The Power of Optimism* (San Francisco: Harper and Row, 1990), 15–17.

CHAPTER ELEVEN
SPIRIT-CONTROLLED CHURCH MEMBERS

1.   Grace Noll Crowell, "To One in Sorrow," quoted in David Jeremiah, *The Power of Encouragement* (Sisters, Ore.: Multnomah Publishers, Inc., 1997), 178.
2.   Reuben Welch, "We Really Do Need Each Other" (Grand Rapids, Mich.: Zondervan Publishing House, 1982).

CHAPTER TWELVE
SPIRIT-CONTROLLED MARRIAGES

1.   Bill and Lynne Hybels, *Fit to Be Tied* (Grand Rapids, Mich.: Zondervan Publishing House, 1991). Used by permission of the publisher.

CHAPTER FIFTEEN
WHEN THE HOLY SPIRIT CONTROLS YOUR LIFE

1.   Data taken from a survey conducted by the Barna Research Group of Oxnard, California, in January 1997.
2.   Raph Spaulding Cushman, "The Secret," *Masterpieces of Religious Verse,* James Dalton Morrison, ed. (New York: Harper and Brothers Publishers, 1948), 408–9.